PHYSICALISM

Physicalism, the thesis that everything is physical, is one of the most controversial ideas in philosophy. Its adherents argue that there is no more important doctrine in philosophy, while its opponents claim that its role is greatly exaggerated. In this superb introduction to the problem Daniel Stoljar focuses on three fundamental questions: the interpretation, truth, and philosophical significance of physicalism. In answering these questions he covers the following key topics:

- a brief history of physicalism and its definitions
- what a physical property is and how physicalism meets challenges from empirical sciences
- 'Hempel's dilemma' and the relationship between physicalism and physics
- physicalism and key debates in metaphysics and philosophy of mind, such as supervenience, identity, and conceivability
- physicalism and causality.

Additional features include chapter summaries, annotated further reading, and a glossary of technical terms, making *Physicalism* ideal for those coming to the problem for the first time.

Daniel Stoljar is Professor of Philosophy at the Research School of Social Sciences, Australian National University.

New Problems of Philosophy
Series Editor: *José Luis Bermúdez*

The New Problems of Philosophy series provides accessible and engaging surveys of the most important problems in contemporary philosophy. Each book examines either a topic or theme that has emerged on the philosophical landscape in recent years, or a longstanding problem refreshed in light of recent work in philosophy and related disciplines. Clearly explaining the nature of the problem at hand and assessing attempts to answer it, books in the series are excellent starting points for undergraduate and graduate students wishing to study a single topic in depth. They will also be essential reading for professional philosophers. Additional features include chapter summaries, further reading, and a glossary of technical terms.

Also available:

Fiction and Fictionalism
Mark Sainsbury

Noncognitivism in Ethics
Mark Schroeder

Analyticity
Cory Juhl and Eric Loomis

Forthcoming:

Consequentialism
Julia Driver

Embodied Cognition
Lawrence Shapiro

Perceptual Consciousness
Adam Pautz

Semantic Externalism
Jesper Kallestrup

Moral Epistemology
Aaron Zimmerman

Self Knowledge
Brie Gertler

Folk Psychology
Ian Ravenscroft

Representational Artifacts
John Kulvicki

PHYSICALISM

Daniel Stoljar

Routledge
Taylor & Francis Group

LONDON AND NEW YORK

This edition published 2010
by Routledge
2 Park Square, Milton Park, Abingdon, Oxon, OX14 4RN

Simultaneously published in the USA and Canada
by Routledge
270 Madison Ave, New York, NY 10016

Routledge is an imprint of the Taylor & Francis Group, an informa business

© 2010 Daniel Stoljar

Typeset in Joanna and Scala Sans by Bookcraft Ltd, Stroud, Gloucestershire

Printed and bound in Great Britain by TJ International, Padstow, Cornwall

British Library Cataloguing in Publication Data
A catalogue record for this book is available from the British Library

Library of Congress Cataloging in Publication Data
Stoljar, Daniel.
Physicalism / by Daniel Stoljar.
p. cm. — (New problems of philosophy)
Includes bibliographical references and index.
1. Materialism. I. Title.
BT825.S83 2010
146'.3—dc22
2009036227

ISBN10: 0-415-45262-7 (hbk)
ISBN10: 0-415-45263-5 (pbk)
ISBN10: 0-203-85630-9 (ebk)

ISBN13: 978-0-415-45262-5 (hbk)
ISBN13: 978-0-415-45263-2 (pbk)
ISBN13: 978-0-203-85630-7 (ebk)

Every era has its Weltanschauung and in much contemporary philosophy the doctrine of 'physicalism' plays this role.

(Gillett and Loewer 2001: ix)

'Weltanschauung' is, I am afraid, a specifically German concept, the translation of which into other languages might well raise difficulties. If I try to give you a definition of it, it is bound to seem clumsy to you. In my opinion, then, a Weltanschauung is an intellectual construction which solves all the problems of our existence uniformly on the basis of one overriding hypothesis, which accordingly, leaves no question unanswered and in which everything that interests us finds its fixed place. It will easily be understood that the possession of a Weltanschauung of this kind is among the ideal wishes of human beings.

(Freud 1995: 783)

For my mother

CONTENTS

ACKNOWLEDGMENTS

I would like to thank the students in my proseminar at Harvard University while I was visiting there in Fall 2007, and in the Foundations Reading Group at ANU June–July 2008, to whom I presented early versions of this material and who gave fantastic feedback. I presented drafts of various parts of the book to audiences at Rutgers, ANU, Harvard, MIT, Otago, Ohio State, University of Illinois at Champagne-Urbana, Sun-Yat Sen University, Cambridge (HPS), Birmingham, and National Yang Ming University. I am very much indebted to all who took part in the discussion on those occasions. I owe particular debts of one form or another to direct comments from David Bourget, Selim Berker, Ben Caplan, David Chalmers, Andy Egan, Alan Hájek, Ole Koksvik, Daniel Korman, Holly Lawford-Smith, Stephan Leuenberger, John Matthewson, Kelvin McQueen, Bernard Nickel, Nico Silins, Declan Smithies, Jonathan Schaffer, and Wen Fang Wang, I am sure I should record other debts; let me apologize in advance to those I have missed out.

Two anonymous readers for Routledge gave very good advice, in particular on the presentation of the material. My editors, Adam Johnson and Tony Bruce, were very professional: prompt, direct, and polite. Jonathan Farrell was extremely helpful with preparing a late-stage manuscript for publication;

and Jacek Brzozowski was very helpful with bibliographical help at a much earlier stage.

Some of the material in Chapter 5 has been adapted from my article 'Hempel's dilemma,' which appears in Heather Dyke (ed.), From Truth to Reality: New Essays in Logic and Metaphysics (2009: 181–97). At various points throughout the book I have also drawn on and adapted some materials from my article 'Physicalism' in the Stanford Encyclopedia of Philosophy (Stoljar 2009b).

The inspiration for the example of the super-tasters in Chapter 10 is the song "John Lee Supertaster" by They Might Be Giants. (They use it for a different purpose.)

Since this book appears in a series aimed in part at graduate students and upper-level undergraduates, it is probably appropriate for me to say that over the years I have learnt an embarrassingly large amount from both teachers and students at Sydney, MIT, Colorado, and ANU. Of these the present work owes a big debt to Noam Chomsky, who first asked me what on earth I thought physicalism was anyway, and to Judith Jarvis Thomson, who first suggested I write a book on the subject.

INTRODUCTION

In 1925 Bertrand Russell wrote the preface to Friedrich Lange's *The History of Materialism*. Lange's monumental work, which had been published in German sixty years before Russell's preface, is a grand survey of materialism from the earliest times to the nineteenth century. What Russell says in his preface about materialism—for present purposes, for 'materialism' read 'physicalism'; I will explain the terminology in a moment—is instructive. He writes:

> Materialism as a theory of the nature of the world has had a curious history. Arising almost at the beginning of Greek philosophy, it has persisted down to our own time, in spite of the fact that very few eminent philosophers have advocated it. It has been associated with many scientific advances, and has seemed, in certain epochs, almost synonymous with a scientific outlook. ... A system of thought which has such persistent vitality must be worth studying, in spite of the professional contempt which is poured on it by most professors of philosophy. (Russell 1925: v)

Russell goes on to say that Lange's book appeared "at the height of the period often described as 'the materialist '60s'"—that is, the eighteen-sixties. This period is remarkable from Russell's point of view because it is a brief period in which materialism became influential. For most of the rest of the history of philosophy, he thinks, materialism is a minority view. Even Lange, whose book is sympathetic to materialism, is no materialist.

Russell's suggestion that the 1860s are exceptional in the history of philosophy is, because of its scope, difficult to assess; *any* claim about the entire history of philosophy is difficult to assess. But there is no doubt that he is right both about the period in which he was writing, and the period immediately preceding it. Toward the end of the nineteenth century, almost all professional philosophers were idealists of one sort or another; that is, they held that the world was in some fundamental sense spiritual or mental, rather than being in some fundamental sense physical or material (see Stove 1991). Russell himself was extremely influential in destroying idealism, but the kind of philosophy that replaced idealism was not materialist. For example, what is perhaps the central work in philosophy of mind of the period, C.D. Broad's *The Mind and its Place in Nature*, contains a famous and influential critique of materialism (see Broad 1925), and Broad himself was an active member of the (definitely non-materialist) Society for Psychical Research (see Broad 1960).

If materialism wasn't popular in 1925, however, the contrast between then and now could not be more extreme. Far from being viewed with professional contempt, materialism became something like a consensus position within analytic philosophy in the 1960s and has remained so, or very nearly so, ever since. Philosophers such as Quine, Smart, Lewis, Armstrong, Fodor, and many others are all materialists. Some philosophers, such as Jaegwon Kim, were materialists and have since changed their minds; while others, such as Frank Jackson, were anti-materialists and have since relented. But as we will see as we proceed, even the anti-physicalism espoused by (then) Jackson and (now) Kim is deeply inflected by physicalism, sharing large parts of its content and philosophical context. As Carl Gillett and Barry Loewer say in one of the passages I selected as an epigraph for this book, physicalism is in many ways the Weltanschauung of modern analytic philosophy. (For an explanation of the German word 'Weltanschauung,' see the other passage I selected as an epigraph.)

Our questions

This book is about that Weltanschauung. We will focus in particular on three sets of questions. The first concerns the *interpretation* of the thesis of physicalism. In slogan form the thesis is easy enough to understand: it says that everything is physical, just as the idealists of the nineteenth century said that everything is mental. But, as we will see, it is difficult to interpret that slogan in a precise way. What is this condition—being physical—that according to physicalism everything has or is? And what is it for *everything* to have this condition?

The *second* set of questions concerns the truth or falsity of physicalism, and, of course, the arguments for or against its truth or falsity. Physicalism is sometimes thought to be part and parcel of the scientific world-view; "synonymous with a scientific outlook" as Russell put it. But what is 'the scientific world-view'? Is there one? And what is the connection between it and physicalism? In recent times philosophers have advanced responses to these questions. We will need to discuss what those responses are.

The *third* set of questions concern the *philosophical significance* of physicalism. Even if physicalism were an interesting thesis that had arguments for and against it, this would hardly justify talk of a 'Weltanschauung.' What justifies this talk in my view is not the thesis of physicalism itself, nor the particular arguments for or against it, but rather the fact that in contemporary philosophy the idea of physicalism structures and informs many different questions and debates. In philosophy of mind, for example, philosophical problems about conscious experience or representation are routinely viewed as problems about finding or fitting or placing or locating—the metaphors differ with different authors—conscious experience or representation in a purely physical world, that is, in a world in which physicalism is true. These sorts of problems, often called 'placement problems,' are viewed as a template for other philosophical problems, e.g. problems about ethics, so that the philosophy of mind becomes a sort of laboratory for the rest of philosophy. But it is far from obvious that this way of viewing philosophical problems is necessary or desirable, and it is a very distinctive feature of this period of philosophy—i.e. from roughly 1960 to the present—that it falls so naturally into this way of thinking.

Other questions

The three questions that we are going to focus on—interpretation, truth, and significance—are by no means the only questions that one might raise about physicalism. It will be helpful for what follows to explicitly set aside three others.

The first concerns the relation of physicalism to its intellectual and social context. Philosophy does not operate in a vacuum, and it is reasonable to suppose that the prevalence of physicalism in philosophy is part of larger currents in intellectual life in the twentieth century and after. For example, it is difficult to believe that the prestige of the sciences in intellectual culture had or has nothing to do with the popularity of physicalism among professional philosophers. Nor is it credible that the extraordinary success of Western medicine, with its largely materialistic or physicalistic outlook, has nothing to do with it. (Is it an accident that one of the central defenders of materialism in the eighteenth century, Julien de La Mettrie, was also a medical doctor?) However, while there are books to be written about the connection between materialism and medicine, and between the social prestige of science and the assumption of physicalism, this book is not an exercise in intellectual history. Rather it is a philosophy book, and questions that I will raise about physicalism have a distinctively philosophical flavor.

Second, one might ask about the relation of physicalism to issues of a fairly technical kind within physics, or perhaps the philosophy thereof—that is, issues whose discussion requires specialized knowledge in physics or philosophy of physics. Indeed, you might think it impossible to discuss one without the other. However, while there are no doubt questions to be raised about the connection between physicalism and physics, there will be no discussion either of physics or philosophy of physics in what follows—apart that is, from very general points about physics that require no specialist knowledge at all. What is the reason for this? Well, for one thing, talking about physics in detail is not something I am competent to do. So if discussions of physicalism in philosophy required technical knowledge in physics, this book would be considerably shorter than it is. Another and more important reason is that something has gone wrong if it is assumed that talking competently and in detail about physics were a requirement on talking competently and in detail about physicalism. For physicalism is a very abstract proposal about the nature of the world, a proposal that does not depend on the details of particular physical theories. True, words like 'physics' and 'physical theory' crop up a lot in discussions of physicalism, and what follows will be no exception. But talking about physics (physical theory, and so forth) in very general terms is one thing and talking about it in detail is quite another.

Finally, there is a legitimate set of questions to ask about the relation between physicalism of the kind that we find in modern philosophy, and various versions of physicalism or materialism to be found throughout the history of thought. Lange's first sentence is "Materialism is as old as philosophy, but not older" (1925: 3). One might therefore ask about its history, not only in philosophy but in science as well. However, while again there are books to be written on these themes—Lange's remains one of the best I know of—and while I will make occasional comments about this, the primary emphasis of this book is not on history so much as on philosophy itself. Contemporary philosophers talk about physicalism in a certain sort of way, and they assume that this thesis plays a certain sort of role in the structure of philosophical problems. Our questions are mainly what that thesis is, whether it is true, and whether it does or should play that role; whether famous materialists or physicalists of the past, such as Lucretius or Gassendi or d'Holbach or Marx or Neurath, held similar views is not our primary concern.

Organization

Our questions concern the interpretation, truth and significance of physicalism; my plan in answering those questions is as follows.

I begin, in Chapter 1, with an exposition of what I take to be the standard picture of physicalism and its role in contemporary philosophy. I set out the standard picture as the conjunction of five theses, noting that these theses form a system. I suggest in addition that this system is attractive because it removes a fundamental obstacle to the very existence of philosophy, and portrays philosophical problems as being highly unified. In my view, it is largely the role that physicalism plays in this way of thinking about philosophical problems that best explains its current popularity.

In Chapter 2 I begin to discuss the interpretation question, starting with some preliminary issues about the logical form of the thesis to be discussed and what its alternatives might be. As we will see, the sentence 'everything is physical' doesn't quite capture what is intended. Most physicalists do not mean that absolutely everything is physical or that every particular is physical or even that every property is physical. What they mean instead is (something like) every instantiated property is necessitated by some physical property. But charting the course from 'everything is physical' to 'every instantiated property is …' is instructive.

In Chapters 3 to 6 I turn to the heart of the interpretation question: the issue of what a physical property is. In Chapter 3 I set out one particular view about what a physical property is which I call 'the Starting Point View.' The Starting Point View provides an adequate formulation of some classical versions of physicalism, but it cannot be what contemporary physicalists have in mind because physicalism as defined by the Starting Point View is false, and for empirical reasons that have little to do with the distinctive concerns of philosophy, and which are in any case accepted by contemporary physicalists.

In Chapter 4 I discuss the prospects of liberalizing the Starting Point View, and so of reinterpreting the notion of a physical property in such a way that physicalism might be true, at least in so far as empirical science is concerned. The most common way to do this is to adopt what I call 'the Theory View.' The problem with this view is that defining physicalism in terms of it 'gets the cases wrong,' i.e. it either has physicalism being true in imagined or possible cases where no version of physicalism should be true, or it has physicalism being false in imagined or possible cases where no version of physicalism should be false. At the end of the chapter, I distill the line of thought presented in Chapters 3 and 4 into an argument whose conclusion is a metathesis about physicalism, viz. that there is no version of physicalism that is (a) true and (b) deserves the name.

In Chapter 5, I discuss an argument that has something in common with, but is also rather different from, the argument of Chapters 3 and 4, viz. Hempel's dilemma. Hempel's dilemma is that if physicalism is defined with reference to contemporary physics, it is false (for no one thinks that contemporary physics provides the whole truth about the world), but if physicalism is defined with reference to an ideal physics, then it is unclear what it is says, and in particular it is unclear that what it says rules out various possibilities inconsistent with physicalism as usually understood. I discuss various objections to Hempel's dilemma, and suggest that the most powerful one is that the dilemma proceeds from implausible assumptions about how physicalism is to be defined, assumptions which have already emerged in our discussion.

Chapters 3 to 5 concern various proposals about what a physical property is, and some consequences of these proposals. In Chapters 6 to 8 I turn to the issue of what relation must hold between every (instantiated) property and a physical property if physicalism is to be true. In Chapter 2 I adopted a particular proposal about this relation without much elaboration and defense, viz. that the relation in question was necessitation understood in the way that Kripke explains it in *Naming and Necessity*. In Chapter 6 I set out this 'Necessity View,' as I call it, in more detail, showing how it is one sort of modal definition of physicalism, and compare it to various non-modal definitions stated in terms of identity, synonymy, realization, and fundamental properties.

In Chapter 7 I turn to the assessment of the Necessity View, focusing in particular on whether it follows from the truth of physicalism that necessitation holds between every property and physical properties. On the one hand, a suggestion along these lines seems mandatory if one wants to distinguish physicalism from standard forms of dualism, according to which there is a lawful but contingent connection between the mental and the physical; indeed, as I understand them, all reasonable definitions of physicalism are in agreement on this point, and so even non-modal definitions of physicalism will have this modal consequence. On the other hand, explaining physicalism in terms of all possible worlds looks in stark contrast with the contingent and empirical nature of the doctrine. In the chapter I examine various ways to develop and resolve this conflict. I also draw a connection between the Necessity View and some widely discussed issues about physicalism, viz. whether physicalism requires there to be psycho-physical laws, and the distinction (as it is often expressed) between 'a priori physicalism' and 'a posteriori physicalism.'

In Chapter 8 I turn from the issue of whether necessitation is necessary for physicalism to the issue of whether it is sufficient, focusing in particular on the objection that, if the Necessity View is correct, physicalism cannot be distinguished from various kinds of non-physicalist positions—I focus on (what I call) 'necessitation dualism.' I discuss a number of proposals about how to distinguish these doctrines, concluding with the suggestion that in order to formulate physicalism it will be required that physicalists move beyond logical and modal considerations, and confront the distinctively metaphysical content of their doctrine. It is here that the conflict between modal and non-modal definitions of physicalism becomes acute; indeed, the upshot of discussion in the chapter involves a sort of compromise between these two styles of definition.

Taken as a whole, our discussion of the interpretation question—the question of what physicalism means or is—puts considerable pressure on the thesis normally called 'physicalism': Chapters 3 to 5 argue that it is not physicalism; Chapters 6 to 8 point out it is no clearer than the metaphysical notions required to explain it. In Chapters 9 to 11 I examine the ways in which philosophers have sought to respond to these problems.

As I see it, the literature on these matters is dominated by two loud and opposing voices. The first, that of the skeptic, accepts that there is no true genuine version of physicalism, and draws a negative consequence for the standard picture and indeed for large parts of philosophy itself. The second, that of the true believer, takes it to be obvious that the standard picture is legitimate, and looks around for a thesis of physicalism that can play the role assigned to it by that picture. The debate between the skeptic and the true believer looks intractable, so it is attractive to seek to avoid it by rejecting a presupposition shared by both sides. In Chapter 9 I critically discuss three such proposals. The first suggests that the problem is generated by the forlorn attempt to analyze the notion of physicalism—doesn't the history of philosophy suggest that attempts at analysis are always a failure? The second suggests that the problem is generated by the mistaken assumption that there is a *thesis* here in the first place—doesn't the physicalist hold a characteristic *attitude* rather than believe a characteristic thesis? The third suggests that the problem is generated by a failure to distinguish the thesis of physicalism and various philosophical uses of a thesis—surely a thesis might be illegitimate or objectionable even while various philosophical uses of a thesis are not. I argue that the first two of these suggestions don't survive scrutiny, and so we are left with the third.

The main consequence of this third view is that if the various philosophical problems associated with the standard picture are legitimate, then in a sense they cannot be about physicalism—references to physicalism in their formulation must be inessential. In Chapters 10 to 11, therefore, I assess whether this consequence is correct. Chapter 10 reviews the arguments against physicalism, the most famous of which occur in philosophy of mind, in particular the conceivability or modal argument against physicalism. These arguments require books unto themselves, and so I focus mainly on what the role of physicalism is in each of the arguments. The conclusion is that physicalism does indeed play an inessential role, and so that the arguments can survive the observation that there is no version of physicalism that is both genuine and plausibly true.

In Chapter 11 I consider the arguments in favor of physicalism, of which the most famous is the so-called causal argument. This argument seeks to infer the truth of physicalism from a principle about causation called 'the exclusion principle' together with the theses that the world is a physically closed system and that the mental is efficacious. I suggest that, once we factor in the question about interpretation into this argument, it too emerges as an argument which is highly abstract and which has nothing to do with physicalism *per se*.

In conclusion, I return to the standard picture and ask what our discussion has revealed about it. The standard picture combines both a philosophy of nature and a philosophy of philosophy. Its philosophy of nature is that physicalism is a high-level empirical hypothesis that we have considerable reason to believe. Its philosophy of philosophy is that many contemporary philosophical problems may be viewed as attempts to place (or find, or …) various items in the world as portrayed in this philosophy of nature. Our discussion shows that this general picture is unsustainable. Contra the standard picture's philosophy of nature, the thesis that seems reasonable to hold about the nature of the world does not deserve the name 'physicalism.' Contra the standard picture's philosophy of philosophy, stating a whole series of philosophical problems in terms of physicalism imposes a uniformity on these problems that is both inaccurate and problematic. It is inaccurate simply because when one looks at a whole range of problems, it is hard to believe that they all have the structure that the standard picture interprets them as having. And it is problematic because the structure often blinds us to ways in which the problems can be solved.

The view I arrive at by the end of the book is a kind of 'bad news/good news' view. The bad news is that the skeptics about the formulation of physicalism are right: physicalism has no formulation on which it is both true and deserving of the name. The good news is that this does not have the catastrophic effects on philosophy that it is often portrayed as having in the literature. For physicalism itself plays an inessential role in the many philosophical problems that are formulated in terms of it, and so the fact that physicalism has no reasonable formulation does not entail that philosophical problems stated in terms of it have no reasonable formulation. In sum, the very considerable influence of physicalism on contemporary philosophy is largely without foundation, but appreciating this points us toward a better understanding of the philosophical problems that confront us.

A word of warning

Well that is the view that I arrive at anyway. Whether it will be your view too remains to be seen. And indeed, at this point it is worth issuing a word of warning about the discussion to follow. This is that while I certainly take myself to be a reliable narrator I am not an unopinionated one. And my opinions have certainly affected how I present the issues, what I think is plausible and not plausible and so on. Whether my opinions are correct or not is a matter about which you will have to make up your own mind. My best advice—though here again I am being opinionated!— is to follow up the readings I have suggested at the end of each chapter (and the references contained in those readings) and, even more importantly, to think through the issues yourself.

Having got that word of warning out of the way let me close this introduction with some brief comments on terminology.

Terminology

The word 'physicalism' was introduced into philosophy in the 1930s by Otto Neurath (1931a, 1931b) and Rudolf Carnap (1959, first published 1932/33), both of whom were key members of the Vienna Circle, a group of philosophers, scientists, and mathematicians active in Vienna prior to World War II. It is not at all clear that Neurath and Carnap conceived of physicalism in the same way, but one thesis that is often attributed to them (e.g. by Hempel 1949) is the linguistic thesis that every statement is synonymous with (i.e. is equivalent in meaning with) some physical statement. On the other hand, 'materialism' is traditionally construed as denoting, not a linguistic thesis, but a metaphysical one, i.e. it tells us about the nature of the world as such. Hence Neurath and Carnap had a good reason for distinguishing physicalism (a linguistic thesis) from materialism (a metaphysical thesis). Moreover, this reason was compounded by the fact that, according to official positivist doctrine, metaphysics is nonsense.

It is sometimes suggested that 'physicalism' is distinct from 'materialism' for a reason quite unrelated to the one associated with its Viennese origins, viz. that 'physicalism' has a certain generality that 'materialism' does not. The root notion of materialism is 'matter' and historically the notion of matter is quite constrained: matter is the stuff that fills up space, is inert, senseless, hard, impenetrable, and so on; a materialist is someone who holds that everything is fundamentally material in this sense of 'matter.' The problem with this version of materialism is that physical science has itself shown that it is untrue; modern physics postulates events and properties that are non-material in this sense (see Chapter 3). Because of this, some contemporary philosophers prefer to speak of 'physicalism' on the grounds, first, that the root notion of physicalism is 'physics' and, second, that 'physics' includes more than simply 'matter.'

Neither of these two reasons for distinguishing the terms is particularly persuasive. As regards the distinction invoked by Carnap and Neurath, the background philosophy that held that in place has for the most part been rejected. As regards the idea that the word 'physicalism' is somehow connected to 'physics', it remains the case that it is as closely related to 'physical object' as it is to 'physics' and, since 'physical object' is synonymous with 'material object,' it is quite unclear that a terminological division between 'physicalism' and 'materialism' is well motivated.

Not only is it difficult to pinpoint any clear rationale for distinguishing 'physicalism' from 'materialism,' it is also the case that, while some physicalists prefer the term 'physicalist,' others most definitely do not. David Lewis, one of the most influential physicalists of the twentieth century, writes as follows:

> [Materialism] was so named when the best physics of the day was the physics of matter alone. Now our best physics acknowledges other bearers of fundamental properties: parts of pervasive fields, parts of causally active spacetime. But it would be pedantry to change the name on that account, and disown our intellectual ancestors. Or worse, it would be a tacky marketing ploy, akin to British Rail's decree that second-class passengers shall now be called 'standard class passengers.' (1994: 293)

And Lewis here is plausibly interpreted as following the terminology of Smart's 1963 paper, one of the key documents of the modern version of the thesis, which had a simple title: 'Materialism.'

In view of the fact that there is no consensus about how exactly to use these words, I will proceed here by stipulation. First, I assume that 'physicalism' and 'materialism' are interchangeable but will generally use the first rather than the second. Where other authors use 'materialism'—as we have seen Russell does—I will paraphrase what they say by using 'physicalism.' Second, and relatedly, I will hereby cancel any implication about the difference between physicalism and materialism. Of course, no up-to-date philosophical thesis can rely on an outmoded science, but the mere use of the terminology should not prejudice questions like this one way or the other.

In addition to 'physicalism' and 'materialism,' another word that is sometimes used is 'naturalism.' Once again, there is no consensus about how to use this word, but in what follows I will use 'naturalism' to mean not a thesis about the nature of the world, and so not physicalism, but rather a methodological thesis. According to this thesis, the best methods that we have for finding out about the world are the methods, whatever they are, that one finds in the natural sciences. As I understand it, methodological naturalism is a pretty thin doctrine. It says that we should think about the world in the way that those people think about the world, where the demonstrative expression 'those people' picks out a particular class of people, viz. scientists. This idea is completely silent on whether people who are not normally regarded as scientists (detectives, for example) use the same methods or not. Likewise it is silent on whether methods employed by such people are justified or not, or even what such methods are. For example, it is sometimes suggested that naturalism is in some way opposed to a priori reasoning (see, e.g. Devitt 1996). But one could only establish this if one could establish that the people demonstrated did not employ a priori reasoning. That seems unlikely, in view of the role of logical, mathematical and conceptual thinking in the sciences. At any rate, I will not assume here that methodological naturalism entails that there is no such thing as a priori reasoning.

Summary

In this introduction, we have set out three questions to focus on: the interpretation, truth (or falsity), and philosophical significance of physicalism, and set aside three others: the relation of physicalism to broader social currents, the relation of physicalism to technical questions in physics or philosophy of physics, and the history of the subject. We have also noted the origins of the word 'physicalism' in the positivism of the Vienna Circle, and made some comments on the relation between the words 'physicalism,' 'materialism,' and 'naturalism.'

Further reading

Two classic works in the history of physicalism are Dijksterhuis's *The Mechanization of the World-Picture* (1961) and Lange's *The History of Materialism* (1925). For a much less forbidding account, see Vitzthum 1995. For physicalism as it appears in positivism, see the further readings for Chapter 1. The Lewis quotation at the end is from 'Reduction of mind' (1994) the first part of which provides an excellent summary of Lewis's views on physicalism. (As I noted in the text, Lewis calls it 'materialism.')

1

THE STANDARD PICTURE

1.1 Introduction

There is a view about physicalism and its place in philosophy that is accepted by enough contemporary philosophers to be called 'the standard picture.' To put it very roughly, the standard picture is as follows.

On the one hand, physicalism is a thesis about the nature of the world that we have considerable and perhaps even overwhelming reason to believe. Physicalism is not an a priori doctrine, like a doctrine in ethics or mathematics. People who deny it are not thereby making any conceptual or logical error. Rather the status of physicalism is more like the status of the theory of evolution or of continental drift; in the words of Hartry Field, one prominent physicalist, "it functions as a high-level empirical hypothesis, a hypothesis that no small number of experiments can force us to give up" (1972: 357). Those who deny physicalism are not making a conceptual mistake, but they are, nevertheless, flying in the face not merely of science but also of scientifically informed common sense.

On the other hand, while physicalism is a thesis we have overwhelming reason to believe, believing it without qualification is no easy matter. For physicalism is on the face of it incompatible with, or at least is in some tension with, various claims that are central to ordinary or common sense views about humans and what they are like, views which in various ways are presumed also in the sciences. Some of the claims which physicalism might be thought to be inconsistent with or in tension with are:

- that people perceive things and have bodily sensations of various kinds, e.g. tastes, cramps, itches, nausea;
- that people speak and think about the world and about each other;
- that at least some words have meaning;
- that people's bodies, and physical objects in general, are colored, textured, have various tastes, and emit sounds and smells;
- that people's bodies, and physical objects in general, are solid or have bulk or fill in space;
- that people have reasons for thinking and acting as they do, and that those reasons may be subjected to normative (including moral) scrutiny;
- that people sometimes act and think freely;
- that people participate in group decisions and actions, and in turn the actions of these groups impact on the individuals who constitute them;
- that there are mathematical and logical truths (e.g. "$5 + 7 = 12$"), and that people can come to know these mathematical and logical truths.

In order to appreciate the importance of these claims, try to think for a moment how things would be if they were false—that nobody thinks or feels, or says anything meaningful, or that ordinary physical objects are not solid or colored, or that there is no freedom of action or social agency or mathematical knowledge. It is obvious when you think about it that these claims and others like them are central to life as we live it; they are, as I will say, *the presuppositions of everyday life*. So in effect what we are being asked to accept by the standard picture is the idea that there is a prima facie conflict between the presuppositions of everyday life on the one hand, and a thesis we have overwhelming reason to believe—i.e. physicalism—on the other.

In view of the conflict or apparent conflict between physicalism and the presuppositions of everyday life, we are faced with a number of options. One is to abandon or modify physicalism. But that seems implausible if physicalism really is, as proponents of the standard picture say it is, a thesis for which we have considerable evidence. Another is to abandon some or all of these presuppositions. But that too seems implausible. Even if we wanted to deny these claims, it is not clear that we could do so. (If a philosophy professor convinces you in a seminar that nobody is in pain and that no physical object is solid, you will forget both the moment you stub your toe

on the doorframe as you leave the room.) The third option is to compromise, i.e. to propose ways to understand these presuppositions so as they are
not incompatible with the truth of physicalism.

It is the third option that is most central to the standard picture. Indeed,
it is no exaggeration to say that variations on this third option together
make up large parts of what analytic philosophy is about. Large parts of
analytic philosophy, that is, involve proposing and assessing ways of interpreting the presuppositions of everyday life so as they are compatible with
the truth of physicalism. Famous philosophers are often associated with
particular proposals about how to do this. For example, Gilbert Ryle in
The Concept of Mind (1949) is famous for saying that psychological claims
are logically in a different category from other kinds of claim, and that if
that is true, the conflict between physicalism and psychological claims is
merely apparent. Similarly, J.J.C. Smart's paper 'Sensations and brain processes' (1959) is famous for saying that we might exploit Frege's distinction
between the sense of an expression and its referent in order to remove
the source of tension between ordinary talk about mental states such as
sensations and physicalism. Finally, Kripke's (1980) discussion in *Naming and
Necessity* of the necessary a posteriori looks like it is interesting in part at least
because it permits us to say that physicalism makes the presuppositions of
everyday life true without committing ourselves to various proposals about
how these claims are to be interpreted and analyzed. As David Lewis once
remarked, Kripke's discovery of the necessary a posteriori looks from this
point of view like a "godsend" (Lewis 2002: 95).

1.2 The generality of physicalism

The standard picture does not view physicalism as true merely for selected
bits of the world—merely for human or sentient or living beings, for
example. Rather it is intended be a very general and abstract doctrine that is
true of the world as a whole. It is, as we saw in the introduction, a world-
view or Weltanschauung.

One way to bring this out is to think of the world as a huge complicated structure, emanating out in various dimensions from the point at
which you exist. There is the history of the world: human history both
recorded and unrecorded; the history of living organisms, the history of
the planet, the solar system and the universe itself. There is the future of
the world (assuming the future exists) both for you, and for the universe
in general. There is the composition of the world: almost any part of it is

made up of smaller and smaller parts: your body, the organs of your body, the cells that make up the organs, the molecules that make up the cells; and so on. Correlatively, almost any part of the world forms larger and larger wholes: your family, your country, your species, the environment, and so on. Still other dimensions of the world are harder to capture in spatial or temporal terms. Every part of the world has various characteristic features and patterns of development. You in particular have various capacities to grow and decay, and to reproduce; you have various sensory and cognitive faculties and potentialities, some of which can be broken down into smaller faculties, and some of which constitute larger ones; there are various social and physical forces operating on you, and in turn you are an actor in a social and physical environment; you are subject to, and critic of, moral, aesthetic, prudential, and epistemic pressures of various kinds; and so on.

Physicalism has something to say about every aspect of this complicated structure. It says that everything here is physical, or to put it more cautiously (for reasons we will examine in the next chapter) that everything here is necessitated by the physical. It is this very general idea that, according to the standard picture, we have considerable and perhaps overwhelming reason to believe. But it is also this very general idea that, according to the standard picture, is inconsistent with, or in tension with, the presuppositions of everyday life.

1.3 Physicalism and the mind–body problem

Physicalism is a general thesis, but it is also very closely associated with the mind–body problem; indeed, the work of the three philosophers I mentioned a moment ago—Ryle, Smart and Kripke—was in each case a contribution to (among other things) the mind–body problem. This connection to the mind–body problem is important for the standard picture in two respects; first, it provides perhaps the clearest example of the general tension between physicalism and the presuppositions of everyday life; second, it provides a template for how to think about many other philosophical problems.

We will turn to this second issue—the way in which the mind–body problem provides a template for others—more fully as we proceed. But, first, how is the mind–body problem an instance of the general tension? Well, you might naturally think that the mind–body problem is a problem about the relation between two things, the mind, and the body. In fact in contemporary philosophy of mind, the problem is almost always conceived of as a problem about the apparent incompatibility of physicalism, on the one hand, and the existence and nature of various mental phenomena, on the other. If physicalism is true, humans and other sentient creatures are themselves wholly physical. But many philosophers think that there are arguments which if successful would show that the apparent fact that we sometimes have (e.g.) sensations is incompatible with the claim that we are wholly physical. (These arguments are usually called conceivability or modal arguments. I will set out these arguments in Chapter 10.) Since it seems obvious that we do have sensations—when we stub our toes, for example—the soundness of these arguments entails that physicalism is false. But as I have said, physicalism is something that, according to the standard picture, we have overwhelming reason to believe. So the mind–body problem in contemporary philosophy presents a sort of paradox in our thinking: apparently persuasive arguments like the conceivability argument show that two things we strongly believe cannot both be true.

If we have an apparently persuasive argument showing that two things we believe cannot both be true we must give up something—but what? Well, to abandon or modify physicalism is in the philosophy of mind case to become a *dualist*. Dualism may be developed in various ways, as we will see in the next chapter. But however it is developed, a dualist is someone who says that physicalism is at best mostly true, rather than being true outright. Maybe physicalism is true of most of the complicated structure I mentioned in the previous section—maybe it is true of rocks and planets and plants—but it is not true of people and other sentient creatures. The option of giving up the presuppositions of everyday life is in philosophy of mind called *eliminativism*. The eliminativist holds that since physicalism is true, and since physicalism is incompatible with sensations, then sensations do not exist. Finally, just as it does in the general case, the compromise option occupies most of the attention of philosophers of mind. There are two broad strategies here. One is to work out an account of what sensations are which makes it clear that the existence of sensations is compatible with physicalism. (Ryle, for example, is often interpreted as proposing a so-called behaviorist analysis of sensations according to which to have a sensation is to exhibit a certain characteristic pattern of behavior; Smart, on the other hand, is often interpreted as proposing a functionalist or topic-neutral analysis according to which to have a sensation is to have an inner state that plays a certain causal role, i.e. is caused by certain things, and in turn causes certain behavior and other mental states of a distinctive sort.) The other strategy, which is inspired by part of Kripke's discussion (though was not endorsed by

Kripke himself), is to argue directly that the conceivability argument is not persuasive, even in the absence of any functionalist or behaviorist analysis of sensations. As we will see in Chapter 10, it is most often this second sort of strategy that philosophers of mind have employed in recent discussions.

1.4 Philosophy within science

We have so far seen that, according to the standard picture, physicalism is a thesis we have overwhelming reason to endorse but is also in tension with the presuppositions of everyday life. We have also noted the generality of physicalism and its connection to the mind–body problem. But why did the standard picture become the standard picture? What is attractive about it?

One reason is that it solves, at least in part, the problem I will call—somewhat grandly—'the problem of philosophy.' Richard Rorty gives a vivid statement of this problem in the following terms:

> If philosophy becomes too naturalistic, hard-nosed positive disciplines will nudge it aside; if it becomes too historicist, then intellectual history, literary criticism and similar soft spots in the 'humanities' will swallow it up. (Rorty 1979: 168)

Rorty might be read in this passage as if he were saying that the problem of philosophy were one about social power, i.e. about whether philosophy construed as a discipline will survive a competition with other disciplines to attract funding from a dean or a rich benefactor. But to my mind the problem is mainly an intellectual one about the very nature of philosophical problems. If philosophical problems are at bottom scientific ones, they seem not to be the sort of thing that philosophers, with their special talents and training, can study. On the other hand, if they are at bottom unscientific ones, then it seems most likely that they should be grouped together with problems about the historical development and cultural expression of ideas; that is, the sorts of problems discussed mainly in history or literature departments rather than in philosophy departments. What then could philosophy possibly be about?

This dilemma has been close to the heart of a lot of philosophy at least since the onset of logical positivism in the 1930s and perhaps much earlier. How to solve it? Well, one option is not to solve it but to embrace it; that is, give up on philosophy and become either a scientist or a person of letters—to become (or try to become!) either Einstein or Nietzsche, as it is sometimes put. If one wants to defend philosophy against this dilemma, however, it is necessary to find something for it to do that is neither science nor literature. The standard picture we have been discussing provides an apparently simple and decisive answer to the problem. Physicalism is a thesis about the world that, on the face of it, has impeccable scientific credentials. But physicalism also looks to be in conflict with the presuppositions of everyday life. In the light of this conflict, we seem inevitably to face the intellectual project of resolving it. Such a project seems important, since we can give up neither physicalism nor everyday life, and yet it is not in any straightforward way either scientific or literary. In summary, physicalism solves (in part, at least) the problem of philosophy.

We may put the basic point differently by connecting the problem of philosophy with the idea of a placement problem, and related to this, with the idea of a Weltanschauung, both of which I mentioned in the introduction. As Freud says in the passage I quoted, a Weltanschauung is a relatively simple thesis or proposal that applies to everything; we may think of it as a relatively simple thesis about the world that aspires to completeness, i.e. that aspires to tell us something about every instantiated property in the world. On the other hand, any Weltanschauung worth its salt is going to generate a series of placement problems. For a world picture with any content is going to place some constraints on what is in the world, and these constraints will render some claims about what is in the world initially implausible. From this point of view, philosophers emerge as those who police the world-view—the Weltanschauungpolizei, i.e. those who seek out sites of conflict and make those conflicts disappear.

Now physicalism is a Weltanschauung in Freud's sense, or at any rate is often thought of in that way. And, from a philosopher's point of view, the beauty of this particular Weltanschauung is, first, that it is one with scientific backing and, second, that the placement problems it generates involve the presuppositions of everyday life. In consequence, the task of policing this particular Weltanschauung could not be more important. So the standard picture is popular in part because it solves this problem of what philosophy is about, and solves it with considerable aplomb.

1.5 Philosophical problems as placement problems

The standard picture is attractive because it provides an answer to the problem of philosophy. But it is attractive also because it makes us think about philosophical problems, or at any rate a large class of philosophical problems, in a remarkably unified way. Consider this passage from Huw Price:

> Like coastal cities in the third millennium, important areas of human discourse seem threatened by the rise of modern science. The problem isn't new, of course, or wholly unwelcome. The tide of naturalism has been rising since the seventeenth century, and the rise owes more to clarity than to pollution in the intellectual atmosphere. All the same, the regions under threat are some of the most central in human life—the four Ms, for example: Morality, Modality, Meaning and the Mental. Some of the key issues in contemporary metaphysics concern the place and fate of such concepts in a naturalistic worldview. (Price 1997: 247)

In the first part of this passage, Price is describing the standard picture roughly in the terms I have done. (He does use 'naturalism' rather than 'physicalism', but I think we can interpret him as meaning the latter inter alia). In the final sentence, however, Price goes on to identify "the key issues in contemporary metaphysics" as concerning "the place and fate of such concepts in a naturalistic worldview." In short, what Price is suggesting is that philosophical, or any rate metaphysical, problems in many domains should all be thought of as questions about whether and how to place or fit or locate or find (as I said in the introduction, the metaphors differ with different authors) various items or claims in a physical world. In the rest of his article, Price goes on to propose an interesting way to deal with these placement problems, a way that owes a considerable amount to Ryle's denial that many claims of philosophical interest are in the fact-stating business. Whether Price is right to endorse this Ryle-inspired view is an interesting question. But for the moment the point I want to emphasize is something implicit rather than explicit in what Price says: the apparent thematic unity of the different issues he mentions, and, related to this, the idea that one can generalize about the key issues in metaphysics in the way that he does.

For in fact it is quite unobvious that there is or should be any thematic unity here. For example, it is quite unobvious that questions in science exhibit any genuine unity, except perhaps in the very general (and so unhelpful) sense that in science people are interested in explaining things. So why should we assume that metaphysical questions about morality, meaning, mind, and modality (to take Price's examples) are similar insofar as all of them represent questions about how to place or fit or locate or find these phenomena in the natural or physical world? Has Price conducted a study of these problems and concluded on the basis of the study that they are all placement problems? Of course not—rather he has, implicitly or explicitly, a theory about what these problems consist in, a theory that entails that they are placement problems, and moreover that they are placement problems of the same sort. This is not to deny that Price is right to assume there is some kind of unity here—perhaps he is. It is simply to remark on the fact that he, and proponents of the standard picture, do assume this, and that this is one reason why the standard picture is attractive.

1.6 Neurath and Carnap

When did the standard picture become the standard picture? As I have already mentioned, it was Otto Neurath and Rudolf Carnap who introduced the word 'physicalism' as a piece of philosophical shoptalk in the 1930s. (One of Neurath's papers is entitled (in English) 'Physicalism: the philosophy of the Vienna Circle.') However, not only did the philosophers of this period use the term differently to the way it is employed today, there were differences in usage even among themselves.

For Rudolf Carnap, perhaps the most influential member of the Vienna Circle, physicalism was explicitly a thesis about meaning or translation. The "general thesis of physicalism," he wrote, is that "physical language is a universal language, that is, a language into which every sentence may be translated" (1959/1932: 165). For Carnap, physicalism was a variation on a more familiar positivist doctrine of phenomenalism. According to phenomenalism, the universal language, i.e. the language into which every sentence may be translated, is an observation language rather than a physical language, where an observation language is one whose basic sentences concern observation or experience.

Why adopt physicalism in this sense as opposed to phenomenalism? In some parts of his writing, Carnap suggests that the choice is pragmatic (1947: 207–8). But elsewhere he seems to suggest that physicalism has an advantage over phenomenalism, viz. that physical language is intersubjective—in particular it is a language suitable for co-operative scientific enquiry (1959/1932: 166). Neurath agreed with Carnap over the intersubjectivity of the physical language, but he nevertheless had a version of physicalism that was different from Carnap's. While Carnap thought that the relation of physical statements to other statements would be one of translatability, Neurath seemed to endorse a much looser conception. For Neurath, commitment to physicalism was a way of being committed to the connection and integration of the various sciences, without assuming that one science was the dominant one. In later work (1946), Neurath used the image of an orchestra for the different sciences—physicalism was part of the background conditions for the orchestra. (Actually the interpretation of Neurath's position is a difficult matter which we will set aside here; for discussion see Cartwright et al. 1996.)

While Carnap and Neurath differed over the interpretation of physicalism, they nevertheless agreed that the notion of a physical language is central to it; to this extent, both held linguistic versions of physicalism that differ from the metaphysical doctrines current today. (As I mentioned in the introduction, for Neurath, and indeed for Carnap, the word 'physicalism' is reserved for a linguistic doctrine quite different from any metaphysical thesis like materialism.) But what is a physical language and what is physical about it? Carnap sometimes writes as if what he means by 'physical language' is the language of physics (e.g. 1959/1932). However, it is unlikely that the language of physics could have played the role that either Carnap or Neurath wanted the idea of a physical language to play. Physics can scarcely be thought of as a lingua franca available to any scientist as Neurath envisioned, and nor is the language of physics plausibly a foundational language in the epistemological program presented by Carnap.

Carnap also seems to suggest (e.g. 1947) that the physical language is not physics but a language of ordinary physical objects and their distinctive properties. This is certainly better from his point of view, but now the distinction between phenomenalism and physicalism looks very subtle indeed. As we have seen, the phenomenalist has the observation language where the physicalist has the physical language. What then is the observation language? One interpretation is that it is the language of things observed, i.e. ordinary physical objects and their properties; another interpretation is that it is the language of events of observation, i.e. observings of physical objects. But observings of physical objects look as if they are best explained by mentioning the physical objects observed. So either way of introducing the idea of an observation language makes it look very closely related to the language of ordinary physical objects. Of course that the distinction between phenomenalism and physicalism (in this sense) is subtle is an objection to neither but is striking in view of the fact that physicalism and phenomenalism are often thought of as radically different doctrines.

The distinction between two accounts of what a physical language is that we have seen at play in Carnap—the language of physics, on the one hand, and the language of ordinary physical objects on the other—will be in one form or another with us throughout our discussion. It is always a good question to ask any physicalist whether they have in mind the idea of a physical object in an ordinary sense or a physics (often the answer is that they have both). So it is interesting to note that Neurath took a quite independent path on this question. He wrote:

> [Physicalism] ... starts from everyday language, which avoids elements which the various peoples of the earth do not have in common. The assumption is, that Melanesian tribes and European explorers can start to talk on cows and calves, pains and pleasures without difficulties, whereas difficulties appear when expressions like 'cause,' 'punishment,' 'mind,' etc. enter the talk. In this part of our everyday language which physicalism acknowledges one formulates questions with 'where, when, how.' And physicalism suggests to drop discussion which do not allow these three questions reasonably made [sic]. (Neurath, quoted in O'Neill 2004: 435)

That Neurath includes 'pleasure' and 'pain' in the physical language is striking, and suggests that what he has in mind by 'physicalism' is something quite remote from contemporary concerns.

1.7 Quine and Smart

The versions of physicalism promoted by Carnap and Neurath were not universally popular with the Vienna Circle and associated philosophers. Wittgenstein, who many in the Circle revered, thought the *name* at least of the doctrine was horrible (Stern 2005). And Moritz Schlick, another member of the Circle, criticized Neurath's version of physicalism on philosophical grounds (see Schlick 1932, 1934). Schlick argued that it was implausible to assign physical language and statements any kind of foundational role in epistemology. Presumably one can be mistaken about whether a certain physical object statement is true in a way that one cannot be mistaken about whether a certain observation statement is true. It is doubtful that Neurath would have been overly concerned with this criticism since for him the whole idea that knowledge has a foundation was something to be rejected.

While their influence on other members of the Vienna Circle was limited, both Carnap and Neurath were extremely influential on W.V. Quine, perhaps the most prominent physicalist of the twentieth century. In the 1950s Quine produced a series of works that defended physicalism in something like its current form. In 'The scope and language of science,' for example, Quine starts as follows:

> I am a physical object sitting in a physical world. Some of the forces of this physical world impinge on my surface. Light rays strike my retinas; molecules bombard my eardrums and fingertips. I strike back, emanating concentric airwaves. These waves take the form of a torrent of discourse about tables, people, molecules, light rays, retinas, airwaves, prime numbers, infinite classes, joy and sorrow, good and evil. (1954: 22)

Such passages seem fairly clearly to formulate a version of physicalism, but the philosophical setting that Quine gave physicalism was quite different from that provided by Carnap or Neurath. In particular, for Quine, as for more contemporary philosophers, physicalism is a very general thesis about what the world is and what it is like, rather than a thesis in semantics or epistemology. For Quine, in short, it was a piece of metaphysics.

Quine took physicalism to be a hypothesis about what the world is and what it is like, but the philosophy of philosophy that is associated with physicalism by the standard picture seems to me at least hinted at in Quine rather than developed fully. In *Word and Object* (1960), the book that culminated the series of physicalist articles in the 1950s, Quine did discuss the question—to borrow Price's words—of the place and fate of the notion of *meaning* in a physical world. And the position he ended up with was a negative one that objective sense could not be made out of ordinary semantic notions. (Indeed, Quine's famous skepticism about semantic notions was a major reason for him to reject the linguistic version of physicalism associated with Carnap.) Nevertheless, the general idea that philosophical problems, or at least a very large class of philosophical problems, can be thought of as placement problems doesn't seem to me explicit in Quine. Indeed, in some parts of his writings, Quine veers surprisingly close to the scientific end of Rorty's dilemma mentioned earlier (Quine 1969).

In the early 1960s a number of philosophers who were attracted to Quine's criticism of positivism as well as his physicalism began to formulate the idea that various philosophical problems are best viewed as problems about how to place or find or locate various items in a purely physical world. A particularly frank and clear statement of this position is given by J.J.C. Smart both in *Philosophy and Scientific Realism* and in the article 'Materialism' (1963, 1963a; see also Sellars 1962). Smart opened the book with the statement that "This book is meant as an essay in synthetic philosophy, as the adumbration of a coherent and scientifically plausible world view" (1963: 1). He went on to defend a materialistic conception of nature, and then to articulate a role for philosophy that is very close to the one that we saw in the passage from Price. Smart took himself to be deeply influenced by Quine, and so he was. But what we find in Smart quite explicitly is something we find (or I find, anyway) only implicitly in Quine, viz. the standard picture, the idea that physicalism is a doctrine about the world that we have overwhelming reason to believe, and yet it is prima facie in conflict with the central claims of human life. The task, or at any rate a key task, of philosophy is to resolve this conflict. Smart himself wrote at a time in which many people would have rejected this picture of what philosophy was about. But it seems reasonable to say that since the 1960s the picture, or something like it, has come to dominate not only the way that philosophers think about the world but also in many cases how they think about philosophy.

The sort of philosophy, and the sort of physicalism, that we find in positivists such as Neurath and Carnap is obviously very different from the sort of philosophy, and the sort of physicalism, that we find in post-positivists such as Quine and Smart. But there is also a sense in which they are quite similar, and it is worth having this similarity clearly before us for what follows. For what the linguistic version of physicalism does is provide a condition on something's being a meaningful sentence; that is, something is a meaningful sentence only if it is translatable into a physical language. The project for philosophers who hold this version of physicalism is then to divide sentences into the meaningful and the non-meaningful, with, hopefully, intuitively correct (or at least interesting) results. On the other hand, what the metaphysical version does is provide a condition on something's being a fact; that is, something is a fact just in case it bears the right kind of relation to physical facts. The project for philosophers who hold this version of physicalism is then to divide putative facts into genuine facts and non-facts with, hopefully, intuitively correct (or at least interesting) results. From a certain point of view, therefore, this post-positivist position on philosophy seems to have more in common with positivist thought than is often supposed.

1.8 The standard picture in a nutshell

Drawing together what we have said, the standard picture may be expressed as the conjunction of five theses:

1   Physicalism is true—the *basic thesis*.
2   Physicalism summarizes the picture of the world implicit in the natural sciences—the *interpretative thesis*.
3   It is most rational to believe the picture of the world implicit in the natural sciences, whatever that picture happens to be—the *epistemological thesis*.
4   Physicalism is, prima facie, in conflict with many presuppositions of everyday life—the *conflict thesis*.
5   The way to resolve these conflicts is to propose views about how to interpret the presuppositions of everyday life so that they are compatible with physicalism—the *resolution thesis*.

These claims form a system. The interpretative thesis and the epistemological thesis together articulate a reason to believe the basic thesis. The conflict thesis then articulates a problem for the basic thesis, and the resolution thesis sets out a strategy whereby we might seek to solve the problem. As we have seen, the picture is attractive because it provides a rationale for philosophy itself, and because it suggests that there is some sort of underlying unity in many, but certainly not all, philosophical questions.

It is the standard picture, I think, that provides the answer (or better: the framework for an answer) to one of the three questions we distinguished in the introduction, the question of the significance of physicalism. Physicalism as it appears in the standard picture certainly looks a significant thesis. But of course physicalism would only be significant in this sense if the picture were correct. And is it? Well, that is the question I hope we will be in a position to answer at the end of the book. But we should certainly not rush to an answer. To begin with, we will need to learn a good deal about what physicalism says before we will be in a position to assess the truth of any of the constituent claims of the standard picture. So it is to that interpretative question we will turn next.

Summary

In this chapter, we have seen that, for philosophers who hold what I called 'the standard picture' there is a conflict or apparent conflict between physicalism, on the one hand, and many of the presuppositions of everyday life on the other. And we have also looked briefly at the attractiveness of the standard picture and (even more briefly) at its origins in the physicalism of Carnap, Neurath, Quine, and Smart.

Recommended reading

For classic presentations of philosophical problems as placement problems involving physicalism, see Smart 1963 and Sellars 1962; later, more sophisticated developments of the idea can be found in Lewis 1986b and Jackson 1998. A paper written from a different perspective but which is nonetheless in agreement with the general idea is Price 1997, from which I took the quotation about the "M-worlds" above. For physicalism as it was expressed by the positivists, see Carnap 1959, original date of publication 1932/33, and Neurath 1931a. The best place for Quine's view is the opening chapter of Quine 1960; see also Friedman 1975. A paper which discusses physicalism and connects it both to Quine and to Neurath is Field 1972.

2

FORM AND ALTERNATIVES

2.1 Introduction

The initial claim of the standard picture is this: physicalism is true. But what is physicalism exactly?

You might think that the answer to this question is easy. Physicalism is the thesis that everything is physical. Since we normally take ourselves to understand what 'everything' means, and what 'physical' means, we should easily enough understand what 'everything is physical' means. But things are not so simple. For one thing—this point will emerge in detail in later chapters—it is far from clear what 'physical' means in the context of physicalism. And even before we get to the question of what 'physical' means, there is the prior question of what 'everything' means. The word 'everything' is a universal quantifier, and so another way to put the question is to ask what the intended application of this quantifier is: every *what* thing is physical exactly? So I want in this chapter to begin our discussion of the interpretation question—the question of what physicalism means or is—by examining this aspect of the issue. As we will see, while the statement 'everything is physical' is fine as a rough and ready slogan, it needs to be replaced with something structurally more sophisticated in order to provide a clear view of our topic.

2.2 Unrestricted quantification

Some philosophers think that the phrase 'everything' may be used in an unrestricted sense according to which it means (to put it a bit roughly) *absolutely* everything: every thing in the entire world (or worlds) whether abstract or concrete, property or particular, animal, vegetable or mineral. The sort of example used to motivate this reading is a sentence like 'everything is self-identical.' It seems reasonable to suppose that absolutely everything that exists is identical to itself; hence, one might think, here the quantifier is being used in an absolutely unrestricted sense.

Actually, even examples like this one are subject to dispute; it is a controversial issue whether 'everything' has or even could have this interpretation in English or any other natural language (see e.g. Rayo and Uzquiano 2006). But we need not enter this controversy here. Rather, I want to ask, assuming that such an unrestricted sense is available, whether the term 'everything' in 'everything is physical' *should* be interpreted as having that sense. The suggestion that it does permits us to formulate the first of many formulations of physicalism that we will consider in this book. According to this formulation:

(1) Physicalism is true if and only if absolutely everything whatsoever is physical.

Should we adopt this formulation? That is, is physicalism the thesis that everything is physical where 'everything is physical' applies to absolutely everything, just as 'everything is self-identical' does or seems to?

Well, the first thing to say here is that if we do interpret physicalism in this way it is an exceedingly strong thesis. One way to make this point is to consider the number two. This is something that exists, or at least exists according to many philosophers. Hence, if the statement 'everything is physical' applied to anything whatsoever, and if this were what physicalism meant, then physicalism would be true only if the number two is physical. But do physicalists really want to say that the number two is physical? It would seem initially odd to suppose so. Certainly the number two is not physical if by this we mean something like an ordinary physical object that we might in principle bump into or see or manipulate with our hands.

One might respond to this that examples involving numbers are hard to adjudicate because it is so difficult to think philosophically about numbers at all. Moreover, as we will see ourselves in the following chapters, there are ways to understand the concept of the physical—roughly, ways that prioritize physical theory over physical objects—that might permit even the number two to be physical. Fair enough, but the key point about (1), i.e. that it renders physicalism exceedingly strong, can be made with less controversial examples. Take the US Supreme Court. This is something that exists, or at any rate exists according to many philosophers. So again, on the interpretation we are considering, physicalism would be true only if the Supreme Court was physical. But do physicalists really want to say that the US Supreme Court is physical? Again, it sounds odd to suppose so. The Supreme Court is not a physical object in the ordinary sense, nor has it anything much to do with physics. It seems odd, to put the point a different way, to interpret physicalism so that a physicalist might be refuted by the existence and nature of the Supreme Court.

Of course you might dig your heels in even at this point. "If physicalism is true," you might say, "then either the US Supreme Court is physical after all, or it does not exist!" However, while this position is certainly possible, it is not on the face of it a very attractive one for a physicalist to take, and this is particularly so when we notice that a different response is available. This different response is to say that what the example of the court shows is not that physicalism is false but that (1) is false, and that 'everything is physical' should not be interpreted as having the unrestricted reading, or, rather, should not be interpreted this way if it is intended as a formulation of physicalism. Instead it should be interpreted as having a restricted reading of some kind. It should be interpreted, that is, as saying, not that everything whatsoever is physical, but rather that everything in a certain relevant or salient class is physical. And in fact, this is usually how one talks in ordinary English. If I am packing the car for a weekend away, I might come inside and say 'everything's in the boot.' But presumably I don't mean that absolutely everything whatever is in the boot. (The number two is not in the boot, for example, nor is the US Supreme Court.) Rather what I mean is something like 'all of our bags are in the boot' or 'all of the stuff that I wanted to pack is in the boot' or more generally 'everything of a certain salient class is in the boot.' Likewise, when the physicalist says 'everything is physical,' what is intended is not that absolutely everything is physical, but rather that everything of a certain salient class is physical.

2.3 Restriction to particulars

But what class? How, in particular, should we restrict the quantifier in the phrase 'everything is physical' so as to obtain a reasonable formulation of physicalism? The next proposal I want to consider is that 'everything is physical' should be interpreted not on the model of what 'everything is self-identical' means (or seems to mean) but rather on the model of what something like 'everything is red' means. What 'everything is red' means or seems to mean is that every concrete thing is red. This suggests a rendering of physicalism as follows:

(2) Physicalism is true if and only if every concrete particular is physical.

Before going on to assess the plausibility of (2) as a formulation of physi-calism, however, we need to be clear on what a concrete particular is.

When philosophers talk in general about particulars (or individuals—I will use these phrases interchangeably), they often have in mind a contrast with properties. Particulars are things like computers, desks, the Supreme Court, the number two, and so on; properties are things like being red, being square, being powerful, being odd, and so on. So, for example, my computer is a particular that has or instantiates the property of being owned by a university; the Supreme Court is also a particular, but does not instan-tiate this property, for no university owns the court. The precise way to characterize the particular/property distinction is a difficult matter, but need not concern us. For our purposes it suffices to say that something is a property only if it is capable of being instantiated, e.g. in a particular or in another property, while something is a particular only if it is not capable of being instantiated in this sense. There are many things that might be true of my computer: it might exist, it might be red, and it might be owned by a university. But one thing that cannot be true of it is that it is instantiated, for it is not the kind of thing that can be instantiated. By contrast, any property, such as being red or being owned by a university, is the kind of thing that can be instantiated.

So much for the distinction between particulars and properties—what is it to say of a particular that it is concrete? When philosophers talk of concrete particulars, they often have in mind a contrast with abstract particulars. The precise characterization of this distinction is also a difficult matter, but again will not concern us. For our purposes it suffices to say that if we consider the class of particulars there seems to be a division between those that have a (perhaps rough) location in space and time and those that do not. The number two, if it is exists, is presumably not located in space and time (where would it be precisely?) but my computer, if it exists, presumably is. What marks a particular as a concrete particular is that it is of the second sort, and so has a location in space and time, while what marks a particular as an abstract particular is that it does not.

In restricting attention to concrete particulars, therefore, a proponent of (2) is directing our attention, first, away from properties and to particulars, and second, to particulars of a certain sort, viz. the concrete sort. But how plausible is it to say that physicalism is true just in case every particular of that sort is physical?

The answer is 'not plausible'. The problem with (1) was that it is too strong, but the problem with (2) is that it is too weak. It is too weak because it does not rule out all forms of dualism. Dualism, especially in the eighteenth century, meant a commitment to the existence of a soul, which, for example, might go to heaven when the body dies. Traditionally, the soul was conceived of as a special sort of particular, a substance, where a substance is a particular capable of independent existence. Now (2) certainly has physicalism being inconsistent with the existence of souls, since (2) has physicalism ruling out the existence of non-physical particulars. So (2) might do as a statement of the physicalism (or materialism) that, for example, the eighteenth-century French materialist Baron d'Holbach intended. But dualists these days often do not believe in the existence of a soul (for an exception see Swinburne 1997). What they believe rather is that physical objects like bodies have non-physical properties. This is often put by saying that contemporary dualists are often property dualists rather than substance dualists. (One might also have said property dualists rather than particular dualists.) But the problem is that (2) is quite consistent with the truth of property dualism. It says that every particular is physical, but it leaves open that some particulars may have non-physical properties. So (2) will not do as a formulation of physicalism.

2.4 Restriction to properties

If (2) won't do, can we adjust it? The next proposal I want to consider replaces (2) with (3):

(3) Physicalism is true if and only if every property is physical.

This is a definite step in the right direction. For one thing the property dualist will clearly want to deny that the right-hand side of (3) is true: the property dualist will say that there are some properties of people that are non-physical; the right-hand side of (3) denies this. Moreover, even the substance dualist, i.e. the dualist who thinks that there are non-physical mental objects such as souls, will also think that such objects have non-physical properties. (For example, a soul will at least have the property of *being a soul*, and surely this is a non-physical property if souls are non-physical.) So they will want to deny the right-hand side of (3) as well. In short, it looks as if formulating physicalism in terms of properties is precisely the thing to do if we want to have a thesis that makes sense of contemporary disputes about physicalism.

However, while (3) is a step in the right direction, nevertheless it like (1) represents physicalism as too strong. For one thing, according to many philosophers there are uninstantiated properties. For example, consider the property of being the Democratic President of the US in 2001. This seems like a perfectly good property for a person to have. Al Gore nearly had it, and would have had it if things had gone slightly differently. As it turns out, however, Gore doesn't have it, and in fact nobody does. So the property is uninstantiated. On the other hand, while it is uninstantiated, it nevertheless exists or at least exists according to many philosophers. But now consider the property of having a soul. If there are no souls, then the property of having a soul is uninstantiated, just like the property of being the Democratic President in 2001. But presumably the property of having a soul still exists, or, at any rate, would exist according to those philosophers who believe in uninstantiated properties. But is it plausible to suppose that this property is physical? Surely not, but if (3) is the formulation of physicalism, it must be physical if physicalism is to be true.

One might seek to avoid this problem by restricting attention still further: not simply to properties as such but to instantiated properties. On this proposal (3) goes over into:

(4) Physicalism is true if and only if every instantiated property is physical.

But (4) is still too strong, and for reasons that have already emerged. Consider again the US Supreme Court and consider some property of it, e.g. its having the power to prescribe rules of procedure to be followed by lower courts. If (4) is physicalism, and if physicalism is true, this property is physical. Now as before it is possible to imagine a physicalist who is happy about this but, again, on the face of things, it is very implausible that a property such as this is a physical property: just as the court itself is a social or legal object rather than a physical one, so too its powers over lower courts are social or legal properties rather than physical ones.

2.5 Fundamental properties

The idea that we should restrict attention to properties seems like a good idea, but the previous proposal is still too strong. An obvious move here is to restrict attention still further to instantiated properties of a certain kind— but what kind? It is clearly no good to talk about properties of the *physical* kind, because then physicalism becomes the thesis that every instantiated property of the physical kind is physical. But the idea that every physical property is physical is an analytic truth, and physicalism, even if true, is not supposed to be an analytic truth.

At this point, it is tempting to reach for the notion of a metaphysically fundamental property in something like the sense described and defended by David Lewis. While the notion of a fundamental property occurs a lot in Lewis's philosophical writings, here is a particularly vivid passage:

> This world, or any possible world, consists of things which instantiate fundamental properties and which, in pairs or triples or ..., instantiate fundamental relations. Few properties are fundamental: the property of being a club or a tub or a pub, for instance, is an unnatural gerrymander, a condition satisfied by miscellaneous things in miscellaneous ways. A fundamental, or 'perfectly natural,' property is the extreme opposite. Its instances share exactly some aspect of their intrinsic nature. Likewise for relations. I hold, as an a priori principle, that every contingent truth must be made true, somehow, by the pattern of coinstantiation of fundamental properties and relations. The whole truth about the world, including the mental part of the world, supervenes on this pattern. If two possible worlds were exactly isomorphic in their patterns of coinstantiation of fundamental properties and relations, they would be exactly alike simpliciter. (Lewis 1994: 292)

We might bring out the basic idea here by thinking of fundamental properties as the ingredients of the world. Imagine God as a divine cake maker: to make the cake of the world what he would have to do would be to arrange the basic ingredients in the right way, and everything else would follow immediately. (The theological metaphor in these contexts is due to Kripke 1980.)

Suppose now we permit ourselves the notion of a fundamental property in something like this sense; then a version of physicalism like the following becomes possible:

(5) Physicalism is true if and only if every instantiated fundamental property is physical.

This idea is clearly better than the previous ones. Consider again the property of the Supreme Court considered earlier, its power to prescribe rules of procedure. Since this property is (a) instantiated and (b) is (plausibly) not a physical property, it entails that physicalism is false if (4) is true. But it does not entail that physicalism is false if (5) is true. Having the power to prescribe rules of procedure is not a candidate for a fundamental property in Lewis's sense.

On the assumption that there are fundamental properties, therefore, it is tempting to say that (5) or something like it is the statement of physicalism. Still, the assumption that there are fundamental properties looks speculative in at least two ways. In the first place, it seems empirically speculative. It is natural to read Lewis in the passage we quoted as saying that the world (i.e. our world) has a fundamental physical level which physics either has told us about or at least will tell us about. However, it may well be that it is an open scientific question whether there is a fundamental level in this sense (Schaffer 2003). If so, we do not want to define physicalism as entailing that there is a fundamental level in this sense. In the second place, it is metaphysically speculative. Lewis says he believes as an a priori principle "that every contingent truth must be made true, somehow, by the pattern of coinstantiation of fundamental properties and relations," and tells us also that "few properties are fundamental." Since he presumably means that this is (according to him) true at every possible world, what he is saying is that, for any possible world at all, every truth is made true by a pattern of co-instantiation of a small group of fundamental properties. But imagine you are a philosopher who doesn't hold this; for example, imagine you are a philosopher who thinks that at least some possible worlds are such that the objects in them instantiate many, rather than few, fundamental properties, and so it is not the case at such worlds that the contingent truths there are made true by a few fundamental properties. It is quite unclear how to resolve this disagreement between you and Lewis. After all, why should it be true that there is a very small set of properties that make true all the contingent truths of every world at all? To put the point another way: the denial of what Lewis says is an a priori principle is not a contradiction; i.e. we could deny what he says without contradicting ourselves. Why then believe what he says?

2.6 Metaphysical necessitation

The notion of a fundamental property might be speculative but it is certainly useful; indeed this is one of Lewis's reasons for defending the notion. And we ourselves will sometimes use the notion in the discussion to follow. But it remains the case that, since a commitment to fundamental properties is speculative, it would be desirable if we had a formulation of physicalism that proceeded without it.

The way forward here is to look back at (4):

(4) Physicalism is true if and only if every instantiated property is physical.

We noted earlier that (4) is attractive but also too strong. We therefore examined one way to adjust it, viz. to restrict attention to fundamental properties.

But there is also a different way to adjust (4). In general, if you have a thesis of the form 'everything is F' which is for one reason or another too strong, it is quite natural to weaken it so that what it says is that 'everything is either F or G,' where G is some property distinct from F. This move is certainly available in the case at hand. The problem for (4) is that it has physicalism requiring that certain mathematical or legal properties are physical. But even if physicalism does not require that, it *does* require that such properties bear a certain relation to physical properties. To put it differently, if physicalism is true there must be some relation that every instantiated property bears to a physical property. Suppose, just to frame this proposal, we name this relation 'R.' Now the following version of physicalism comes into view:

(6) Physicalism is true if and only if every instantiated property is either physical or bears a certain relation R to an instantiated physical property.

This idea avoids the problems we have been discussing. The property of having the power to prescribe rules of procedure is not a physical property but it might bear a certain relation to a physical property. So (6) avoids the problem about the Supreme Court. On the other hand, (6) does not

appeal to the notion of a fundamental property, and so avoids the speculative nature of the suggestion that there are fundamental properties.

But of course, while (6) might avoid these problems, it faces the obvious
problem that it does not tell us what the relation R is. As we will see later
(in Chapter 6), different philosophers have made different suggestions here
about what R could be: metaphysical necessitation, supervenience, realization, and others. For most of our discussion in this book, however, I am
going to make the working assumption that the relation is the first of these:
metaphysical necessitation, or necessitation for short. On the assumption,
therefore, that necessitation is the relation R that appears in (6), we can
replace (6) with (7):

(7) Physicalism is true if and only if every instantiated property is either physical
     or else is necessitated by some instantiated physical property.

Like (6), (7) avoids the problems we have been discussing. The property of
having the power to prescribe rules of procedure is not a physical property
but might nevertheless be necessitated by a physical property; at any rate we
have at present no argument that it is not. On the other hand, like (6), (7)
does not appeal to the notion of a fundamental property.

The assumption that R is the relation of metaphysical necessitation is at
this point just that: an assumption. It will need to be discussed and defended
in detail later. But it is also a reasonable assumption at this point, for at least
three reasons: first, we need to focus on some relation or other just to fix
ideas; second, the precise choice of relation here will not affect the argu-
mentation in Chapters 3 to 5 or indeed in most of the book; third, as I
will argue in Chapters 6 to 8, necessitation is a rather plausible assumption
about what the relation is: even if the relation is not necessitation, it will be
something that entails it.

Before we adopt this assumption at all, however, we need first to understand it. What is the relation of necessitation and what is metaphysical about
it? Well, what I have in mind here is the notion made prominent by Kripke in
Naming and Necessity (1980). In this sense, one property F necessitates another
property G just in case, necessarily, if F is instantiated, then G is instantiated;
equivalently, if F is instantiated then G must be instantiated. This notion of
necessity here is commonly spelled out in philosophy in terms of possible
worlds. So, for example, the property of being red necessitates the property
of being colored because, in all possible worlds, if the first is instantiated,
i.e. if something is red, then the second is too, i.e. something is colored.

Likewise, the property of being red necessitates the property of being either red or square because in all possible worlds if the first is instantiated the second is.

The key phrase in thinking about metaphysical necessity is 'in *all* possible worlds.' The point is not merely that in *some* possible worlds, or in all possible worlds *of a certain class*, if F is instantiated, G is. The claim is meant to extend to any world at all. To put the point another way, if F metaphysically necessitates G, there is no possibility at all in which F is instantiated but G is not. Again: if being red metaphysically necessitates being colored, then there is no possibility in which being red is instantiated and yet being colored is not.

Now, often when we talk about possibility and necessity, it is not plausible that what we say could be explicated in terms of *all* possible worlds, and so it is not plausible that we are talking about metaphysical necessity. For example, if I say, 'It is impossible that I buy a house with a harbor view,' I am presumably not saying that in *no* possible world could I do this. Of course it is metaphysically possible that academics are better paid than they actually are, or that houses with harbor views lose their cachet. What then do I mean? The most natural thing to say is that what I mean is that it is financially impossible that I do, where, in turn, this means something like 'In no possible world where the financial facts are roughly as they are could I buy a house with a harbor view.'

The point here is connected to the one mentioned earlier about quantification: in ordinary talk, we usually restrict the domain of quantification in various ways. So too, in ordinary talk about necessity and possibility we usually restrict attention to possible worlds of a certain sort. But this is not to deny that in some contexts (for example, certain philosophical contexts) it might be that we have an unrestricted notion in mind, and so have metaphysical necessity in mind. In some contexts, that is, what might be intended is not a restricted class of possible worlds but any possible world whatsoever. Such at any rate is the suggestion implicit in the idea of metaphysical necessitation.

Turning back now to (7), what (7) says is that, while various legal or numerical properties might not be physical, if physicalism is true they must nevertheless be necessitated by the physical; that is, if physicalism is true there must be some physical properties which necessitate legal or numerical properties. Indeed, if (7) is true, and if physicalism is true, then every instantiated property at all must be either physical or necessitated by the physical.

2.7 Commentary

I began this chapter by noting that while 'everything is physical' is fine so far as it goes, it would need to be replaced with something more sophisticated in order to provide a clear view of our topic. For most of our subsequent discussion (7), or its right-hand side, will be that more sophisticated thing. So, for most of our discussion, physicalism will be the thesis that every instantiated property is either a physical property or else is necessitated by some instantiated physical property.

By itself, this does not answer the interpretation question. We still need to be told what a physical property is, and we still need to defend and explain the assumption that physicalism is stated in terms of necessitation. We will come to all this in subsequent chapters. What (7) does do however is provide us with the logical form of the thesis of physicalism. We need now to interpret that form.

Before turning to this issue in earnest, however, I have two further tasks in the remainder of this chapter. First, I need to make a number of clarifying comments on what has already been said. (These points raise questions of a somewhat technical sort; if you are happy with the discussion so far, I recommend skipping them.) Second, I want to compare physicalism with its rivals.

2.7.1 Do properties exist?

First, isn't it problematic to assume that properties exist in the way that I have been assuming they do? After all, there is a big traditional dispute in philosophy over the question of whether properties exist. One side in this dispute—the nominalist—holds that they don't; the other side—the realist—holds they do. Presumably, then, the nominalist will agree that trivially every instantiated property is necessitated by some physical property—for the simple reason that there are no properties at all! In what follows, however, I am going to set nominalism aside. True, if one is a nominalist who denies that properties of any sort exist one will not be able to formulate physicalism in the way that I have. But if one is a nominalist one will not be able to formulate a lot of things. The fact is that reference to properties (characteristics, attributes, and so on) is routine not only in philosophy and science but in ordinary talk as well. Nominalists are obliged to make some sense of that sort of talk. Either they will succeed, in which case they will be able to adapt what they say to the special case of physicalism; or they will not, in which case how to formulate physicalism is the least of their problems.

2.7.2 *Abundant and sparse properties*

Second, even if one sets nominalism aside, it remains true that there are (at least) two very different conceptions of what it is to be a property, and it might be thought unclear which notion we have in mind (cf. Lewis 1983). According to what is sometimes called the abundant conception of a property, for any set of things at all, there is a property that every member of that set has. So on this conception, the property of being a club or a tub or a pub (to borrow Lewis's example in the passage I quoted above) is a perfectly good property, since there is a set of things that have this property. On the other hand, according to what is sometimes called the sparse conception, properties are by definition Lewis's fundamental properties, i.e. properties conceived of as fundamental constituents of reality. Which conception is in operation here? The answer is that for us what is at issue is the abundant conception, unless otherwise stated. So in particular, when I say 'every instantiated property is necessitated by some instantiated physical property' what is at issue is the abundant conception of a property. For one thing, only then would the thesis have anything like the generality that it is intended as having. For another, the whole point of appealing to this formulation was to avoid the idea of a fundamental property, and this means avoiding the idea of properties on the sparse conception.

2.7.3 *Properties and relations*

Third, in emphasizing properties I am not de-emphasizing relations. When we speak of properties we typically have in mind one-place properties, such as being bent or being red. But we might generalize this idea to two-place (or in general n-place properties for any n) such as the property of being two feet to the left of or the property of giving, as in 'John gave a ball to Mary.' In other words, a relation can be conceived of as simply a property of a special sort. If that is so, then our account will apply to relations just as much as to properties.

2.7.4 *Properties, states of affairs, and truths*

Fourth, one might think that the emphasis on properties (even understood as abundant properties and relations) is under-motivated. Perhaps it is true that any version of physicalism that restricts itself to *particulars* is going to be too weak. But why jump directly to properties? For example, some philosophers suppose that physicalism is a thesis not about properties but about states of affairs, where a state of affairs consists in an object's having a property, or two (or more) objects standing in a relation; for them, it is the thesis that every state of affairs is necessitated by some physical state of affairs, where for one state of affairs to be necessitated by another means that necessarily if the first obtains the second does too. Still other philosophers suppose that physicalism is a thesis not about properties but about truths (or, if this is different, about facts); for them, it is the thesis that every truth is necessitated by some physical truth, where for one truth to be necessitated by another means that necessarily, if the first is true, so is the second. Both the state of affairs formulation and the truth formulation do not limit themselves to particulars—why then prefer the property formulation to these? My reason for focusing on property as opposed to states of affairs or truths is really procedural rather than anything else; some of the issues about what it is to be physical that I will focus on come out somewhat easier (at least I find them easier) if one focuses on properties as opposed to states of affairs or truths. But I have no doubts that one could conduct the discussion in either way. The important point is physicalism is not limited to a thesis about particulars—if it were, the basic questions about physicalism could not be raised.

2.7.5 *Properties and laws*

Fifth, one might think it strange that the formulation of physicalism I have adopted makes no mention of scientific or physical laws. Presumably, we could imagine a world which is exactly like this one in terms of the properties that are instantiated there but differs from this world in terms of other properties—and the reason is that the laws that govern this imagined world are quite different from the laws that govern our world. Isn't it then important to include reference to the physical laws in addition to the physical properties? One might respond to this by agreeing to include a reference to the physical laws in any statement of physicalism that we will operate with. But another way to respond is to say that in a sense we have already included reference to laws, just by being very relaxed about what a property consists in; that is, by adopting the abundant conception mentioned above. On this conception, if a law L obtains at a world, then a property that is instantiated at that world is being such that L obtains.

2.7.6 *Properties and particulars*

Sixth, one might think it strange that our basic formulation of physicalism makes no mention of the particulars which have the properties in question. Presumably when we talk about properties being instantiated we have in mind the idea that there are particulars that instantiate them. So for example we are imagining people being in pain or feeling an itch, and again people (or their brains) instantiating various physical properties. But physicalism as we have set it out so far makes no mention of this. However, while this is so I don't think it will affect the discussion that we will have to any great extent, and for the most part I will ignore it. One reason for this is the distinction between substance dualism and property dualism mentioned before. Our focus in what follows will be on property dualism rather than substance dualism, and to keep the contrast between property dualism and physicalism clear it is sufficient to focus on properties. Another reason is that the abundant notion of property that I have adopted makes it quite easy to translate talk of particulars into talk of properties since, for any particular there is the property of being that particular.

2.7.7 *One property or many?*

Seventh, one might think it unlikely that, if physicalism is true, there is *one* physical property that is such that if it is instantiated then the Supreme Court has various powers. Presumably there is a huge series of properties each of which has to be instantiated. However, it is no part of the idea behind (7) to deny this. Perhaps the easiest way to see this is to repeat the point that we are being very relaxed about what a property is; again, that is the point of adopting the abundant conception. The physical property that is such that if it is instantiated the Supreme Court has various powers might be very complicated indeed, and may include reference to various physical laws obtaining. Nevertheless it is still one property.

2.7.8 *Two ways to simplify*

Finally, (7) says that physicalism is the thesis that every instantiated property *either* is a physical property *or else* is necessitated by an instantiated physical property. But there are two ways in which this might be simplified. First, the 'either is a physical property' part is strictly speaking redundant, and you may have noticed that I have left it off already in our discussion. To be a physical property is just to *be identical to* a physical property, and if a property F is identical to a physical property G then of course G necessitates F. Second, I will often leave implicit that we are talking about *instantiated* properties rather than properties whether or not they are instantiated.

2.8 Alternatives

Physicalism is the thesis that every abundant instantiated property (or relation) is either physical or is necessitated by a (perhaps hugely complicated) abundant instantiated physical property or relation—for short that every property is necessitated by a physical property. What then are the alternatives to physicalism?

2.8.1 Idealism

As I noted in the introduction, a thesis that was dominant in the period before physicalism was idealism. Idealism is not much in fashion today (see, however, Foster 1982), but it does function as one of the main alternatives to physicalism. Like physicalism, idealism may be expressed in slogan form as 'everything is mental,' and, again like physicalism, the idealist might initially be read as saying that 'every instantiated property is necessitated by a mental property' or, on the assumption that there are fundamental properties, that every fundamental property is mental.

Now, actually such a claim is not by itself inconsistent with physicalism, for the reason that it is possible for a property to be both mental and physical (cf. Lewis 1983). For example, consider what is called in philosophy of mind the 'mind–brain identity theory.' On this view, the property of being in pain is identical to some physical property—the property of having c-fibres firing, to adopt the usual (unrealistic) example. Now consider the property of being in pain (a.k.a. the property of having c-fibres firing). Is it a mental property? Surely yes—being in pain is a paradigmatic example of a mental property. Is it a physical property? Again: surely yes—the whole point of the identity theory is to identify a mental property with a physical property. So this property at least is both mental and physical. But now consider the possibility that every instantiated property is necessitated by some property of this kind, i.e. the kind we just noticed being in pain is if the identity theory is true: both mental and physical. The possibility might be far-fetched but it does not seem impossible. But now let us ask: is physicalism or idealism true in this case? The answer would seem to be that both are true, or at any rate that both are true as we have so far been developing them. So what we have here is an argument that physicalism and idealism are not incompatible.

In my experience, this argument provokes two different reactions. The first accepts the argument, saying it shows only that it is not contradictory to suppose that both physicalism and idealism are true. Of course, a proponent of this reaction might go on to say, physicalists do in *fact* deny idealism—by asserting that every property is necessitated by a non-mental property—just as idealists do in *fact* deny physicalism, by asserting that every property is necessitated by a non-physical property. But in both cases this is strictly speaking a further commitment, not something that follows from the very meaning of the theses to which they committed.

The second reaction insists that idealism and physicalism must be understood in such a way that they are mutually exclusive, and so the 'possibility' in which they are both true must be illusory. In some ways, this second reaction is the more natural one. However, setting out this reaction in detail proves extremely difficult. In particular, the most natural way to develop this second reaction is to suggest that the contrast between the mental and the physical is somehow built into the very meaning of the terms. On this view, a physical property is one that is non-mental, while a mental property is one that is non-physical. This move certainly does result in idealism and physicalism being mutually exclusive. But unfortunately it also makes the mind–brain identity theory obviously contradictory! If not being mental is part of what it is to be physical then how could being in pain be both mental and physical? Of course, a lot of philosophers think that the mind–brain identity theory is *false*, but very few regard it as contradictory, and certainly not as obviously so.

2.8.2 Dualism

One way to deny physicalism is to say that every property is necessitated by a property that isn't physical; another is to say that *not* every property is necessitated by a physical property, i.e. that some properties are and some properties aren't. That is the position of the traditional opponent of physicalism, the dualist. In particular, dualists say that some *psychological* properties are not necessitated by anything physical.

Dualism may be developed in various forms. One distinction, as we have already seen, is that between substance dualism and property dualism. Another distinction, which we will turn to in Chapter 8, is the distinction between a necessitarian dualist and a more standard sort of dualist. A third distinction, which we will turn to more fully in Chapter 11, is between the interactionist, the epiphenomenalist, and the over-determinationist dualist. As we will see, the interactionist dualist says that mental events and properties play a causal role in the world just as physical events and properties do. The epiphenomenalist denies that mental events and properties have any effects at all, or at any rate any physical effects—the epiphenomenalist denies the causal efficacy of the mental. And the over-determinationist dualist says that mental events, when they do cause physical events, are always parts of causal sequences that involve what philosophers call over-determination—roughly the idea is that physical events can sometimes have two quite independent causes, a mental cause and a physical cause.

However exactly it is developed, dualism is traditionally opposed to physicalism, and indeed the two are often construed as being in some kind of titanic struggle. But in fact they have a considerable amount in common. Physicalists hold that every property is necessitated by a physical property. Dualists of the standard sort don't hold that because they think that some properties, psychological properties, are not necessitated by any physical property. Nevertheless, dualists of the standard sort hold that physicalism is nearly or mostly true. With the exception of the psychological realm, they might be physicalists. Indeed, this is an important fact about the contrast between physicalism and dualism of a standard sort. I have been emphasizing the connection between physicalism and the standard picture. But suppose now that one tweaked physicalism slightly so that it is mostly true. On this sort of position, large parts of the standard picture would remain. It is for this reason, I believe, that in contemporary philosophy you often find dualists and physicalists on the same side on matters of philosophical method, even if not on the question of whether physicalism (or dualism) is true. And it is for this reason that philosophers seem to shift their position from physicalism to dualism (and vice versa) without shifting their basic philosophical outlook. (As I read them this is true in the cases of Jackson and of Kim, whose shifts of position I noted in the introduction: see Jackson 1998 and Kim 2007.) The underlying point is that physicalism and dualism of the standard sort agree on many things. Logically speaking their disagreement is like the disagreement between a physicalist who thinks that there are four fundamental properties and a physicalist who thinks that there are five.

I have been talking of dualists of the standard sort. However, it is possible to be a dualist of a non-standard sort too. In particular, while dualists of a standard sort hold that the properties not necessitated by the physical are psychological, it is in principle possible to hold this of other sorts of properties too. For example, vitalists in biology held that there are biological properties not necessitated by the physical. In the eighteenth century it was held that some facts about chemistry would be of this sort. And some contemporary philosophers have held the view that facts about colors are of this sort—this position is sometimes called primitivism about colors. All of these views share a basic structure with dualism because they all agree that while some fundamental properties are physical, not all are. While I will talk mostly of dualism in this classic sense, it is important to note that the view might be developed in these other ways too.

Finally, the suggestion that the basic strategy of the dualist can be extended from psychological properties to biological and chemical properties and to colors as well, has a logical extension, which I will call 'pluralism.' The pluralist extends the basic strategy of dualism to all, or at least many, instantiated properties. So, according to pluralism, many properties are neither physical properties nor necessitated by any physical properties. This position too might be classified as a sort of dualism, but of course it is very remote from dualism of the standard sort.

2.8.3 Coherentism

The positions I have described so far—physicalism, dualism (including pluralism), and idealism—all have something in common. All have ambitions to describe absolutely everything, or at least every instantiated property, in the world. But there is an important kind of fourth position, which I will call coherentism, which regards this aspiration to completeness with extreme skepticism. According to this view, there are different accounts of the world, and it is a mistake to try to decide between them. The problem with the standard positions is that they all make this mistake.

In *Ways of Worldmaking*, Nelson Goodman, one of the most prominent coherentists of the twentieth century, writes, "many different world-versions are of independent interest and importance, without any requirement or presumption of reducibility to a single base" (1978: 4). The coherentist, he continues,

> far from being anti-scientific, accepts the sciences at full value. His typical adversary is the monopolistic materialist or physicalist who maintains that one system, physics, is preeminent and all-inclusive such that every version must eventually be reduced to it or rejected as false or meaningless. If all

right versions could somehow be reduced to one and only one, that one might with some semblance of plausibility be regarded as the only truth about the only world. But the evidence for such reducibility is negligible, and even the claim is nebulous since physics itself is fragmentary and unstable and the kind and consequence of reduction envisaged are vague. (How do you go about reducing Constable's or James Joyce's world-view to physics?) (1978: 4–5)

In this passage we see a number of themes that we will go into in more detail later on. One is whether physicalism requires reducibility of the sort Goodman describes; we will come back to this in Chapter 8; another concerns the 'instability' of physics, a theme we will look at directly in Chapter 5, and in a different way in both Chapters 3 and 4. But for the moment what I want to focus on is Goodman's suggested contrast between the physicalist, according to whom physicalism is the 'only truth about the only world' and the coherentist, according to whom there are many truths about many worlds.

In fact this contrast is somewhat obscure. In my view, the best way to make sense of Goodman's coherentism is to see it as involving what philosophers usually call a 'coherence theory' of truth; indeed, this is my excuse for using the label. (Goodman himself uses the word 'pluralism' for his own position, but since I have just used that for a different view, I will not follow him in this.) According to a coherence theory of truth, a proposition is true if and only if it is part of a coherent set of propositions (or, on some developments of the view, a coherent set of propositions that one might hold in the ideal limit of inquiry). Since there can be more than one such set of propositions, the coherence theory permits, but does not require, the possibility that a proposition might be true with respect to one set of propositions but not true with respect to another. Hence it permits, but again does not require, the idea that there are various different world versions.

But if that is what coherentism is, Goodman's contrast between it and physicalism is elusive. For physicalism is not a theory of truth! In particular physicalism is strictly speaking consistent both with the denial of the coherence theory and its assertion. Of course, some physicalists—perhaps even most physicalists—might combine their view with a denial of the coherence theory of truth. For such physicalists it is certainly hard to see how they would be friendly to coherentism. On the other hand, it is perfectly possible to combine physicalism with a commitment to a coherence theory of truth; indeed, Neurath himself, the person who introduced the word 'physicalism,' is perhaps best interpreted as doing just this. On such a view, physicalism is true for the reason that it is part of a coherent set of propositions that one might hold in the ideal limit of enquiry. Of course, it might be that dualism is also true in this sense, which certainly sounds odd. But the oddity here is a consequence of the coherence theory of truth, and has nothing in particular to do with physicalism or dualism *per se*.

One might reply on Goodman's behalf that while this might be true in theory, it is not true in practice; in practice, that is, all physicalists deny the coherence theory. As we have just seen this is probably false—witness Neurath. But be that as it may, it remains true that, while some philosophers such as Goodman contrast physicalism with coherentism, and while we can make sense of what they say, the contrast here is nevertheless quite unlike the contrast between physicalism and dualism or idealism. Indeed, the point that I have just made about physicalism—that it may be associated with any theory of truth at all—also holds good for dualism and idealism. What is true is that traditionally the dispute between these theories plays itself out against the background of a particular theory of truth, or rather, against the background of the tacit denial of a particular theory of truth. But that does not mean that there is any internal connection between these theories and theories of truth.

2.8.4 Naturalistic platonism

What makes coherentism attractive is that it proposes a way to avoid the apparently endless metaphysical debates represented by the traditional alternatives of dualism, materialism, and idealism. On the other hand, what makes it unattractive is precisely its commitment to a coherence theory. If you hold a theory of truth according to which there could be two incompatible but true sets of propositions, it is hard to avoid the objection that what you are talking about is not truth any longer but something else. So it is desirable to articulate a further position that, like coherentism, offers an alternative to the standard options of idealism, dualism, and physicalism, but unlike coherentism operates without a coherence theory of truth. The fourth and final alternative to physicalism I will consider is just that. There is no standard name for a position like this, so I will call it 'naturalistic platonism.'

Earlier I considered the possibility that a property might be both mental and physical. As we saw, the mind–brain identity theory incorporates this idea, a fact that shows that, at least as a matter of definition, idealism and physicalism are not incompatible. A related point is that it is possible for a property to be neither mental nor physical. Now, when one thinks of properties that are neither mental nor physical, one might reasonably think of biological properties or color properties—these are neither mental nor physical in any ordinary sense. However, when speaking of naturalistic platonism, this is not what I mean. What I have in mind rather is the thought that the underlying nature of the world, whatever it is, is quite different from how it is presented to us in common sense, i.e. in ordinary thought and perception—this is the 'platonist' part of naturalistic platonism. On the other hand, the nature of the world might be discovered, assuming that it might be discovered at all, by naturalistic methods—that is the 'naturalistic' part of naturalistic platonism. As against the coherentist, the naturalistic platonist need not hold any particular theory of truth; as against the idealist, dualist, and physicalist, the naturalistic platonist thinks that whatever descriptions are true of the fundamental facts, they are not going to be descriptions drawn from ordinary thought, like the contrast between the mental and the physical.

One might think that the right phrase to describe this sort of position is 'neutral monism.' After all, a 'neutral' property might well be a property that is neutral between mental and physical, i.e. neither mental nor physical. But there are two reasons against adopting this terminology. In the first place, the term 'neutral monism' has historically been used for positions more like idealism (see e.g. Russell 1917 and, for discussion, Stubenberg 2008) than anything I am describing here. In the second place, the 'monist' part of neutral monism suggests that the fundamental properties of the world are all of a single sort, but naturalistic platonism need make no suggestion along these lines.

One might also find the contrast between physicalism and naturalistic platonism a bit elusive at this point. After all, contemporary physics also tells us that the underlying nature of the world, whatever it is, is quite different from how it is presented to us in ordinary thought and perception. Hence, if physics has something to do with physicalism, then one might think that physicalism is itself a kind of naturalistic platonism. However, while it is true that some versions of physicalism might count as versions of naturalistic platonism, there are still reasons to distinguish them, and these reasons will become clearer as we proceed. First, while physicalism has something to do with physics, it also has something to do with the notion of a physical object, and ordinary physical objects precisely *are* the sorts of things presented to us in ordinary thought and perception. Second, traditional versions of materialism do not go much beyond common sense because they represent the world as being made up of things that are physical by common sense standards. To the extent that physicalism is a position that is deeply connected to traditional materialism, it too will be informed by common sense. Finally, as we will see there is a serious question about whether there is any thesis of physicalism that is both true and deserving of the name; but there is no parallel problem for naturalistic platonism.

Summary

In this chapter, we have traced a path from a very simple formulation of physicalism ('everything is physical') to a more sophisticated one ('that every instantiated property is either physical or is necessitated by some physical property'). That sophisticated statement is the one we will mostly operate with, though in a sense it raises more questions than it answers. In particular it raises the question of what a physical property is, what necessitation is, and why necessitation should be necessary and sufficient for physicalism. We have also contrasted that thesis with various others such as idealism, dualism (including pluralism), coherentism, and finally naturalistic platonism.

Recommended reading

For necessitation, see Kripke 1980. On necessitation and fundamental properties, see Lewis 1994, as well as Schaffer 2003. A contemporary defense of idealism is Foster 1982. A contemporary defense of dualism is Chalmers 1996; for the classic defense see Descartes 1641. For pluralism, see Crane and Mellor 1990; Searle 1992; Dupré 1993. On coherentism, see Goodman 1978, and also Price 1997. On neutral monism of the traditional kind, see Russell 1917 and Stubenberg 2008. There are very few discussions of naturalistic platonism but, for an overly brief discussion in a different terminology, see Stoljar 2006: 31–3.

3

THE STARTING POINT VIEW

3.1 Introduction

We provisionally agreed in the previous chapter that physicalism is the thesis that every instantiated property is necessitated by a physical property. But we also noted that agreeing to this does not by itself solve the interpretation question—the question of what physicalism means or is. For one thing, we need to be told what it is for a property to be a physical property. It is that question that will be our topic for the next three chapters.

To motivate the question 'what is it for a property to be a physical property?' it suffices to point out that replacing 'physical' with something else in our formulation changes things considerably. For example, consider the (fanciful) thesis of *financialism*, viz. that every instantiated property is necessitated by some instantiated financial property. This thesis is false; no multinational put the moons of Jupiter in place. By contrast, consider the thesis of *fundamentalism*, viz. that every property is necessitated by some fundamental property, where a 'fundamental property' is the sort of property discussed by Lewis in the passage I quoted in the previous chapter. This thesis is necessarily true, if it is true at all, and in fact follows immediately from the assumption that there are fundamental properties in Lewis's sense. But physicalism is neither financialism nor fundamentalism. It is intended to be the potentially true and contingent thesis that every property is necessitated by a physical property; it is neither the false thesis that every property is necessitated by a financial property, nor the necessary (if true) thesis that every property is necessitated by a fundamental property. In short, when physicalists say that every property is necessitated by some physical property, they must mean something quite specific by 'physical property.' What then is it that they mean? What is it about a property that makes it a physical property?

3.2 Physical objects v. physical properties

In approaching this issue, it is convenient to start by assuming that we *do* understand what it is to be an intuitively physical *object*, such as a rock or a washing machine. If you doubt this, I ask you to conduct the following experiment. Go home, walk into your laundry, and slam your fist (or your head) against your washing machine as hard as you can. The thing that you will then be confronted with is a physical object, and moreover you know that it is a physical object. Hence you know what it is to be a physical object.

Not only do we know what it is to be a physical object on the basis of presented exemplars, it also seems possible to give a definition of a physical object, at least of a rough and ready sort. The definition goes like this:

> *x* is a physical object if and only if *x* has (or has enough of) the following properties: it has size, shape, extension in space, the capacity to move and be moved, the capacity to undergo various processes such as bending, breaking, and burning, and perhaps most importantly it has solidity or bulk—that is, it is intrinsically such that it resists or would resist pressure from other physical objects, for example, pressure from human bodies.

This definition certainly is rough and ready. For one thing, it is circular. Moreover, it might be possible to explicate some of these features in terms of others. Finally, not all intuitively physical objects have *all* of these properties; some physical objects in this ordinary sense are more liable to break than others. But the general idea of a physical object is clear enough for most purposes, or so anyway I will assume.

Now, from the fact, assuming it to be a fact, that we have the notion of a physical *object* it does not follow that we have a corresponding notion of a physical *property*. Objects and properties are items of different ontological categories, and you can't assume that a predicate, such as 'physical,' that applies to items in one category, will apply in a similar way to items in the other, nor can it be assumed that knowing what it is for a thing to be a physical object suffices for knowing what it is to be a physical property. To illustrate this, notice that, while we may take ourselves to know what it is for an object to be yellow, it does not follow that we know what it is for a property to be yellow. Properties are the wrong kind of thing to be yellow. To say that a property is yellow is a bit like saying that a number or a proposition is yellow, which they clearly are not. Hence it is not a trivial matter to extend the idea of physicality from objects to properties.

3.3 Over before it begins?

Not only is it not a trivial matter to extend the idea of physicality from objects to properties, some philosophers have presented positive arguments that this *cannot* be done (see, e.g. Stroud 1986; Daly 1998). Suppose we assume that we know what a physical object is, and that we try to introduce the idea of a physical property on that basis. How might we proceed? We seem to be confronted with three very unappealing options:

1   The first option is to say that a property is physical in just the same way that an object is, i.e. that physical properties *are* those that have or have enough of the properties that define what it is for an object to be physical. But this option is no good, for properties themselves do not have these properties. On any ordinary conception, properties are not extended in space, for example.

2   The second option is to say that a property is physical just in case it is instantiated by a physical object. But this option is no good—for physical objects might have various properties not all of which are physical. For example, according to property dualism, every object is physical but some properties had by physical objects are not physical. So the hypothesis that any property had by a physical object is a physical property destroys the difference between physicalism and property dualism.

3   The third option is to say that a property is physical just in case it is instantiated by a *purely* physical object. But this option is no good—for purely physical objects are objects that have only physical properties, and even if we agree that some explanations might be circular and illuminating, this one is circular and un-illuminating.

If this catalogue of options is exhaustive, there is a *logical* barrier to the project of explaining the notion of a physical property via the notion of a physical object. Conclusion: 'physical' really does behave like 'yellow'; physicality in objects is clear enough, but physicality in properties is nonsense.

The problem at issue here—the problem of extending the notion of physicality from objects to properties—threatens to be an extremely serious one for the project of clarifying physicalism. Physicalism is the thesis that every instantiated property is necessitated by some instantiated physical property; clearly this thesis makes no sense if the notion of a physical property makes no sense. On the other hand, if the argument just considered is sound, that notion does indeed make no sense. Is the project of clarifying physicalism over before it has begun?

Fortunately, the answer is 'no,' for the argument we just considered is not sound, and the reason is that the enumerated options are not exhaustive. True, we cannot say that a property is physical in quite the same way that an object is. But we can say that a property is physical in a related or derivative way. For example, for all that the argument just considered says, it remains open to us to say that a property is physical if and only if it is one of the distinctive properties of an intuitively physical object. (Likewise it remains open to us to say that a truth or fact is physical if and only if it is one that concerns physical objects and their distinctive properties.) These suggestions might at first sight look problematic: isn't it objectionably circular to explain the idea of a physical property in terms of the idea of a physical object? On reflection, however, it is not, and the reason is that physicality in an object is not quite the same thing as physicality in a property. Indeed, that is the lesson of the argument we just considered.

3.4 Cluster concepts

Even if we might say that a physical property is one of the distinctive properties of a physical object, it doesn't follow that we must say this, or that this is all we can say about a physical property. In other words, the precise interpretation of a physical property is yet to be supplied. How then is it to be supplied?

When faced with a difficult concept, it is often useful to assume that the concept is what is sometimes called a 'cluster concept.' Like many ideas in philosophy, the notion of a cluster concept can be understood in various ways. But what I will mean here might best be illustrated with an example. Suppose we come across a group of people who speak English just as we do, but who use a word we have never heard before, a word that seems to be somewhat special to them—let the word be 'glubbing.' How are we to go about finding out what these people mean by the word 'glubbing,' or (which is in this context more or less the same question) what their concept of glubbing is? The natural thought would be to ask them to tell us some of their beliefs about glubbing. Suppose we do this, and that members of the community tell us the following: glubbing is a kind of tuba music, which happens only on a Tuesday, and which is exclusively performed by people called 'Michael.' It seems reasonable to conclude at least tentatively that the concept of glubbing is just the concept of something that is a kind of Tuba music, is performed on a Tuesday, by someone called Michael. That is, these three features—Tuba, Tuesday, Michael—are necessary and suffi-cient for something to glub or to be an instance of glubbing.

So far so good—we have one definition of what the concept of glubbing is. But suppose now that on further investigation it turns out that there is a disagreement among members of this community, a disagreement we didn't notice before. On being presented with our proposal about how to define the concept of glubbing, some members of the community object. "It is true," they say, "that glubbing is performed by people called Michael. But this is not part of the definition of the word: it is simply an empirical gener-alization about glubbing that is itself sustained by the empirical fact that only the Michaels have tubas on Tuesdays." Other members of the commu-nity don't object in this way to our proposal, and are happy to say that being performed by people called Michael is 'analytic to' (as some of them say) glubbing. There doesn't seem much point in this sort of case to insist that some members of the community are right while others are wrong. The better thing to say is that there are various legitimate ways to spell out the concept of glubbing. On some ways, it is necessary that glubbing be performed by someone called Michael; but on other ways of spelling it out, this is not necessary and might even be false.

What goes for glubbing goes too for the concept of a physical property, or at any rate so I will assume. Here too we have a concept or word used by a group of people—for example, professional philosophers, and associates of professional philosophers—and our question is: 'what is this concept?' The obvious place to start is with the relevant beliefs that philosophers have about the physical, and the obvious thing to bear in mind is that there might be alternative legitimate ways of spelling out the concept in the light of these beliefs. (Objection: "How can you be sure what the relevant beliefs of this community are—isn't that an empirical question?" Reply: "Yes it is an empirical question, but I am a paradigm instance of the community in question, a naturalized speaker of the language of physicalism. So my own sense of what being physical is can be taken as fairly representative, at least in the first instance. In any case, we will be considering various different ideas about what the physical is as we proceed.")

3.5 The concept of the physical as a cluster concept

On the assumption that the concept of a physical property is a cluster concept, among the elements that might legitimately be included in the cluster are these:

Object: Physical properties are the distinctive properties of intuitively physical objects.

Theory: Physical properties are those expressed by the predicates of physical theories.

Objectivity: Physical properties are objective or intersubjective (i.e. one can know that they are instantiated from more than one point of view—creatures with very different background psychologies and histories can come to know that they are instantiated).

Method: Physical properties are those we could come to know through an application of the methods distinctive of the natural sciences.

Contrast: Physical properties are *not* the distinctive properties of souls, ectoplasm, psi-phenomena, ESP, etc.

Of these five theses, only Object has so far been introduced; as we have seen, on the assumption that we have the notion of an intuitively physical object, we may introduce the idea of a physical property as one of the properties that is distinctive of a physical object. The other four elements—Theory, Objectivity, Method, and Contrast—raise problems of their own. For the moment, however, I am going to proceed with the bald statements above; we will examine them as the need for this arises in the course of the discussion.

3.6 The Starting Point View

Having placed Object, Theory, Objectivity, Method, and Contrast in this way rather baldly on the table, I want first to focus on a particular view both about what physical properties are, and about what physicalism is—I will call it 'the Starting Point View.' The Starting Point View has two parts. The first is the following definition of what a physical property is:

(1)   *F* is a physical property if and only if:
   (a)   *F* is one of the distinctive properties of physical objects; and
   (b)   *F* is expressed by a predicate of a physical theory; and
   (c)   *F* is objective; and
   (d)   *F* is a property we could come to know about through the methods of science; and
   (e)   *F* is not one of the distinctive properties of souls, ectoplasm, ESP, etc.

It should be clear that the Starting Point View takes all of Object, Theory, Objectivity, Method, and Contrast and treats them as jointly necessary and sufficient for something to be a physical property. If we call a physical property so defined a 'starting point physical property,' this part of the Starting Point View says that physical properties are starting point physical properties.

One part of the Starting Point View provides a definition of what a physical property is; the other provides the following definition of what physicalism is:

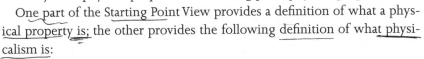

(2)   Physicalism is true if and only if every instantiated property is necessitated by some instantiated starting point physical property.

So this part of the Starting Point View simply takes the definition of physicalism with which we have been working and plugs into it the Starting Point View of a physical property. If we call the version of physicalism here defined 'starting point physicalism' this part of the Starting Point View says that physicalism is starting point physicalism.

It is important to notice here that the Starting Point View does not say that physicalism is true or false or that any physical property is or is not instantiated. Somebody could perfectly well agree with the Starting Point View of what physicalism is and nevertheless insist that it is false. Rather, the Starting Point View is a thesis about what it is for a property to be a physical property and, correlatively, what it is for a thesis to be physicalism.

Is the Starting Point View correct? Well, how are we to go about deciding whether it is correct? Earlier we introduced one methodological idea, the idea of a cluster concept. Another idea, which often goes together with that of a cluster concept, is what is called in philosophy 'the method of cases.' Again, like many philosophical ideas, the method of cases can be understood in various ways. But as I will understand it here, the method of cases is a method whereby we test various proposed analyses of concepts or theses. In particular, what the method of cases asks us to do is consider a variety or range of possibilities and then ask a pair of questions concerning each of them: 'Would the concept *on the proposed analysis* apply in this case?' and 'Would the concept *as we normally understand* it apply in this case?' To the extent that our answers to these questions coincide across the range of cases at issue, we have confirmation of the proposed analysis.

That is the strategy I will use in what follows, but with a twist. Rather than focusing on an analysis of the concept of a physical property, it is preferable in this case to focus directly on the thesis of physicalism, and in particular on the proposal of the Starting Point View that physicalism is starting point physicalism. The reason for this is roughly as follows. It is not at all obvious that we have a stable range of judgments about what it is for a thing to be a physical property, and about whether various proposed concepts of a physical property apply in particular cases; though we certainly have some judgments along these lines. On the other hand, it does seem reasonable to assume that we have a stable range of judgments about under what possible conditions physicalism is true or false. At any rate, in the history of philosophy of mind, people tend to agree across a wide range of cases about whether materialism would in those cases be true or false. The idea is to exploit those judgments to figure out whether the Starting Point View is true. In sum, what I am going to do now is to consider various possible cases and ask the following pair of questions about each: 'Is physicalism as we normally understand it true in this possible world?' and 'Is starting point physicalism true in this possible world?' Our methodological assumption is that, to the extent that our pattern of answers line up, we have confirmed the Starting Point View.

3.7 Classical atomism

If we apply the method of cases so understood to the hypothesis that physicalism is starting point physicalism, the initial results are promising. Consider:

> THE ATOMIST WORLD: this is a possible world at which every instantiated property is necessitated by some property distinctive of classical atoms. The properties instantiated at this world duplicate whatever properties are instantiated at the actual world, insofar as this is possible.

To motivate the possibility being described here, we may need to remind ourselves at least in general terms what atoms are supposed to be. To start with, what I have in mind here are the atoms of antiquity, the atoms of Democritus or Lucretius rather than anything that might get called an 'atom' in modern physics. Now, atoms in this sense might be understood, at least very roughly, as rather like rocks only much, much smaller. Like rocks, atoms have the properties that intuitively physical objects have—location, shape, size, solidity, ability to collide with other objects, and so on—and yet they may have these properties in ways a bit different from ordinary physical objects. For example, a key feature of the atoms of antiquity is that they enter into causal interactions, when they do, only by direct contact, i.e. by one atom colliding with, or banging into, another. This is presumably not true of ordinary rocks that can influence in other ways too, e.g. by way of gravitational attraction. Nevertheless—and this is the key point—atoms are basically ordinary physical objects. For example, if you were magically shrunk down to the size of an atom (or an atom magically grew so that it were the size of you) you would perform an experiment analogous to the one I asked you to perform in the case of your washing machine. You could bang your fist (or your head) as hard as you could against the atom. And once again, the object that you would then be confronted with is a physical object in the same intuitive sense that your washing machine is.

Now, as I will understand it here, an atomist is not just a person who believes the existential claim that there are atoms; rather an atomist is someone who draws on this claim to explain various features of the world. So, for example, the atomist believes that the earth is just a big arrangement of atoms, and that the distinct properties of the earth, its size and shape, say, are a function of the properties of the atoms that make it up. The more ambitious an atomist is the more phenomena he or she will apply this strategy to. An atomist in chemistry holds that the chemical properties of (e.g.) water are a function of the arrangement of its constituent atoms. An atomist in biology holds that the growth of plants, the reproduction of organisms, and so on are likewise a matter of the arrangement of atoms. At the limit, an atomist believes that the actual world just is the atomist world I just described, that is, a world at which *every* property is necessitated by some property distinctive of atoms. So if it is true that Napoleon retreated from Moscow, or that I have a pain in my toe, or that Venice is beautiful, then these facts are necessitated by some highly complex fact about atoms.

Now actually the atomist world raises a number of interesting and perplexing questions: I will come back to one of them at the end of this chapter. For the moment, however, I want to concentrate on variations of the two questions we identified earlier: (a) 'Is starting point physicalism true at the classical atomist world?'; and (b) 'Is physicalism as we normally understand it true at the classical atomist world?' (Before you go on, take a moment to answer these questions yourself.)

When we ask these questions, I think it is clear that the answer to both is 'yes.' That is, at the classical atomist world, both physicalism and starting point physicalism are true; moreover, this provides evidence for the Starting Point View. Indeed, not only is the answer to both of these questions 'yes,' it is also true that the atomist world that I have described is something like the paradigm case of a world in which physicalism is true. That is, physicalism is not only true at the atomist world, the fact that it is true there seems to a very large degree to define what it is to be a version of physicalism. It is completely routine when explaining what materialism is to use phrases such as 'it's all atoms and the void,' and to mention the fact that philosophers like Hobbes and Lucretius were materialists. So it is hard to see how any thesis could deserve the name 'physicalism' *unless* it were true at the atomist world.

3.8 Gravity

Reflection on the classical atomist world confirms the hypothesis that physicalism is starting point physicalism, but reflection on other cases does not, or at any rate does not so clearly. Consider:

> THE ATOMIST WORLD WITH GRAVITY: this is a possible world at which every property is necessitated by some property distinctive of classical atoms, with this twist: at this world atoms instantiate the further property of universal gravitation, a property that makes them behave in peculiar ways. The properties instantiated at this world duplicate whatever properties are instantiated at the actual world, insofar as this is possible.

To motivate the possibility described here, we may note some general features of the historical shift from earlier forms of atomistic or Cartesian physics to Newtonian physics. Newton was an atomist in something like the sense just described. (Newton in fact believed that atoms were perfectly spherical.) But in addition to the properties mentioned in the previous section, Newtonian atoms were subject to forces such as universal gravitation between atoms. Atoms affected each other not only by colliding with each other, according to Newton, but also by gravitation.

Now both Newton and his contemporaries held this view to be extremely controversial. Consider this passage from Lange's *The History of Materialism*, the book I mentioned in the introduction:

> We have in our own days so accustomed ourselves to the abstract notion of forces, or rather to a notion hovering in a mystic obscurity between abstraction and concrete comprehension, that we no longer find any difficulty in making one particle of matter act upon another without immediate contact. We may, indeed, imagine that in the proposition 'No force without matter,' we have uttered something very Materialistic, while all the time we calmly allow particles of matter to act upon each other through void space without any material link. From such ideas the great mathematicians and physicists of the seventeenth century were far removed. They were all in so far still genuine Materialists in the sense of ancient Materialism, that they made immediate contact a condition of influence. The collision of atoms or the attraction by hook-shaped particles, a mere modification of collision, were the type of all Mechanism and the whole movement of science tended toward Mechanism. (Lange 1925: 1.308)

To put things in our terms, what Lange seems to be telling us in this passage is that there is a very great distinction between the atomist world and the atomist world with gravity, and that as a corollary to this, there is a very great distinction between the "ancient Materialist" suggestion that the world is the atomist world, and the Newtonian suggestion that the world is (with the exception perhaps of humans and God) the atomist world with gravity. In the atomist world, causal interactions are limited to collision and contact. But the atomist world with gravity includes something over and above this, and indeed something over and above any feature of traditional atomism. Indeed, it is quite natural to read into Lange's passage the suggestion that the Newtonian world-view is committed to something that logically speaking is a bit like property dualism. The property dualist might well hold that in order to account for certain psychological phenomena, the atomist world would need to be enriched with mental properties that are distinct from any properties had by atoms. Likewise, the Newtonian (at least as interpreted by Lange) seems to hold that in order to account for certain causal phenomena, the atomist world needs to be enriched with certain gravitational properties that are distinct from any had by atoms.

Once again there are different questions we might ask about the atomist world with gravity. But for our purposes the questions are (a) 'Is starting point physicalism true at the atomist world with gravity?'; and (b) 'Is physicalism as we normally understand it true at the atomist world with gravity?' (Once again: before going on, ask yourself how you would answer these questions.)

I think the answer to the second question is 'yes.' At any rate most contemporary physicalists would, I believe, unerringly say that the classical atomist world with gravity is a world at which physicalism is true. Indeed, such a world is a simple variation on the world that they take as the actual world. But the answer to the first question is 'no,' at least it is 'no' if one thinks it is reasonable to suppose that gravity is *not* a feature of an ordinary physical object.

Of course, the persuasiveness of this last answer depends on the extent to which gravity is *not* intuitively physical. As Lange observes, we have become so accustomed to the idea that gravity is physical we might have some difficulty not including it among the ordinary physical properties of ordinary physical objects. But in recent work in psychology it has seemed plausible to suppose that the ordinary notion of a physical object is governed by properties that rule out gravity. The psychologist Elizabeth Spelke, for example, holds that in our naïve or pre-scientific understanding of physical objects, humans spontaneously assume that they are subject to a principle she calls "contact," according to which one object influences another only if it collides with it (see Spelke 1994). If Spelke is right, then it is plausible to suppose that gravity as it is understood in Newtonian physics is not an intuitively physical property.

3.9 Modern physics

Perhaps it is best to say, not that starting point physicalism is false at the atomist world with gravity, but that it is unclear whether it is true—the lack of clarity deriving from whether universal gravitation counts as one of the distinctive properties of ordinary physical objects. If so, the case does not provide a refutation of the Starting Point View. Nevertheless, there are other cases that do seem to provide such a refutation. Consider:

THE MODERN PHYSICS WORLD: this is a possible world at which every property is necessitated by properties distinctive of the things postulated by modern physics. The properties instantiated at this world duplicate whatever properties are instantiated at the actual world, insofar as this is possible.

Of course, to describe the modern physics world only to this extent is to seriously underdescribe it. What are the objects and properties postulated by modern physics? Are they fields or quantum wave-function states or super-strings? Clearly, one might fill out the description of the modern physics world in a myriad of ways depending on which particular physical theory you had in mind. For our purposes, however, the crucial point about the modern physics world is not so much what the basic properties of this world *are* as what they are *not*. In particular, what they are not are properties distinctive of ordinary physical objects—they are not starting point physical properties.

Actually, this point—that modern physics provides a set of properties that are not starting point physical properties, and not necessitated by starting point physical properties—has been made by a number of different people in different ways. Here are three passages making basically this point, from (the late nineteenth-century German philosopher) Friedrich Nietzsche, from (early twentieth-century physicist) Sir A.S. Eddington, and from (the twentieth-century philosopher) W.V. Quine:

> As for materialistic atomism, it is one of the best refuted things there are; and perhaps no scholar in Europe is still so unscholarly today as to accord it serious significance expect for handy everyday use (as an abbreviated means of expression) – thanks above all to the Pole Boscovich who, together with the Pole Copernicus, has been the greatest and most triumphant opponent of ocular evidence hitherto. For while Copernicus persuaded us to believe, contrary to the senses, that the earth does not stand firm, Boscovich taught us to abjure belief in the last thing on earth that 'stood firm,' belief in 'substance,' 'matter,' the earth-residuum and particle atom: it was the greatest triumph over the senses achieved on earth. (Nietzsche 1973: 43)

> I have settled down to the task of writing these lectures and have drawn up my chairs to my two tables. Two tables! Yes; there are duplicates of every object about me – two tables, two chairs, two pens. ... One of them has been familiar to me from earliest years. It is a commonplace object of that environment which I call the world. How shall I describe it? It has extension; it is comparatively permanent; it is coloured; above all it is substantial. By substantial I do not merely mean that it does not collapse when I lean upon it; I mean that it is constituted of "substance" and by that word I am trying to convey to you some conception of its intrinsic nature. It is a thing; not like space, which is a mere negation; nor like time, which is – Heaven knows what! ... Table No. 2 is my scientific table. It is a more recent

acquaintance and I do not feel so familiar with it. It does not belong to the world previously mentioned, that world which spontaneously appears around me when I open my eyes, though how much of it is objective and how much subjective I do not here consider. It is part of a world which in more devious ways has forced itself on my attention. My scientific table is mostly emptiness. Sparsely scattered in that emptiness are numerous electric charges rushing about with great speed; but their combined bulk amounts to less than a billionth of the bulk of the table itself. (Eddington 1928: 5–7)

Physicists regale us with yet further testimony ill fitting the notion of a particle. There is talk of cyclic resolution of particles, as if particles could be components of components of themselves. Furthermore there is the well-established convertibility of matter and energy. Manifestly the physicists' age-old attachment to matter has relaxed. Matter is quitting the field, and field theory is the order of the day. ... What then of our physical objects? They were to have been the material contents of portions of space-time. But must we now take as our objects simply those portions of space-time themselves, subject to whatever distributions of local states they happen to be subject to? (Quine 1976: 499)

In my view, all of these passages contain elements that are mistaken or confused. Notoriously, Nietzsche says that Boscovich was a Pole when in fact he was born in Dubrovnik. More seriously, consider Nietzsche's suggestion that Boscovich's physics entails that there are no solid objects. This is clearly a very exciting sounding claim. It entails, for example, that there are no washing machines, since washing machines are presumably solid, or at least seem so when you bang your head on them. Unfortunately for Nietzsche, however, (though perhaps fortunately for Boscovich) Boscovich's theory does not entail that there are no washing machines. Boscovich held (to put it very roughly) that the world consists of a series of points, each of which is the centre of an energy field. Certainly it is true that points themselves are not physical objects in the ordinary sense, since they are not extended, or solid etc. But it does not follow that there are no solid things, such as washing machines or rocks. For, even if Boscovich's theory is true, it remains possible that washing machines and rocks are made up of points and energy fields in Boscovich's sense.

The exciting but mistaken suggestion that modern physics entails that there are no washing machines is also present, though perhaps in a more oblique way, in the passages of Quine and Eddington, or so it seems to me. Quine says that "matter has quit the field" suggesting perhaps that a physicist who postulates fields or similar entities is committed to the non-existence of matter, at least in the form of ordinary bodies. But this is not so; features of fields might simply make up ordinary bodies. Similarly, Eddington goes on elsewhere in his book (311) to say that table #1 is an "illusion" and more generally that solidity is an illusion, "a fancy projected by the mind into the external world" (306). But the fact that a solid object like a table is made of things that are not themselves solid hardly entails that tables are illusory.

However, even if we set aside the claim that Boscovich's or indeed any other physical theory entails that there are no washing machines, there is also a different point in all of these passages which seems, if not quite as exciting, then certainly exciting enough and also perhaps true. This is that according to contemporary physics there are properties instantiated in the world that, whatever else they are, are not intuitively physical and are not necessitated by the intuitively physical. Of course physical theories of any sort will tell us that there are various things, and that these things have properties and stand in relations to one another. And different physical theories will tell us different things: Boscovich's view tells us that there are force fields; quantum mechanics tell us that there are quantum wave-function states; string theory tells us something else. But, at least if we take the lead of such luminaries as Nietzsche, Eddington, and Quine, the things that modern physics tells us about are not intuitively physical objects, and do not have the properties distinctive of intuitively physical objects. The conclusion to be drawn from this is that, however we fill out the details of the modern physics world (again, it could presumably be filled out in various ways), the fundamental properties at such a world (assuming there are such properties) are not starting point physical properties.

As in the case of the other possibilities we have considered, there are many questions we might ask about the modern physics world. But, again, for our purposes the questions are (a) 'Is starting point physicalism true at the modern physics world?'; and (b) 'Is physicalism as we normally understand it true at the modern physics world?' (Once again: how would you answer these questions?)

I think it is clear that the answer to the first question is 'no.' If starting point physicalism were true at the modern physics world, then every property necessitated there would have to be necessitated by a starting point physical property. But this is not so; at this world there are properties—e.g. the ones postulated by modern physics—which not only are not starting point physical properties but are not necessitated by them. Indeed, if anything, the truth is the other way around: at the modern physics world, the starting point properties are necessitated by others. So starting point physicalism is not true at the modern physics world. As regards the first question, however, it would seem as if the answer is yes. At any rate, there is a straightforward argument that physicalism is true at this world. This argument is that contemporary physicalists hold that the modern physics world is (near enough) the actual world. And since they think that physicalism is true at the actual world, it follows that physicalism is true at the modern physics world. But if that is right we have a refutation of the thesis that physicalism is starting point physicalism: the modern physics world is a world at which physicalism is true but starting point physicalism is not. Hence physicalism is not starting point physicalism.

3.10 Is atomism possible?

We have been using the method of cases to test the hypothesis that physicalism is starting point physicalism. What we have been led to is the conclusion that while the hypothesis gets some important cases right, e.g. those associated with classical atomism, it does not get other cases right, e.g. those associated with developments of physics away from classical atomism, and in particular those associated with modern physics.

What points may be drawn from this exercise? One point is that the Starting Point View is false: physicalism is not properly interpreted as starting point physicalism, because there are worlds at which physicalism is true and starting point physicalism is false. But another point is just that if physicalism is starting point physicalism, then it is false, and moreover, it is false for reasons that have very little to do with philosophy: developments within physics itself suggest that starting point physicalism is false. But it doesn't follow that physicalism itself is false. Whether physicalism itself is false depends on whether physicalism is starting point physicalism. If physicalism can be interpreted in a different way, then it will not follow that physicalism is false. In the next chapter we will consider the project of doing precisely that. Meanwhile I will close this chapter with some further reflections on atomism.

As Nietzsche said in the passage above, materialistic atomism is one of the best-refuted things there are—or as we would put it somewhat more soberly, there are empirical reasons for thinking that the atomist world is not the actual world. One interesting point to be made about this is that when physicalists say that physicalism is true they can't mean that the dream world of the classical materialist, the paradigm case for physicalists, is the actual world. For, as we have seen, that paradigm case is the atomist world, and it is quite clear that the atomist world is not the actual world. So the actual world can't quite be as the physicalist dreams that it is.

But there is a further point to be made here. I have been assuming so far that, even if the atomist world is not actual, it is at least a possible world: atomism might be false, but it remains a possibility. However, there is a famous line of argument that would show, if it were successful, that the atomist world is not simply non-actual but impossible as well. The argument, which I have elsewhere called the categorical argument, focuses on the notion of a dispositional property, where (at least for our purposes) a dispositional property is one that if an object has it then a corresponding counterfactual is true of the object. For example, being uncomfortable is a dispositional property of a chair because if you were to sit in it, you would feel uncomfortable, and being yellow is a dispositional property of a lemon because if you were to look at it you would have a certain sensation. Dispositional properties are of interest to philosophers for a number of reasons, but one main reason is that they seem to require (what are called) categorical grounds. A categorical ground is a non-dispositional property which grounds or necessitates the dispositional property in question. So if a chair is uncomfortable, there must be some non-dispositional property or properties which are such that if they are instantiated, then the chair is uncomfortable.

What have dispositional properties to do with the atomist world? Well, on the face of it one of the key properties instantiated at the atomist world, solidity, is itself a dispositional property. For if an atom is solid, then it would resist pressure and penetration were it to come into contact with other objects. If solidity is dispositional property, however, then by the principle that dispositions require cateogorical grounds, there had better be a categorical property of an atom that grounds its solidity. But at the atomist world there seems to be no candidate for such a property! The shape, size and position of atoms cannot ground their solidity because it is possible for a vacuum, i.e. a region of space devoid of any matter at all, to have these properties and not be solid. And nor can solidity ground itself, for it is a dispositional and not a categorical property. But this suggests that solidity is both instantiated and not instantiated at the atomist world. Conclusion: the atomist world is impossible.

Actually, there are some moves in that argument which are difficult to adjudicate but we will not go into these issues in this book. The main point is merely to note that, if the argument I just reviewed is sound, then falsity is only the start of the problem for starting point physicalism, and the dream world of the materialist is an impossible dream.

Summary

In this chapter we have been considering the pros and cons of a very simple definition of physicalism offered by the Starting Point View. We have seen that if the Starting Point View is true, and physicalism is starting point physicalism, then physicalism is false and for reasons that are accepted by contemporary physicalists. We have also taken the time to introduce two methodological ideas, the idea of a cluster concept and the notion of the method of cases.

Recommended reading

A very good example of the method of cases is Johnston's 1992 paper 'How to speak of the colors'. A famous dispute on the nature of the physical and the impact of modern physics is that between Eddington 1928 and Stebbing 1958/1937. An accessible modern discussion of the nature of matter is Trusted 1999; see also Keith Campbell's *Metaphysics: An Introduction* (1976), unfortunately now out of print, but available in most libraries. A discussion that influenced both Lewis and Smart is Feinberg 1966. On the categorical argument, see Russell (1927) Unger (1998) and for discussion see Stoljar (2006), chapter 6 and the references therein.

4

THE THEORY VIEW

4.1 Introduction

The intellectual situation with which we were confronted in the previous chapter is similar in outline to one we confront in discussing other topics of philosophical interest. Take, for example, color; in a famous paper, Mark Johnston (1992) argued that, on the assumption that concepts of color are cluster concepts, it will turn out that there are no colors (lemons not yellow, etc.), at least if we assume certain things about the elements of the relevant cluster. Should we in fact assume those things? Johnston said no: there are various legitimate conceptions of what colors are and what we should do instead is investigate ways of understanding the concept of color so that we may say truly that there are colors. The basic idea is simple. "Of course if you mean *that* by 'color'," Johnston in effect imagines the color realist as saying, "there are no colors. But why mean that? Why not mean something else?"

Indeed, this situation might arise even when the concept under discussion has no philosophical interest at all. So, returning to our example of glubbing from the previous chapter, imagine that it turned out that all of the people who claim to be called Michael are in fact called something else—Philip, for example. In that case, if we operate with the conception of glubbing according to which it is analytic to glubbing that it is done by someone called Michael, we would be forced into anti-realism about glubbing. After all if glubbing is *defined* as a kind of tuba music, which happens on a Tuesday, and which is performed by people called Michael, then being performed by people called Michael is a necessary condition on the existence of glubbing; no Michaels, no glubbing. At this point, however, it seems natural to play the 'various legitimate conceptions' card. Sure, if that is what you mean by 'glubbing,' there is no glubbing, but what about if we operate with a different conception?

Could we not say the same thing about the concept of a physical property? Could we not say, in other words, that while the Starting Point View, when combined with agreed-on empirical facts, has the result that physicalism is false, there is also a distinct view that does not have this result? That is surely what contemporary physicalists have in mind when they say that physicalism is true. "Yes," a contemporary physicalist might say, "what I believe is not physicalism in the sense of starting point physicalism. But what I believe is still close enough to deserve the name." This idea involves liberalizing physicalism so that it does not have the result that, because of developments in science itself, the thesis is false. This liberalization project is the topic of this chapter.

4.2 Liberalizing the Starting Point View

How would this liberalization project go? Well let us look again at the five things that have a legitimate claim to be included in the cluster that defines what it is to be a physical property:

Object: Physical properties are the distinctive properties of intuitively physical objects.

Theory: Physical properties are those expressed by the predicates of physical theories.

Objectivity: Physical properties are objective or intersubjective (i.e. one can know that they are instantiated from more than one point of view—creatures with very different background psychologies and histories can come to know that they are instantiated).

Method: Physical properties are those we could come to know through an application of the methods distinctive of the natural sciences.

Contrast: Physical properties are *not* the distinctive properties of souls, ectoplasm, psi-phenomena, ESP, etc.

As we saw in the previous chapter, the Starting Point View builds all of these features into its concept of a physical property, and so into physicalism. However, what gets the Starting Point View into trouble is not so much that it builds *all* of these elements into the concept. What gets it into trouble is that it builds the first of them in, i.e. it builds Object in. In particular, the Starting Point View entails that something is a physical property only if it is a distinctive property of an intuitively physical object, and hence that physicalism is true only if all instantiated properties are necessitated by physical properties in this sense. But, as we have seen, this seems to be shown false by the method of cases, and would, anyway, have the result that physicalism is false at the actual world. In consequence, when we seek to liberalize the Starting Point View, we should investigate potential conceptions of the physical (and *mutatis mutandis* of physicalism) that dispense with Object: while any conception that incorporates Object is in trouble, a conception that dispenses with it might not be.

Obviously there are various forms that this proposal might take. For most of this chapter, however, I want to focus on a view about physical properties and physicalism I will call 'the Theory View.' The Theory View has two parts. The first provides the following definition of what a physical property is:

(1) *F* is a physical property if and only if *F* is expressed by a predicate of a physical theory.

So the Theory View takes one element of the cluster, Theory, and treats it as necessary and sufficient for something to be a physical property. If we call a physical property so defined a 'theory-based physical property,' this part of the Theory View says that physical properties are theory-based physical properties.

One part of the Theory View provides a definition of what a physical property is. The other provides the following definition of what physicalism is:

(2) Physicalism is true if and only if every instantiated property is necessitated by some instantiated theory-based physical property.

So the Theory View takes the basic definition with which we have been working and plugs into it the notion of a theory-based physical property. If we call the version of physicalism here defined 'theory-based physicalism' this part of the Theory View says that physicalism is theory-based physicalism. (It is important to notice that, like the Starting Point View, the Theory

View is a view about what physicalism is, and what physical properties are; it is not a view about whether physicalism is true or whether any physical properties are instantiated.)

The Theory View is obviously a much more liberal conception of what a physical property is than the Starting Point View. Why focus on something this weak? This is for three reasons. First, the Theory View is pretty much the standard view about these matters in contemporary philosophy. If you ask a philosopher what he or she means by 'physical property' the answer you are most likely to get is one or another version of the Theory View. Hence, in focusing on the Theory View, we are focusing on the most common theory of the physical.

Second, when you think about the elements in the original cluster that putatively defines what it is to be a physical property, it is reasonable to draw a distinction between Object and Theory, on the one hand, and Objectivity, Method, and Contrast on the other. If you look up 'physical' in the dictionary, one sense you will find listed is something like 'pertaining to the body.' It is the 'pertaining to the body' sense that Object is getting at, for a body precisely is a physical object in the intuitive sense. But another sense you will find is something like 'pertaining to physics.' It is the 'pertaining to physics' sense that Theory is getting at: a property is physical if it is distinctively had by the sort of thing that pertains to physics or, as I have put it, if it is expressed by a physical theory. So Object and Theory together provide something like the dictionary definition of the physical. On the other hand, Objectivity, Method, and Contrast seem on the face of it to have nothing particularly to do with the concept of the physical in its dictionary definition. Both Objectivity and Method have a procedural or epistemic quality to them, while Contrast is obviously privative, that is, it tells you something about what the physical is not rather than about what it is.

Finally—and this will emerge as we proceed—it is convenient to present the issues by first concentrating on a simple version of the Theory View, and then adding explicitly the further conditions of Objectivity, Method, and Contrast. By the end of our discussion we will be able to address the question whether any reasonable definition of physicalism might be obtained from the elements of the cluster we have put on the table.

4.3 What is a physical theory?

The Theory View says that something is a physical property just in case it is expressed by a physical theory. This idea looks simple on the surface but in fact it is quite complicated. For it is obscure in this context what 'physical theory' is supposed to mean.

On a very simple interpretation, a physical theory is a theory with a particular subject matter, i.e. intuitive physical objects and their distinctive properties. But this cannot be quite what a proponent of the Theory View has in mind. For to say this is no advance on the Starting Point View. Suppose a proponent of the Theory View says that physical properties are those expressed by predicates of physical theories, and then goes on to say that physical theories concern physical objects and their distinctive properties. Putting this together we arrive back at the problematic element of the Starting Point View, namely that physical properties are the distinctive properties of physical objects. But the whole point of switching to the Theory View was to avoid that problematic element.

A different way in which one might try to explain what is meant by 'physical theory' is to appeal to some specific physical theory, for example one actually formulated at some point in time—e.g. medieval impetus physics or modern quantum physics. However, this proposal is unattractive also. For one thing there is the problem that physical theories will change over time—this issue is central to Hempel's dilemma, our topic in Chapter 5. But the more general problem is that physicalism is intended to be an abstract thesis, a thesis that is not tied to the details of any particular physical theory. Suppose you pick some particular formulated theory, and define a conception of physical properties, and so physicalism, in terms of it. In effect, this removes physicalism from its philosophical context. Physicalism is routinely appealed to in philosophical contexts in which people have not specified a particular physical theory (and, quite likely, are in no position to do so).

In the light of these considerations, it would appear that any reasonable development of the Theory View will need to articulate a conception of a physical theory that, on the one hand, moves beyond the properties introduced when we talk about intuitive physical objects, but that, on the other, does not involve specifying a particular physical theory. In my view the way forward here starts from the (admittedly simple-minded) idea that a physical theory is a theory that a scientist advances in the course of trying to explain or describe ordinary physical objects, their distinctive properties, their constitution and behavior, and so on. Such an inquiry is not limited to physical properties in the starting point sense. It may well be that, in the course of describing the constitution and behavior of ordinary physical objects, a scientist is obliged to postulate objects and properties which are not starting point physical. In turn, a scientist might reasonably take it to be part of his or her overall inquiry to provide theories of these (non-starting point physical) objects and properties, and that the theories so provided are also called 'physical theories' because of their scientific connection to physical theories of a more standard sort. More generally, on the more liberal view of a physical theory that I am describing, a physical theory is a certain type of theory, i.e. a theory that a scientist produces in the course of the project of explaining the nature and behavior of ordinary physical objects and in the course of related projects.

It should be clear that this idea of a physical theory is pretty open-ended, and, in consequence, the Theory View itself is open-ended. However, this is neither unexpected nor unwelcome. It is not unexpected because it is reasonable to think that the notion of the physical that is in operation in contemporary philosophy is somewhat open-ended—indeed, the basic problem with the Starting Point View is precisely that it does not acknowledge this. And it is not unwelcome because, if 'physical theory' is interpreted in this more expansive way, the Theory View is an advance on the Starting Point View for it provides us with a class of physical properties larger than those provided by the Starting Point View.

4.4 Two versions of the Theory View

We have seen that the idea of a physical theory that is in operation in the Theory View is an open-ended one, and that this provides much needed liberalization of the Starting Point View. Nevertheless, questions remain about what exactly the Theory View is. In particular, two rather different versions of the view may be distinguished.

In order to distinguish these two different versions of the Theory View, it is helpful to start with a prior question. Suppose we agree that a physical theory is a theory produced by a scientist in the course of the sort of inquiry described in the previous section. Presumably there is a huge number (indeed, a potentially infinite number) of such theories; which one does the proponent of the Theory View intend? Once again, there is a temptation here to appeal to the details of some particular formulated theory, but, as before, this will run into the problem that physicalism is supposed to be a thesis that abstracts away from the scientific detail. However, once we have the very general notion of a physical theory before us, it becomes possible to answer the question of which theory the proponent has in mind in a different way. Instead of appealing to some actual formulated theory, a proponent of the theory view can now say that what is intended is simply the true physical theory whether or not it has been formulated. (Depending on how one counts theories, it might be that there is more than one true physical theory. In my view, we might in this case speak of the conjunction of the true theories, rather than the true theory, but in any event I will ignore this aspect of the issue in what follows.)

Suppose we agree that, as far as the proponent of the Theory View is concerned, the physical theory that is intended is the true physical theory. Then (1) above should be replaced with (3):

(3) F is a physical property if and only if F is expressed by a predicate of a true physical theory.

What (3) says is that a property is physical if it is expressed by a true theory, whatever it is, of the behavior, nature, and constitution of ordinary physical objects, and by any true theories, whatever they are, that scientists feel they need to construct in the course of that inquiry.

Now, if we assume that the basic form of the Theory View is not (1) but (3) we may distinguish two quite different versions of the view. On the one hand, (3) might be understood as saying that a property is a physical property just in case it is expressed by a theory that is true *at the actual world*; indeed, this is a very natural way to take it. On the other hand, it might be understood as saying that a property is a physical property just in case it is expressed by a theory that is true *at some possible world or other*. Taking it the first way results in at what I will call the *actualist* version of the Theory View:

(4) F is a physical property if and only if F is expressed by a physical theory that is true at the actual world.

Alternatively, taking it the second way results in what I will call the *possibilist* version of the Theory View:

(5) F is a physical property if and only if F is expressed by a physical theory that is true at some possible world or other (i.e. not necessarily the actual world).

To bring out the difference between these two versions, imagine a property F that is expressed by a physical theory that is true at some possible world W, but is not expressed by any theory that is true at the actual world. Is this property physical or not? On the face of it, (4) and (5) answer this question differently. According to (5) F is a physical property, because it is a property that is expressed by a physical theory that is true in some possible world or other. On the other hand, according to (4) F is not a physical property, because it is not expressed by a physical theory that is true in the actual world.

So it seems that the Theory View presents us not with one account of what it is to be a physical property but with two. And, since we have two different accounts of what it means to be a physical property, we likewise have two definitions of what it is for physicalism to be true. The first, which I will call 'actualist theory physicalism,' says that every instantiated property is entailed by some instantiated physical property, where a physical property is a property expressed by a physical theory that is true in the actual world. The second, which I will call 'possibilist theory physicalism,' says that every instantiated property is entailed by some physical property, where a physical property is a property expressed by a physical theory that is true in some world or other. In what follows, therefore, I will first consider the hypothesis that physicalism is actual theory physicalism, and then turn to the hypothesis that it is possible theory physicalism. Following the pattern established in the previous chapter, my method for examining these hypotheses will be the method of cases.

4.5 The actualist version

If we apply the method of cases to the hypothesis that physicalism is actual theory physicalism, the initial results are promising. Consider this again:

> THE MODERN PHYSICS WORLD: this is a possible world at which every instantiated property is necessitated by the properties distinctive of the things postulated by modern physics. The properties instantiated at this world duplicate whatever properties are instantiated at the actual world, insofar as this is possible.

As we saw in the previous chapter, this possible world causes trouble for starting point physicalism in two ways: first, at this world starting point physicalism is false but physicalism is true; second, this is a world that most contemporary physicalists believe is the actual world, so starting point physicalism is not a thesis that is true at the actual world by the lights of contemporary physicalists. On the other hand, no such trouble afflicts actual theory physicalism. In fact, actual theory physicalism is designed so as to be true at the modern physics world. It is no wonder, therefore, that reflection on this world confirms the actualist version of the Theory View.

4.6 Twin physics

On the other hand, while the modern physics world confirms the hypothesis that physicalism is actual theory physicalism, there are other cases that do not.

Suppose we agree that contemporary physics tells us that various properties, e.g. mass, spin, and charge, are the fundamental properties, in Lewis's sense. Now imagine a twin-earth or twin-world at which the fundamental properties are some other properties, assumed to be of a quite different character to mass, spin, and charge. I am not imagining here that the properties in question are spiritual or mental or conform to any paradigm we have of a non-physical property. I am simply imagining a world that is similar to our own from an evidential point of view except that the fundamental properties are different. In other words, imagine:

THE TWIN-PHYSICS WORLD: this is a possible world or twin-earth at which every property is necessitated by twin-mass, twin-charge, and twin-spin. The properties instantiated at this world duplicate whatever properties are instantiated at the actual world, insofar as this is possible.

The possible world described here is a variation of a famous story in philosophy due to Hilary Putnam, the twin-earth story (see Putnam 1975; the adaptation to the discussion of the physical is due to Alan Sussman—see Sussman 1981). In Putnam's original case, we are asked to imagine that we are back in 1750 before the development of modern chemistry. In our world, the stuff that we call water, the stuff that fills up the bathtub and falls from the sky as rain (or fails to fall from the sky as rain, if you live in a drought-affected part of the earth) is the chemical compound H_2O. On twin-earth, however, it is a quite different compound that, from the point of view of eighteenth-century science, is indistinguishable. Putnam used the example to argue that the reference of various terms like 'water' is determined not by factors internal to individual speakers (or the bodies of individual speakers) but by the way in which speakers are related to their environment; here we will adapt the basic idea of the example to a different topic, the interpretation of physicalism. (Putnam's example can be told in two kinds of ways: in one way we imagine that our world contains two earths, ours and a twin-earth; in another way, we imagine an alternative possible world that is chemically different. Here our focus is on the second way.)

Now, this adaptation of Putnam's twin-earth scenario raises a number of questions. As before, however, our questions are (a) 'Is actual theory physicalism true at the twin-physics world?'; and (b) 'Is physicalism as we normally understand it true at the twin-physics world?' (Once again: answer these questions yourself before proceeding.)

It seems to me that the answer to the second question is clearly 'yes.' At any rate, it is reasonable to suppose that, to the extent that physicalism is true in our world, it is true in the possible world I just described. One way to bring this out is to recall the point that physicalism is supposed to be an abstract account of the world, not tied to details of any particular physical theory. But the difference between the physics that is true at our world and the physics that is true at this imagined twin-world is in this sense a difference of detail. A different way to bring it out is to notice that the twin-physics world contains counterparts of all of our physicalists and anti-physicalists. Just as we have Hobbes, Smart, Descartes, and Broad, so they have twin-Hobbes, twin-Smart, twin-Descartes, and twin-Broad. It does not seem that the plausibility of the arguments of these twin-philosophers is affected by the fact that the underlying physics is different from the one that happens to be true in our world. To put it differently, if you think that Hobbes and Smart are having the better of their opponents in our world, you should likewise think that twin-Hobbes and twin-Smart are having the better of their opponents at the twin-physics world. So if physicalism is true at our world, it is likewise true at the twin-physics world.

On the other hand, while physicalism is true at the twin-physics world (alternatively: while it is true that twin-physicalism is a version of physicalism) actual theory physicalism is not true at the twin-physics world, and so our answer to the first question—'Is actual-theory physicalism true at this world?'—is 'no'. The reason that actual theory physicalism is not true at the twin-physics world is that it is defined in terms of the physical theory, whatever it is, that is true at the actual world. If the physics of the actual world tells us that mass and spin and charge are the fundamental properties, then actual theory physicalism will be false in any situation at which they are not the fundamental properties. And the twin-physics world is one such case. Hence actual theory physicalism is not true at the twin-physics world.

why not use a
why not use actual theory
view as sufficient but not nec.?

4.7 Could the conclusion have been reached more quickly?

Reflection on the twin-physics world shows that actual theory physicalism is not physicalism. Physicalism is true at the twin-physics world, but actual theory physicalism is not. But you might wonder at this stage whether this conclusion could have been reached in a more straightforward manner, and in particular in a manner that did not involve introducing a variation on one of the more famous thought experiments in modern philosophy.

For example, consider again a possibility discussed in the previous chapter:

> THE ATOMIST WORLD: this is a possible world at which every instantiated property is necessitated by some property distinctive of classical atoms. The properties instantiated at this world duplicate whatever properties are instantiated at the actual world, insofar as this is possible.

As we saw earlier, physicalism is true at the atomist world; indeed the atomist world is the paradigm case of a world in which physicalism is true. On the other hand, it might be argued that actual theory physicalism is not true at the atomist world. After all, the physics of the actual world is presumably not atomist in the sense intended here. But if that is right we reach our conclusion again: physicalism is not actual theory physicalism because it is true at the atomist world, but actual theory physicalism is not.

However, while this line of argument is suggestive, it is doubtful it will be ultimately successful against the actual theory physicalism. (I owe this point to Stephan Leuenberger.) We have so far been concentrating on a very simple version of the Theory View according to which a physical property is a property expressed by a true physical theory. But presumably it is possible to elaborate this basic idea so that what is at issue is not simply the true statements of some physical theory but the language of a physical theory more broadly construed. If we expand the notion of a physical theory in this way, it is unclear that the atomist world would be one at which actual theory physicalism would be false. For it is unclear that properties distinctive of atomism cannot be expressed in the language of actual physics, even if atomism is not true in the actual world. If that is so, we are obliged to use cases like the twin-physics world, and not simply cases like the atomist world, to argue that physicalism is not actual theory physicalism.

4.8 The possibilist version

The actualist version of the Theory View advances the hypothesis that physicalism is actual theory physicalism. As we have seen, that hypothesis runs into a major problem in the form of the twin-physics world. But of course that tells us nothing about the other version of the Theory View, the possibilist version. This version advances the hypothesis that physicalism is possible theory physicalism. What does the method of cases have to say about this hypothesis?

Well, applying again our standard procedure, the initial results are once again promising. Indeed, take *all* of the possible worlds we have so far considered: the atomist world, the atomist world with gravity, the modern physics world, and the twin-physics world. In all of these cases possible theory physicalism is true or at least could be. For in all of these worlds every property is necessitated by a property expressed by a physical theory that is true at those worlds. In consequence, possible theory physicalism is better as an interpretation of physicalism than anything we have come across so far.

However, while possible theory physicalism certainly does well in these cases, there is unfortunately a rather simple explanation of why this is the case, viz. it is an *extremely* permissive thesis. Indeed, this version of the Theory View is so permissive that it will permit physicalism to be true at many worlds at which it intuitively is not. Consider:

THE CLASSICAL DUALIST WORLD: this is a possible world which is exactly like the classical atomist world, but with this modification: when atoms come together to form human bodies, such bodies are yoked together with a soul in such a way that the behavior of the body is explained only on the assumption that it is influenced by soul and its distinctive properties. The properties instantiated at this world duplicate whatever properties are instantiated at the actual world, insofar as this is possible.

Suppose we ask, concerning the classical dualist world, versions of our standard questions: (a) 'Is physicalism true at the classical dualist world?'; and (b) 'Is possible theory physicalism true at the classical dualist world?' As regards the first question, it is obvious that the answer is 'no'. Just as the atomist world is a paradigm case for physicalists, so the classical dualist world is a paradigm case for the dualist: if classical dualism is not in conflict with physicalism, then it is hard to see that anything is.

On the other hand, as regards the second question, the answer would seem to be 'yes': while *physicalism* is false at the classical dualist world, *possible theory physicalism* is, or could be, true there. For consider: a physical theory is (we assumed earlier) a theory that explains the behavior and constitution of ordinary physical objects and related objects. But at the classical dualist world there is such a true theory, it is simply that the theory in question will make reference to souls and hence to irreducible mental properties. So, at such a world, the irreducible mental properties will count as physical because they are expressed by a physical theory that is true at that world. Similarly, at such a world, possible theory physicalism counts as true because, at that world, every property is necessitated by a property expressed by a true physical theory.

4.9 Adjusting the possibilist version

The conclusion to which we are heading is this. According to the Theory View, physicalism is either actual theory physicalism or possible theory physicalism. But it is not the first—for actual theory physicalism is false at a world, the twin-physics world, at which physicalism is clearly true. And it is not the second—for possible theory physicalism is true at a world, the classical dualist world, at which physicalism is clearly false. Hence no version of the Theory View, considered as an account about what physicalism is, could possibly be true.

At this point, you might object that our focus has been much too narrow. Earlier we saw that, in view of the falsity of the Starting Point View, it is necessary to liberalize it, that is, to operate with an account of what it is to be a physical property that draws on some, rather than all, elements of the cluster that defines what it is to be a physical property. The Theory View, which is our version of such a liberalized theory, is very liberal, because it operates with only one element of the cluster. Could one not appeal to other elements of the cluster to strengthen it so that it avoids the objection from the classical dualist world? This suggestion is a perfectly natural one, but on reflection it seems a difficult one to sustain. The problem is basically that there are many cases rather like the classical dualist world, and adjusting matters to deal with this case will not avoid the underlying problem

To illustrate, let us examine this sort of maneuver in what is perhaps its most natural form, in which it takes the possibilist version of the Theory View so far discussed and adds to it the element in the cluster I called Contrast (cf. Wilson 2006). As we saw, Contrast says that physical properties are not the distinctive properties of souls, ectoplasm, psi-phenomena, ESP, etc. If we add this to the Theory View as we have so far discussed it, the resulting proposal is this:

(6) *F* is a physical property if and only if:
    (a) *F* is expressed by a predicate of a physical theory that is true at some possible world; and
    (b) *F* is not one of the distinctive properties of souls, ectoplasm, etc.

Factoring this into physicalism, we arrive at a version of physicalism that will not be true at the classical dualist world, for the simple reason that no distinctive property of a soul could be a physical property.

Now one problem that might be mentioned for this proposal relates to a point already discussed in Chapter 2: the point that there are cases at which both physicalism and idealism are true. There we noted that one way to avoid such cases is to make it analytic to the notion of a physical property that physical properties are not mental. And we also noted that the disadvantage of this view was that it made the mind–brain identity theory not simply false but incoherent. Isn't appealing to Contrast going to run into a similar problem?

The answer is 'no,' and the reason is that, while it would be problematic to define the physical as, inter alia, the non-mental, the idea behind Contrast is much less sweeping. What it says is that there are certain clear cases of things that are both mental and non-physical, and that these clear cases need to be respected by any proposal about how to define the physical. It does not say that *anything* mental is non-physical. For that reason, therefore, it seems to me to be reasonable to build Contrast in to the definition of physicalism, but not reasonable (or, anyway, far less reasonable) to build the notion of the non-mental into the definition.

However, while it might be reasonable to build Contrast in our account of what a physical property is, doing so is not going to solve the underlying problem that possible theory physicalism is too permissive. For consider:

THE PRIMITIVE COLOR WORLD: This is a possible world which is exactly like the classical atomist world, but with this modification: when atoms come together to form objects roughly congruent in size with human bodies, these objects instantiate primitive colors, and the behavior and nature of these objects cannot be explained except on the assumption that they instantiate these properties. The properties instantiated at this world duplicate whatever properties are instantiated at the actual world, insofar as this is possible.

It is quite standard in philosophy of mind to treat this sort of possibility as inconsistent with physicalism. When David Armstrong (1968: 270) remarks that "the conception of secondary qualities as irreducible or unanalyzable properties has led to the greatest problems," he means that this conception has led to the greatest problems *for physicalism*; in particular, to put it in our terminology, he means that physicalism is not true at the primitive color world. Nevertheless, the primitive color world is one at which possibilist theory physicalism is true, just as much as it was at the classical dualist world. So the primitive color world poses a problem directly analogous to the classical dualist world. On the other hand, one cannot avoid the problem by appealing to the idea that physical properties are not mental, because at the primitive color world, the properties that cause the problem are not *mental* properties at all—colors, after all, are not in the mind.

Of course, the possibilist might now appeal to the two remaining elements of the cluster of things that define what it is to be a physical property, Objectivity and Method. Objectivity says that physical properties are such that one can know that they are instantiated from more than one point of view. What this means—to put it roughly but well enough for present purposes—is that creatures with very different background psychologies and histories can come to know that physical properties are instantiated: understanding what a physical property is does not require having a partic- ular sort of psychology or history. The contrast here is with various psycho- logical properties: understanding what the taste of Vegemite is does seem to depend on having a quite particular psychology and history. For its part, Method says that physical properties are those we could come to know through an application of the methods distinctive of the natural sciences. What this means—again: roughly but well enough for present purposes— relates to the notion of naturalism that I set out in the introduction. The thought is that there is a distinctive sort of method that *those* people (i.e. scientists) use, and that physical properties can be found out about using those methods.

Suppose now we add Objectivity and Method to the version of the Theory View we were just discussing. The result would be something that takes all of the elements of the cluster that define what it is to be a physical property except one (Object) and builds them into an account:

(7) *F* is a physical property if and only if *F* is
  (a) expressed by a predicate of a physical theory that is true at some possible world;
  (b) is not one of the distinctive properties of souls, ectoplasm, etc; and
  (c) is objective; and
  (d) is the sort of property about which one could find out using the methods of the sciences.

Factoring this definition of a physical property into our definition of physicalism, we arrive at a version of physicalism that will avoid the problem presented by the primitive color world. Primitive colors, while not mental, are perhaps subjective rather than objective; that is, it is not the case that one can understand primitive colors from more than one point of view. Hence they will not count as physical by the lights of (7).

Once again, however, it seems easy enough to imagine other cases. Consider either of the following:

THE VITALIST WORLD: this is a possible world exactly like the classical atomist world, but with this modification: when atoms come together to form objects which are the counterparts of our plants and animals, these objects instantiate élan vital, a property quite distinct from any associated with atomism, and the behavior and nature of these objects (in particular their growth and reproduction) cannot be explained except on the assumption that they instantiate these properties. The other properties instantiated at this world duplicate whatever properties obtain at the actual world, insofar as this is possible.

THE EMERGENT CHEMISTRY WORLD: this is a possible world exactly like the classical atomist world but with this modification: when combined together atoms instantiate chemical properties which explain the observed behavior of molecules but which are themselves distinct from any property associated with atomism. The other properties instantiated at this world duplicate whatever properties obtain at the actual world, insofar as this is possible.

The first of these examples involves a theoretical possibility, vitalism, which is contrary to physicalism on anyone's view. The second example is less well known to contemporary discussion but in fact had a prominent role in earlier phases of philosophy of mind—e.g. in Broad's *The Mind and its Place* in *Nature* it appears as one kind of anti-physicalism (see Broad 1925). But whichever example is in play the point they make is the same. While both the vitalist world and the emergent chemistry world are cases at which physicalism is false, they are both cases at which possible theory physicalism might well be true, at least if the background notion of a physical property is taken to conform to (7). There is nothing subjective, or mental, or unscientific about élan vital or fundamental chemical properties, it is simply that they are not physical.

4.10 Adjusting the actualist version

I have been talking so far about whether we might strengthen the possibilist version of the Theory View. The other suggestion we need to consider is that the actualist version of the Theory View might be weakened or adjusted so that it can accommodate the various counterexamples we have provided.

The most common suggestion here (e.g. Lewis 1986; Ravenscroft 1997) is to appeal to similarity:

(8) *F* is a physical property if and only if
    (a) *F* is expressed by a predicate of a physical theory that is true in the actual world; or
    (b) *F* is similar to the sort of property that is expressed by a predicate of a physical theory that is true in the actual world.

One problem with the proposal, of course, is that it is plausible only because it is very coy about what the dimensions of similarity are. A priori, anything is similar to any thing else.

However, even if we waive the general problem about similarity, it is hard to see this version of actual theory physicalism as an improvement. For consider the twin-physics world again. Are the properties instantiated at this world similar in the relevant respects to those instantiated in the actual world or not? Either answer to this question leads to trouble. On the one hand, if they are similar, it is unclear that the properties instantiated at the classical dualist world (or perhaps other non-physicalist worlds) are not similar in those respects too. But then a version of physicalism that employs (8) will be true at the dualist world. On the other hand, if they are not similar, the version of physicalism that employs (8) will not be true at the twin-physics world. But as we have seen, there is no justification for that assertion.

4.11 Four further suggestions

We saw earlier that the actualist version of the Theory View is too restrictive and the possibilist version is too permissive. What we have just seen is that adjusting these views does not alter that underlying problem. We may complete our discussion of the Theory View by briefly considering four further suggestions.

4.11.1 Further conditions on physical theories

The first questions the notion of a physical theory with which we have been operating. We have been assuming that a physical theory is a theory with a certain subject matter, the nature, constitution, and behavior of ordinary physical objects and related phenomena. But it might be objected that, while a physical theory certainly has the property of being concerned with this subject matter, it also has some further properties. Moreover, the objection continues, when these further properties are taken into consideration it will become clear that there is a mistake in what we said earlier about possible theory physicalism and the classical dualist world. What we argued earlier was that possible theory physicalism might perfectly well be true at the classical dualist world but no version of physicalism ought to be true there. But the argument for this turned on the idea that there is a true physical theory at the classical dualist world. Now, if a physical theory is simply a theory with a certain subject matter that point goes through. But what if a physical theory is a theory with a certain subject matter and some further feature? Then it is much less clear.

This suggestion is a good one in the abstract, but it becomes less attractive if one asks what this further feature could possibly be. So far as I know the suggestions that have been made about what this further property could be all suffer from the defect that the property in question is either not a property of physical theories as such, or else is true of the physical theory true at the classical dualist world. For example, it is sometimes said that physical theories are comprehensive or apply to all fundamental properties or are universal. But the problem is that this does not seem to be true of physical theories as such. As Jeffrey Poland has convincingly argued (Poland 1994: 120–2), it might be the case that a physical theory has these properties if physicalism is true, but we cannot assume that in the present context. To take a different example, Janice Dowell (2006) argues that a physical theory needs to have the further property of integration, and one might appeal to this property to explain why possible theory physicalism is not true at the classical dualist world. However, there are two things wrong with this idea. The first is that it is not clear that it is essential to a physical theory that it has this feature. (Dowell herself thinks this is only a contingent feature, as I understand her.) Second, it is not clear why the physical theory that is true at the classical dualist world is not integrated in the relevant sense.

4.11.2 *The via negativa*

The second suggestion appeals to what is sometimes called the 'via negativa,' the idea that one may define what a physical property is negatively, as not something else. A simple way to formulate the via negativa is to say that something is a physical property if and only if it is not a mental property. But for reasons that have emerged this is no good; for example, it has the consequence that the mind–brain identity theory is incoherent. A better way to proceed is to define a physical property as not one of the properties mentioned in Contrast. Earlier we considered the idea that Contrast might be added to the Theory View; what proponents of the via negativa hold, as I understand them, is that Contrast will do on its own.

But there are many reasons to resist such a definition. Take the vitalist world again. It seems reasonable to say that in that world plants and animals instantiate a property that is non-physical, i.e. élan vital is not physical. And yet one should not say on this account that plants and animals instantiate a mental property, i.e. élan vital is not mental. In short, élan vital is neither mental nor physical. But the via negativa cannot accommodate that fact.

One might try to meet this objection by building élan vital into Contrast. But the problem now is that just as élan vital is neither mental nor physical, there seem to be properties that are neither mental nor physical nor biological—the properties associated with emergent chemistry, for example. A proponent of the via negativa might at this point suggest adding them to the list on Contrast as well (cf. Papineau 2001). But while such a move is certainly possible—in fact it can be repeated indefinitely—it is quite unclear that it is a good way to tell us what a physical property is. It is perfectly true in principle that one can say what a thing is by listing all the possible things that it is not, but by the same token this is not a good way of explaining what a thing is. Suppose you ask me what a dog is, and I say that it is something that is not a cat (this is the via negativa applied to the property of being a dog). You point out reasonably that according to my

[margin handwritten note, right side:] body of questions

[margin handwritten note, right side:] mind / body questions

[handwritten note at bottom of page:] But if were not in the business of conceptual analysis, then we don't have worry about this. The indefinite ad hoc style is perfect isfine

proposed definition a hamster is a dog, i.e. since it is not a cat. I reply by conceding the point but modifying my original definition: something is a dog if it is neither a cat nor a hamster. You reply by making the same point this time using the example of a donkey. We could of course continue in this vein for an indefinite amount of time, but it is quite unclear what the point of it would be.

✔ To discuss dogish v wily coyotish Problems.

4.11.3 *Microphysicalism*

The third suggestion appeals to what is usually called 'microphysicalism.' (I am indebted to Kelvin McQueen here.) Microphysicalism is a version of physicalism that says that the fundamental physical properties are proper-ties of the relatively small. On the face of it microphysicalism is only one version of physicalism. However, suppose one thought that any version of physicalism was also a version of microphysicalism. Then one would have a reason to rule out the idea that physicalism is true at the classical dualist world—and *mutatis mutandis*, the vitalist world and the emergent chemistry world. For in all of these cases, what we have are cases in which objects that are not very small instantiate non-physical properties.

However, there are at least three things wrong with this suggestion. First, it does not seem hard to imagine cases in which the non-physical properties are likewise properties of the very small—examples involving panpsychism might be of that sort. Second, it is implausible that physicalism entails microphysicalism. For example, imagine a case in which every property is necessitated by properties of individual atoms, plus a macro property—the entire shape of the universe, say. Such a case does not seem in any way contrary to the spirit of physicalism, but it would be if physicalism entailed microphysicalism. Finally, many physicalists believe that microphysicalism is not true at the actual world; on the other hand, since they also believe that physicalism is true at the actual world, it is natural to think that physicalism does not entail microphysicalism. (For discussion, see Papineau 2007.)

4.11.4 *Indexicality*

The final suggestion appeals to indexicality, and in particular to the sugges-tion that 'actual' is an indexical. So far we have talked informally about 'the actual world' as if this was simply a name for the world that we are in. However, it is more common in philosophy to suppose that 'actual' is an indexical expression—that is, an expression semantically like 'I,' 'here,' 'now,' and so on—and one might think that this has an impact on how we are thinking of the twin-physics case.

To illustrate, suppose Smart, in the actual world, says 'I'm hungry' and twin-Smart in the twin-physics world, likewise says 'I'm hungry.' Notoriously, there is a sense in which what they say is the same and a sense in which what they say is different. To borrow David Kaplan's famous distinction between character and content (see Kaplan 1989), we might say that the content of what Smart says is different from the content of what twin-Smart says, while the character is the same. The content of what Smart said is that Smart is hungry, while the content of what twin-Smart said is that twin-Smart is hungry. If we focus on the content of what Smart said, then we arrive at the idea that the two philosophers said something different, and moreover that what Smart said is false at the twin-physics world. On the other hand, it remains possible to say that the character of what they said is the same, since they both said something that was true just in case the speaker who uttered the sentence was hungry.

All right so far; but now suppose that Smart says not something boring like 'I'm hungry' but something exciting (or apparently exciting) like 'actual physics provides a complete description of the world'; and suppose moreover that twin-Smart says the same. If we treat 'actual' as an indexical, we should be able to draw a character/content distinction in this case just as we did in the previous one. And indeed we can. In effect, the content of what Smart says is what I earlier called actual theory physicalism. This theory is different from the content of what twin-Smart says, and moreover is false at the twin-physics world. On the other hand, it remains open to us to say that the character of what Smart said is the same as the character of what twin-Smart said, since both said something that is true (at a world) just in case the physical theory of that world provides a complete description of that world. But this undermines our discussion of the twin-physics case. For suppose we identify physicalism with the character of what Smart said rather than with the content. Then it will turn out that what Smart says and what twin-Smart says is the same, and moreover is true at both worlds. So if we identify physicalism with the character of what is said we avoid the objectionable result that physicalism is false at the twin-physics world.

I think this suggestion does indeed avoid the problem of physicalism being false at the twin-physics world. But unfortunately it does not avoid other problems, and these problems are similar to those we have already looked at. For consider the counterpart of Smart in the classical dualist world, dualist-Smart, and imagine that at that world he says 'actual physics provides a complete description of reality.' The character of what he said at that world is presumably exactly the same as the character of what both Smart and twin-Smart said. Moreover, if we evaluate the character for truth, then it will come out true in the classical dualist world. So the problem here is a version of our basic dilemma. If in the case we have imagined, we identify physicalism with the content of what Smart said, physicalism turns out to be false at the twin-physics world. On the other hand, if we identify physicalism with the character of what Smart says, physicalism will turn out be true at the classical dualist world. But either result is objectionable.

4.12 The argument of the last two chapters in a nutshell

The discussion about physical properties that we have been having over the last two chapters might be stated briefly by noting that it suggests both a metathesis about physicalism and an argument for that metathesis. (A metathesis, in this context, is simply a thesis about a thesis.) The metathesis is:

(9) There is no version of the thesis that is
   (a) true; and
   (b) deserves the name.

The argument for the metathesis is:

P1 In formulating physicalism, we must operate either with the Starting Point View or some liberalized version of the Starting Point View.

P2 If we operate with the Starting Point View, it is possible to articulate a version of physicalism that deserves the name, but that version is false.

P3 If we operate with a liberalized version of the Starting Point View, it is possible to articulate a version of physicalism that is true, but that version does not deserve the name, because either:
   (a) it is true at possible worlds where no version of physicalism should be true; or
   (b) or it is false at possible worlds where no version of physicalism should be false.

C There is no version of physicalism that is both true and deserving of the name.

This argument is clearly valid, so the question is whether its premises are plausible.

But the premises *are* plausible, or at any rate so our previous discussion has suggested. The first premise of the argument flows from the idea that the concept of the physical is a cluster concept that includes the features I introduced in the previous chapter: Object, Theory, Objectivity, Method, and Contrast. What P1 says is that if these are the features then you must define physicalism either in terms of all of them or else in terms of a (proper) subset of them—and this follows immediately if we assume that the concept of the physical is a cluster concept in the way described.

The second premise of the argument is a straightforward consequence of the material discussed in the previous chapter. What it says is that if you adopt the Starting Point View both of what a physical property is, and of what physicalism is, then you will wind up with a version of physicalism that is false, and moreover, is false for philosophically uncontroversial reasons.

The third premise of the argument summarizes the main argument of this chapter. We saw that if you operate with the Theory View, and so operate with an extremely liberal version of the Starting Point View, then the resultant versions of physicalism will be either false at worlds at which no version of physicalism should be false, or true at worlds at which no version of physicalism should be true. We also saw, more briefly, that if you enrich the Theory View with any of the other elements of the cluster this basic problem will not go away.

So it would seem that the premises of the argument are plausible. On the other hand, while the argument is valid and its premises are plausible, its conclusion is somewhat startling at least on first hearing. Should we accept it? And what are the consequences of accepting it if we should? These are questions that deserve an answer. However, before trying to answer them I am going to turn my attention from the reflection on possible cases that has occupied our attention up to now to other questions about how to clarify physicalism.

Summary

In this chapter, we have considered what I called the liberalization project. As I explained at the beginning of this chapter, the liberalization project is the project of finding a version of physicalism that is not false because of developments within science itself. As we have seen, the prospects of the liberalization project look dim, because it is difficult to see how to articulate a version of physicalism that will 'get the cases right,' i.e. is true at possible worlds where physicalism is intuitively true and false at possible world where it is intuitively false. When we combine this point with the main point of the previous chapter, that starting point physicalism is false, we arrive at an argument which I just formulated, an argument we will come back to in detail in subsequent discussion.

Recommended reading

For discussions of the liberalization project which complement the one undertaken in this chapter, see Stroud (1986), Daly (1998), Chomsky (2000, 2009), van Fraassen (2002), and Strawson (2003, 2006). For a recent defense of actual theory physicalism, see Melnyk (2003). For the twin-earth example (though expressed slightly differently), see Sussman (1981). For possible theory physicalism, see Dowell (2006). For possible theory physicalism with Contrast added, see Wilson (2006). For the via negativa see Montero (1999, 2009), Montero and Papineau (2005) and Gillett and Witmer (2001). For microphysicalism see Pettit (1994), Hutteman and Papineau (1999), and Papineau (2007, and the references therein).

5

HEMPEL'S DILEMMA

5.1 Introduction

The argument we just formulated has the form of a dilemma. It tells us, first, that if physicalism is interpreted one way, i.e. as starting point physicalism, something bad happens; second, that if physicalism is interpreted another way, i.e. as some liberalized version of starting point physicalism, something else bad happens; and, third, that these two ways exhaust the field. However, while the argument of the last two chapters is a dilemma that concerns the interpretation of physicalism, it is in fact not the standard dilemma in this area of philosophy. That dilemma is usually called 'Hempel's dilemma.' This chapter focuses on Hempel's dilemma, and compares it with the one we have just been discussing.

5.2 The Theory View again

We may start by looking again at the Theory View, and in particular at its first part, the part that tells us what a physical property is. When suitably interpreted, that said:

(1) F is a physical property if and only if F is expressed by a predicate of a true physical theory.

We have already noted one source of interpretative complexity in (1), turning on whether the physical theory at issue is true in the actual world, or true at some possible world or other. The *actualist* version of the Theory View says that what is at issue is truth in the actual world, the *possibilist* version says that what is at issue is truth in some possible world or other.

However, in addition to the actualist/possibilist distinction, there is also a second source of interpretative complexity in (1). Construed as a discipline, physics is an activity that has been going on for some time. It is going on now, and will presumably go on until the point, if there is such a point, at which scientists reach the end of their inquiries. Now, in view of the fact that physics has been going on for some time, the basic idea behind (1) might be reasonably interpreted in one of two ways: either it could be interpreted as talking about the physical theory *that we currently believe to be true*, or it could be interpreted as talking about the physical theory that will turn out to be true in the ideal case, *whether or not* that coincides with what we currently believe.

On the first interpretation of this idea—I will call it the 'current theory' version—(1) goes over into:

(2) *F* is a physical property if and only if *F* is expressed by a predicate of a physical theory that is true by our current lights.

If we call a physical property so defined a 'current theory property', the current theory version of the Theory View says that physical properties are current theory properties. Likewise, if we call the version of physicalism that might be defined in terms of current theory properties 'current theory physicalism'—I will pass over the precise details of how to do this; it should be clear from the previous discussion—then this version of the Theory View says that physicalism is current theory physicalism.

On the second interpretation—I will call it the 'ideal theory' version—(1) goes over into:

(3) *F* is a physical property if and only if *F* is expressed by a predicate of a physical theory that is true in the ideal limit.

If we call a physical property so defined an 'ideal theory property,' this version of the Theory View says that physical properties are ideal theory properties. Likewise, if we call the version of physicalism that might be defined in terms of ideal theory properties 'ideal theory physicalism'—as above, I will pass over the precise details of how to do this—then this version of the Theory View says that physicalism is ideal theory physicalism.

5.3 What is an ideal theory?

I have expressed the distinction at issue here as one between the physical theory that is currently believed to be true, and the physical theory that is true in the ideal limit. Now, the notion of an ideal limit is often associated with the nineteenth-century philosopher C.S. Peirce, who in turn is often credited with a theory of truth according to which a proposition is true if it is appropriate to assert the proposition at the ideal limit of inquiry. On the face of it, however, it seems reasonable to be skeptical about this idea. What counts as an ideal theory exactly, and in what respects is it ideal? It might be said that an ideal theory is one that is epistemically ideal in the sense that it is formulated by people who have taken all possible evidence into account. But what is all possible evidence, and how should one take it into account? Since the answers to these questions are unclear, one might be concerned that Hempel's dilemma is itself unclear.

One way to avoid this problem is by speaking not of an ideal theory but of a future theory, i.e. a theory that we will believe in the future. However, while this suggestion avoids the problem of ideal theories it nevertheless faces others. For example, what if there is no future? Suppose the end of the universe happens unexpectedly soon—in ten minutes, say. Obviously this would be extremely unfortunate in all sorts of ways, but why should it be extremely unfortunate from the point of view of physicalism? (Would it show that physicalism is *false*, for example?) Moreover, what if the theory that we end up with in the future is worse from an epistemic point of view than the one we have now? While it is sometimes tempting to suppose so, in fact there is no a priori guarantee that the unfolding of time will bring us closer and closer to the truth.

A better way to avoid the problem is by noting that, while it is traditional to formulate Hempel's dilemma in terms of the notion of an ideal theory, in fact this is unnecessary. I have contrasted so far the theory that we currently believe to be true with the theory that is true in the ideal limit. But I could just as well have contrasted the theory that we currently believe to be true with the theory that is in fact true. Indeed, one might think that this is what an ideal theory meant all along—after all, if the ideal physical theory is not simply the theory that is in fact true, what exactly is it? But even if that is not right, it is perfectly possible to formulate the argument in terms of the contrast between what is believed currently to be true, and what is true. However, having noted these alternative ways to formulate matters I will largely continue in the terms I have adopted here. So far as I can see, the main points can be stated whichever distinction is in play.

5.4 The dilemma formulated

We have seen that, in addition to the two versions of the Theory View distinguished in the previous chapter, the actualist versus the possibilist version, we have two further versions, the current theory version versus the ideal theory version. We now turn to Hempel's dilemma itself, which as I understand it is an argument founded on this distinction.

In the course of a commentary on Goodman's *Ways of Worldmaking*, Hempel wrote:

> I would add that the physicalist claim that the language of physics can serve as a unitary language of science is inherently obscure: the language of what physics is meant? Surely not that of, say, eighteenth-century physics; for it contains terms like 'caloric fluid,' whose use is governed by theoretical assumptions now thought false. Nor can the language of contemporary physics claim the role of unitary language, since it will no doubt undergo further changes too. The thesis of physicalism would seem to require a language in which a *true* theory of all physical phenomena can be formulated. But it is quite unclear what is to be understood here by a physical phenomenon, especially in the context of a doctrine that has taken a decidedly linguistic turn. (Hempel 1980: 194–5.)

Hempel here was contrasting Goodman's position with that of Otto Neurath (see Neurath 1931a, 1931b). As we saw earlier, Hempel interprets Neurath's physicalism as being the linguistic doctrine that every statement is equivalent in meaning to—i.e. is synonymous with—some physical statement (see Hempel 1949). And, on its face, Hempel's point is limited to a criticism of physicalists of this type. But as we have already seen, few if any physicalists are of that type now. Nowadays, physicalism is the metaphysical doctrine that, not necessarily but as a matter of fact, every instantiated property is necessitated by some instantiated physical property. So it might appear that, even if Hempel is right about the inherent obscurity of this semantic version of physicalism, this is not something with which a contemporary physicalist need be overly concerned.

For most philosophers, however, the problem Hempel is posing ⌐ a problem not simply for a linguistic version of physicalism but for the metaphysical version as well. Geoffrey Hellman, for example, writing a few years after Hempel, describes it as "perhaps the most serious objection to all efforts in formulating physicalism," and formulates it in the following influential and often-quoted passage:

> current physics is surely incomplete (even in its ontology) as well as inaccurate (in its laws). This poses a dilemma: either physicalist principles are based on current physics, in which case there is every reason to think they are false; or else they are not, in which case it is, at best, difficult to interpret them, since they are based on a 'physics' that does not exist—yet we lack any general criterion of 'physical object, property, or law' framed independently of physical theory. (Hellman 1985: 609).

Moreover, in supposing that the problem is a problem for physicalists in general, Hellman has been followed by many others. Hempel's dilemma has become, as Poland puts it (1994: 157) "the stock objection."

What exactly is the argument here? I think it is best expressed in terms of the distinction just introduced between current theory physicalism and ideal theory physicalism. In particular, Hempel's dilemma says that you must choose one of these options and that neither is any good. The first option is no good because if physicalism is interpreted as current theory physicalism, then it is false. And the second option is no good because if physicalism is interpreted as ideal theory physicalism, then we don't know what it says.

Putting this line of reasoning into premise-and-conclusion form, we arrive at the following argument:

H1 If physical properties are by definition the properties expressed by the predicates of a current physical theory, physicalism is false.

H2 If physical properties are by definition the properties expressed by the predicates of an ideal physical theory, we don't know what physicalism says.

H3 Either it is the case that physical properties are by definition the properties expressed by predicates of a current physical theory, or it is the case that physical properties are by definition the properties expressed by predicates of an ideal physical theory.

HC Either physicalism is false or we don't know what it says.

Understood this way, Hempel's dilemma is a valid argument for a prima facie significant conclusion. What reasons are there for the premises? I will address this question by focusing on each premise in turn.

5.5 The first premise

Suppose we think of a physical theory as a theory that aims to provide a complete inventory of the properties and relations required in the explanation of ordinary physical objects and related phenomena. Surely current physics does not provide a complete inventory; that is, surely we are in the midst of an ongoing investigation, rather than being at the end or close to the end of the investigation. Now, to say that current physics is incomplete is not to say that it is mistaken in any specific suggestion it makes about which properties and relations are required in the explanation of ordinary physical objects and related phenomena. Philosophers sometimes assert that current physics must be mistaken in these ways. Some, for example, argue it is mistaken because it is inconsistent—various parts of it cannot be true together; others argue it is mistaken because, since physical theories have been false in the past, current physical theory is very likely false too. Whatever is the truth of these claims, they are largely irrelevant to Hempel's dilemma as I understand it. The starting point of the dilemma is not that current physics is mistaken about the inventory but that it has not completed the inventory.

Now, if current physics is indeed incomplete, presumably there is a possible future physical theory that is complete, or at least is more complete than current physics is. Let us now imagine such a theory, and in particular imagine that a predicate of such a theory expresses a property—call it 'F'—where, let us also imagine, F is an instantiated property not necessitated by any of the properties expressed by current physics. Now, if physical properties are by definition those that are expressed by the predicates of current physical theory, F is not physical. This is not to say that F is spooky or ethereal, nor that F conforms to any paradigm we might have of what a nonphysical property is; in fact, since we have no idea what F is, F conforms to no paradigm at all. It is just to say that if physical properties are by definition contemporary physical properties, F is not physical.

Now, that F is not physical is not by itself a problem for physicalism. The beauty of Venice is a property of Venice, but not a physical property of

Venice. But that is no problem for physicalism, for as we have seen physicalism is not the thesis that every property is a physical property. It is rather the thesis that every instantiated property is necessitated by some instantiated physical property—and this formulation permits the instantiation of some non-physical properties. However, while F's not being physical is not by itself a problem for physicalism, there is a related consideration that is. For not only is F not physical; it is also not necessitated by any physical property. That in fact was our assumption. But now it does indeed follow that physicalism is false: F is an instantiated property that is neither physical nor necessitated by anything physical; physicalism entails that there is no such property.

In sum the reason for H1 is that current physics is incomplete. If current physics is incomplete, then, if physical properties are by definition those expressed by contemporary physics, physicalism is false.

5.6 The second premise

Suppose that the Peircean limit of inquiry is reached at 5.00 p.m. on November 5, 3027. Presumably the scientists leaving work on that fateful day—of course they may not know that the day in question is the fateful one—will have formulated some physical theory, and the theory in question will say at least that there are various properties, let us call them 'F', 'G,' and 'H,' which do various things. If physical properties are by definition the properties expressed by the predicates of this ideal physics, then the physical properties are F, G, and H. Similarly, if physical properties are by definition the properties expressed by the predicates of ideal physics, then physicalism tells us that F, G, and H necessitate every other (instantiated) property, either singly or in combination. But what then does physicalism say? For those of us who are not at the Peircean limit the answer seems to be that we have no idea. Physicalism says that every property is necessitated by some complex of F, G, and H. But since we don't know what F, G, and H are, we don't know what physicalism says. Of course we can in a sense name these properties and refer to them; I have just done so at least schematically. But naming is different from knowing. Even if we can name the properties, we still don't know what they are, and nor do we know what physicalism says. In effect, we are like the people in Gareth Evans's example who can refer to Julius as 'the actual inventor of the zip,' but do not know who Julius is (Evans 1983).

There is another way to bring out the sense in which if physicalism is ideal theory physicalism we don't know what it says. If physicalism is ideal theory physicalism, then what we *do* know is that a potentially infinite series of conditionals of the following form are true:

> If the properties expressed by ideal physics are those distinctive of classical atoms, then physicalism says that everything is necessitated by the properties distinctive of classical atoms.

> If the properties expressed by ideal physics are those distinctive of quantum wave-function states, then physicalism says that everything is necessitated by the properties distinctive of quantum wave-function states.

> If the properties expressed by ideal physics are those distinctive of Leibnizian monads, then physicalism says that everything is necessitated by the properties distinctive of Leibnizian monads.

> If the properties expressed by ideal physics are those distinctive of pumpkins, then physicalism says that everything is necessitated by the properties distinctive of pumpkins.

> ...

However, while we know that a series of conditionals like this are true, we do not know which of them (if any) have true antecedents. And this means that we do not know what physicalism says. We know that if such and such is true, then physicalism says things are thus and so. But we don't know whether such and such is true.

Suppose then we don't know what physicalism says—what follows? Well, if we do not understand it at all, we are in no position to know it, no position to deny it, no position to believe or disbelieve it with justification. Nor are we even in a position to speculate about whether it is true. In fact the whole project of rationally assessing physicalism—providing reasons for and against it, declaring oneself for it or against it, saying it is a good bet at least in the long run—seems to presuppose that we know what it is, at least in outline. But if that presupposition is false, physicalism is unworthy of assessment.

In sum the reason for H2 is that we don't know what an ideal physics says. If we don't know what ideal physics says, then, if physical properties are by definition the properties expressed by the predicates of ideal physics, we don't know what physicalism says.

5.7 The third premise

The first premise of Hempel's Dilemma says that if physical properties are defined one way, something bad happens, and the second premise tells us that if physical properties are defined some other way, something different but also bad happens. The third premise tells us that these methods of definition exhaust the field: either physical properties are defined in terms of a theory that is current or they are defined in terms of a theory that is ideal. What is there to motivate this premise?

Actually, it is surprisingly difficult to extract from the literature any reason at all to motivate this premise; indeed, this point will be important in our ultimate assessment of Hempel's dilemma. At least as I read them, most contributions to this debate fail outright to provide such considerations, and pass over this part of the argument without comment. Indeed, so far as I am able to judge many people seem to think H3 is just obvious. (To verify this claim, you should look through the articles mentioned in the recommended readings at the end of this chapter.)

Why do people think this? The main reason, I suspect, is that it is easy to confuse H3 with a logical truth. Now presumably it *is* logical truth that physics is either current or it is not; likewise presumably it is a logical truth either physical properties are by definition those expressed by a current physical theory or they are not. If the third premise of Hempel's dilemma were either of these logical truths, it would not require serious defense. But the third premise of Hempel's dilemma is not either of these. For H3 does not say that physics is current or it is not. Nor does it say that either physical properties are by definition expressed by a current physical theory or they are not. What it says is that either physical properties are by definition expressed by a currently believed physical theory or they are by definition expressed by an ideal physical theory, i.e. a theory that is true at the actual world. And this, as we will see in 5.10 below, is an entirely different matter.

5.8 Fallibilism

So far I have set out Hempel's dilemma and said something about the motivation for each premise. Is the argument sound? Well, a common first reaction (though one I have strangely not found in print) is that it is unsound because it fails to appreciate the sense in which the contemporary physicalist is a fallibilist in epistemology. The fallibilist in epistemology holds that, at least for any empirical belief, the evidence that one has for the belief does not entail that the belief in question is true. Fallibilists emphasize that, at least in empirical matters, there is no certainty, no ruling out all possible alternatives. And the contemporary physicalist certainly is by nature a fallibilist. Indeed, the very idea that physicalism is a kind of empirical, but abstract, hypothesis is suggestive of fallibilism.

However, while physicalists may well be fallibilists, what is the connection between fallibilism and Hempel's dilemma? Well, as we have seen, the reasoning in support of both H1 and H2 presupposes that contemporary physics is incomplete. In the case of H1, the incompleteness of current physics supports the idea that if physicalism is defined in terms of it, then physicalism is false. In the case of H2, it supports the idea that we don't know what an ideal physics will say. But perhaps a physicalist could insist that, in their view, physics *is* complete—it is simply that, compatibly with what we know, it *might not* be complete. In sum, fallibilism permits one to respond to Hempel's dilemma by denying the incompleteness of physics. "It is not true that physics is incomplete," you might say, "all that is true is that it might be; that is, it is consistent with our evidence that it is."

Without further development, this response to Hempel's dilemma is unsatisfactory. It is true that both the completeness and the incompleteness of current physics are logically compatible with the truth of what physics tells us about the world now, and it is certainly true that most physicalists are fallibilists and reasonably so. However, this does not mean that it is plausible to believe that current science is complete. On the contrary, there seem a rather large number of reasons for supposing the opposite:

- There may be *cosmological* reasons: we may think of ourselves (or humans in general) as occupying a very small pocket of the universe; it is amazing to think that cognitive mastery could be achieved from such a vantage point.
- There may be *evolutionary* reasons: we may think of ourselves (or humans in general) as evolved creatures whose cognitive capacities have been shaped by millions of years of evolution; surely in that case it is implausible that minds like ours could form a complete picture.
- There may be *psychological* reasons: we may think of our mind (or the human mind in general) as being subject to various kinds of barriers, constraints, or filters; surely it is implausible that minds of our kind are likely to know all, or almost all, the facts.
- There may be *historical* reasons: we may think that the science of our own day is like that of previous epochs in that it contains mistakes,

confusions, wrong turns, and approximations; the natural inference is that present circumstances are no different from previous circumstances in these respects, even if present science is better than, or closer to the truth than, other sciences.

- There may be *methodological* reasons: we may think that the practice of science or rational inquiry presupposes that one doesn't know various types of facts: the very point of scientific inquiry seems to presuppose ignorance.

In summary, while it is true that both the completeness and incompleteness of current physics are logically compatible with what science tells us about the world, it is not hard to motivate the hypothesis that current physics is indeed incomplete. So appealing to fallibilism will not help the physicalist respond to Hempel's dilemma.

Of course, one might respond again that, while these considerations are true enough in their way, they nevertheless do not actually *entail* that current knowledge is incomplete; hence it remains open for an optimist to insist in the face of them that current physics is complete. But at this point the issue seems to degenerate into a stalemate between the optimist and the pessimist about current physics (and current science more generally). The optimist and the pessimist may agree about what is currently known, and may agree about all of the claims just reviewed. And yet it may be the optimist thinks that current knowledge is complete (or very nearly so) while the pessimist thinks it is not.

How do we decide this issue? So far as I can see there is no way (or, at any rate, no practical way) to resolve it. On the other hand, it seems clearly a dispute about a matter of fact. If correct, that is an interesting observation that deserves further discussion, though we will not be able to have that further discussion in this book. But for the moment, the important thing is the connection between the unresolvability of this dispute and the fallibilist response to Hempel's dilemma. In particular, it would appear that fallibilism is not going to provide a successful response to Hempel's dilemma, for the success of that response turns on an unresolvable dispute between the optimist and pessimist about current physics.

5.9 Knowing enough to know

The fallibilist objection says that Hempel's dilemma fails because, while it is possible that we have complete knowledge, in fact this is implausible.

The next objection that I want to consider takes a different tack. We have seen the key observation in the dilemma is the incompleteness of current knowledge, and, moreover, that in some sense or other this is undeniable. Nevertheless, it might be objected that even if we acknowledge that current physical theory is incomplete, the argument may be resisted. "Sure, current physics is incomplete, and in consequence we don't know exactly what the true physics will say," the proponent of this objection will say, "but nevertheless we know enough to know that the true physics will not contain sui generis psychological phenomena, and this is enough for the purposes of philosophy of mind." In sum, the main thrust of this objection is to accept the soundness of Hempel's dilemma but to argue that the conclusion does not have the significance that many have supposed.

What can we say about this objection? The first thing to say about it is that it does contain an important insight, an insight that we ourselves will develop in later chapters. It is common to suppose that Hempel's dilemma is significant because, if it were sound, many famous discussions in philosophy of mind would lose their rationale. For example, take the knowledge argument, which I will discuss briefly in Chapter 10. This is an argument to the conclusion that physicalism is false. And people who debate the argument often describe themselves as 'physicalists' (if they don't like the argument) or 'anti-physicalists' (if they do). On the other hand, if Hempel's dilemma is sound, the whole rationale of this discussion of the knowledge argument seems to have been removed. If Hempel's dilemma is sound, we know— and on grounds that have nothing to do with the knowledge argument— that physicalism is either false or unworthy of assessment. What then would be the point of discussing whether some other argument establishes that it is false?

However—and this is the insight embodied in the response to Hempel's dilemma that we are now discussing—this reason for finding the dilemma significant is mistaken. While it is true that discussions surrounding the knowledge argument go on in the name of physicalism, it is much less clear that this is essential to the enterprise. For the knowledge argument would, if successful, tell us not only that phenomenal facts—such as the fact that I have a pain in my toe—are not entailed by physical facts. It would also tell us that this fact is not entailed by any fact that is not itself a phenomenal fact: that is, it would tell us that phenomenal facts are not entailed by any other facts. But if that is right, physicalism construed as a thesis about the world drops out of the picture. It doesn't matter for the purposes of the knowledge argument whether the contrasting facts are physical or not: what matters is that they are not phenomenal. If this is so, however, physicalism *per se* is inessential to the argument. And that means that, even if the conclusion of Hempel's dilemma were true, it would have a very limited impact on arguments such as the knowledge argument. Indeed we will return to this very point later on in our discussion (Chapter 10).

So there is no doubt that there is an element of truth in this 'know enough to know' objection to Hempel's dilemma. Nevertheless, it is still unsuccessful as a response, and for two reasons. First, the objection assumes that Hempel's dilemma is significant, if it is, for one reason only, viz. because of its impact or alleged impact on arguments in philosophy of mind such as the knowledge argument. However, while this is certainly one way in which Hempel's dilemma is significant it is not the only way. In fact, Hempel's dilemma is incredible on its face (which is not to say that it might not be sound). Philosophers from Hobbes to Smart have endorsed physicalism; and philosophers from Descartes to C.D. Broad have denied it. Surely it is incredible that these philosophers are as confused as they would have to be if the conclusion of Hempel's dilemma were true. In sum, the reason for resisting that conclusion, and so thinking Hempel's dilemma is significant (or at any rate of considerable interest), is this: it is an apparently obvious fact from the history of philosophy that physicalism is a substantive doctrine; hence it is not the case that it is either false or unworthy of assessment. The 'know enough to know' objection says nothing about this aspect of the issue

Second—and in a sense this is the most obvious thing wrong with the objection—it says nothing about what is wrong with the argument! As we have seen, what it says is that even if the argument is sound, we may live the conclusion. But the objection says nothing at all about whether the argument is sound. Moreover, as we have seen there is reason to wonder whether it is sound whatever one thinks about the role of physicalism in philosophy of mind. In sum, if we are interested in a response to Hempel's dilemma we will have to look elsewhere.

5.10 Identifying the mistake in Hempel's dilemma

Neither the fallibilist response nor the 'know enough to know' response provides much of a reason to reject Hempel's dilemma. What then *is* wrong with it? To identify the mistake in Hempel's dilemma, it is necessary to look again at the third premise. That premise, to repeat, is:

H3 Either it is the case that physical properties are by definition the properties expressed by predicates of a current physical theory, or it is the case that physical properties are by definition the properties expressed by predicates of an ideal physical theory.

Earlier we noted that in the discussions of Hempel's dilemma, this premise is almost always overlooked, and we also suggested that many people appear to mistakenly believe that it is a logical truth. What I would now like to point out is that H3 is not only *not* a logical truth: it is not a truth at all, and in fact is a substantive falsehood.

To see that it is not a logical truth, notice that H3 assumes that physical properties must be defined in terms of one of two quite specific physical theories, the theory that is currently believed and the theory that will be believed in ideal circumstances. But even if this is true it is not a necessary (and so not a logical) truth. First, why should physical properties be defined in terms of physical theories of any sort as opposed, for example, to physical objects? Second, even if they are defined in terms of a physical theory, why pick these ones in particular?

To see that the premise is false, let us reconsider some of the material we have already covered in Chapters 2 to 4. The third premise of Hempel's dilemma is a disjunction, and so it is false if both disjuncts are false. Let us look first at the second disjunct, the claim that physical properties are by definition expressed by the predicates of an ideal physical theory. Earlier we saw that what 'ideal physical theory' really amounts to in this context is only the theory that is in fact true. So the second disjunct of H3 says that physical properties are by definition the ones expressed by the physical theory that is true. But reflection on the twin-physics world, which we discussed in Chapter 3, shows clearly that this is false. Properties such as twin-mass and twin-charge seem as physical as their non-twin counterparts; and yet they are not expressed by a predicate of any theory that is true at the actual world. Moreover, the same point applies to the properties expressed by a theory that is currently believed to be true. The properties expressed by a theory that is currently believed to be true do not include properties such as twin-mass and twin-charge. And yet these are physical. So both disjuncts of H3 are false. In consequence, the third premise of Hempel's dilemma is false, and the argument collapses.

5.11 Hempel's dilemma v. our dilemma

Hempel's dilemma is unsound because it presupposes that the proper definition of a physical property makes reference to the theory that is true at the
actual world, or that is currently believed about the actual world. The twin-
physics world shows that this is mistaken. But of course you might wonder
whether the same or a similar problem afflicts the dilemma *we* formulated
at the end of the previous chapter. More generally, you might wonder what
the distinction is between our dilemma (as I will call it) and Hempel's. I
am going to postpone the assessment of our dilemma until Chapter 9, but
meanwhile let me close this chapter by noting some points of contrast.

The main difference between Hempel's dilemma and our own is that Hempel's
dilemma tries to generate a problem for the formulation of physicalism from
within a temporal or historical framework. The key idea of Hempel's dilemma
is that the physical theories that we currently have are different in an important
way both from those that we had in the past, and from the theory that will be
true in the ideal limit. Our dilemma, by contrast, tries to generate a problem
for the formulation of physicalism from within a modal framework, a framework that involves reflection on possible cases. The key idea of our dilemma is
that we have various intuitions about the conditions under which physicalism
is true, and it is impossible (or so the argument claims) to produce a formulation of physicalism that respects those intuitions.

This main difference between Hempel's dilemma and ours brings a
number of other differences in its train. One feature of the discussion of
Hempel's dilemma is that it gets entangled in questions about the history of
science, about how much we have achieved, how much there is to do, and
so on. As we noted when talking about the fallibilist objection, questions of
this sort seem to degenerate into a stalemate between the optimist and the
pessimist about present science. But because our own dilemma is placed in
a completely different framework, we avoid these issues entirely.

Another distinguishing feature of Hempel's dilemma that is less obvious
is this. It is in fact rather odd to raise questions about the definition of a
physical property, or about physicalism, from within a temporal framework.
Suppose we are having a discussion in epistemology about what knowledge
is, and suppose that I am defending the view that to know some proposition p it is necessary and sufficient for a person to believe that p with justification and for p to be true. The standard way of assessing that proposal is
by considering various possible cases and asking whether in those cases
someone can know that p without meeting all of these conditions. On the

other hand, it would be extremely strange to proceed here by concentrating only on claims about knowledge that are currently believed to be true, or that will be true in the ideal limit. This would be a good way to proceed if one were interested in which knowledge claims are true, but it would not be a good way to proceed if one were interested in what knowledge is. Our interest so far has been not in whether physicalism is true but in what it is; it is very natural to pursue that interest using a modal framework as our dilemma does. But Hempel's dilemma and its associated temporal and historical framework are ill suited to this purpose.

Of course, even if we acknowledge this problem with Hempel's dilemma, and the differences between it and ours, one might suggest that the real intention behind Hempel's dilemma is better captured in our dilemma. To properly adjudicate that suggestion we would need to examine the presuppositions and intentions of Hempel and other philosophers who have advanced his dilemma. Such a project would certainly be interesting, but it is not one I will pursue here.

Summary

In this chapter we considered Hempel's dilemma and compared it with the dilemma that we ourselves raised for physicalism at the end of Chapter 4. Hempel's dilemma is widely viewed as the key dilemma for the formulation of physicalism. But as we have seen, when we formulate that argument clearly, it is quite unclear that it is persuasive. The central problem is that the main premise of the dilemma presupposes that physicalism should be defined via the physical theory that is true (or currently believed to be true) at the actual world. But the twin-physics world shows that this is mistaken.

Recommended reading

The key documents for Hempel's dilemma are Hempel's own papers on the subject: Hempel 1969 and Hempel 1980. Hempel's papers are rather rich since he is responding to metaphilosophical themes prominent in both Carnap and Quine; for some discussion see Stoljar 2009a. Hempel's dilemma has generated a rather large literature. Some papers and books similar in broad outlook to Hempel's are Daly 1998; Chomsky 2000; Crane and Mellor 1990; Mellor 1973; van Fraassen 2002; and Montero 1999 and 2009. For responses to Hempel's dilemma different from that presented here, see Smart 1978; Poland 1994 and 2003; Melnyk 1997 and 2003; Wilson 2006; and Dowell 2006b.

6

THE NECESSITY VIEW

6.1 Introduction

Right at the end of *Naming and Necessity*, Saul Kripke writes:

> Materialism, I think, must hold that a physical description of the world is a complete description of it, that any mental facts are 'ontologically dependent' on physical facts in the straightforward sense of following from them by necessity. No identity theorist seems to me to have made a convincing argument against the intuitive view that this is not the case. (1980: 155)

Whether Kripke is right about the "identity theorist" is a question we will come back to later (in Chapter 10). For the moment, let's focus on Kripke's explanation of what physicalism ("materialism") is committed to. What Kripke says is that according to physicalism, mental facts, and presumably any facts, follow from physical facts by necessity, or more briefly, are necessitated by the physical facts. Now, if we interpret this claim as giving necessary and sufficient conditions for physicalism—something which seems to me to move beyond Kripke's text, strictly interpreted—and if we also assume that what he says about facts applies also to instantiated properties, what we have here is the formulation of physicalism that we adopted in Chapter 2. According to this formulation, physicalism is true just in case every instantiated property is necessitated by, or follows by necessity from, some instantiated physical property.

Now, in Chapter 2, we adopted this formulation in a somewhat summary fashion. Strictly speaking all our discussion there led to was the idea that physicalism is the thesis that every instantiated property is either physical or bears a certain relation R to a physical property; we simply *assumed* that the relation in question was one of necessitation. Of course, there were a number of reasons for this assumption; in particular, it made the presentation of the issue in Chapters 3 to 5—that is, the issue of what a physical property is—easier, and did not affect the substantive conclusions of those chapters in any way.

In the next part of our discussion (Chapters 6 to 8), however, I want to go back and consider in some detail the pros and cons of the idea that physicalism is the view that every instantiated property is necessitated by some physical property—the Necessity View, as I will call it. In this chapter we will concentrate on what the Necessity View says, and on the differences between this view about physicalism and various rival views. In the following two chapters I am going to take up, respectively, the question of whether necessitation is necessary for physicalism, and the question of whether it is sufficient. As we will see when we turn in Chapter 8 to the issue of whether necessitation is sufficient for physicalism, the contrast between the Necessity View and its rivals becomes at this point pressing, and raises a number of problems of philosophical clarity and method.

Throughout our discussion of the Necessity View, it is important to keep three preliminary points in mind. First, when we discuss the Necessity View, we can afford to set aside the question of what a physical property is. That question is certainly a difficult one, as we have seen, but it does not affect the issues we will focus on in the next three chapters. Second, as with the Theory View and the Starting Point View, neither the Necessity View nor the rivals to that view that we will discuss entail that physicalism is true or false. Rather they are views about what physicalism *is*. In form at least, physicalism is the thesis that every instantiated property must bear a certain relation to physical properties; the Necessity View tells us what that relation is, viz. necessitation. But you might agree with this, and still think physicalism is false; likewise, you might disagree with it, and still think that physicalism is true. Finally, the issues concerning necessitation that we are going to discuss are extremely complicated and detailed, taking in topics from modal logic, metaphysics and philosophy of language, including the meta-theory of these disciplines. We will simply not be able to follow up all the highways and byways here. So I am afraid that my approach in what follows will be at times reminiscent of a tour guide who points you in the direction of an interesting site, only to say that time is short and we must get back to the hotel.

6.2 The Necessity View formulated

We might begin our discussion of the Necessity View by repeating a point made in Chapter 2, namely, the notion of necessitation that is at issue here is what is called 'metaphysical' (or even 'Kripkean') necessitation, where one property metaphysically necessitates another just in case, in all possible worlds, if the first is instantiated, the second is. As we saw, the key phrase here is 'in all possible worlds.' Metaphysical necessity is not restricted to *some* possible worlds, or all possible worlds of a certain class. The claim is meant to extend to any world at all. So, for example, being red metaphysically necessitates being colored just because, in any possible world at all, if something is red, then it is colored.

However, while the notion of necessitation here is metaphysical necessitation, it might not be immediately apparent how to connect that idea to the Necessity View. In the formulation we adopted in Chapter 2, the Necessity View was something like this:

(1) Physicalism is true if and only if every instantiated property is necessitated by some instantiated physical property.

On the assumption that the notion of necessitation here is metaphysical necessitation, the right-hand side of (1) says that every instantiated property is metaphysically necessitated by some instantiated physical property. But what exactly does that mean?

When thinking about this question, it is helpful to have two features of physicalism before us. The first arises from a fact we have mentioned before (and will mention again), viz. that unlike some philosophical doctrines, physicalism is not a thesis that is intended to be true at, or about, all possible worlds; rather it is intended to be true at, or about, some possible worlds in particular. Physicalism is, as we have seen, a contingent doctrine, if it is true.

We may capture this fact—that physicalism concerns some possible worlds and not others—by explicitly relativizing the statement of physicalism offered by the Necessity View to an arbitrary possible world. The result would be this (where 'w' denotes the world in question):

(2) Physicalism is true at *w* if and only if every property instantiated at *w* is necessitated by some physical property instantiated at *w*.

So the idea behind (2) is this. Suppose we focus on an arbitrary possible world, say the actual world. To determine whether physicalism is true at that world, ask whether every property that is instantiated at that world is necessitated by some physical property that is instantiated at that world. If so, then physicalism is true; if not, then it is not.

The second feature of physicalism that it is helpful to bring out is its quantificational structure. As noted in Chapter 2, physicalism involves quantifying over properties, for it tells us something about the relation between every property and some physical property. To bring this out it is best to replace (2) with (3):

(3) Physicalism is true at *w* if and only if for every property *F* instantiated at *w* there is some physical property *G* instantiated at *w* such that *F* is necessitated by *G*.

Of course, since (2)—and (1)—already involves quantificational structure, the only difference between (3) and the previous formulations is that (3) makes this structure explicit.

It is, therefore, both possible and desirable from the point of view of explicitness to replace (1) with (3); but what of it? Well, with (3) before us, it becomes plain to see how to factor the notion of metaphysical necessity into the formulation of physicalism offered by the Necessity View. As we have seen, one property necessitates another just in case, in all possible worlds, if the first is instantiated the second is instantiated. To factor this in to our basic notion, we simply take (3) and understand its reference to necessitation in Kripkean terms:

(4) Physicalism is true at *w* if and only if for every property *F* instantiated at *w*, there is some physical property *G* instantiated at *w* such that, for all possible worlds *w**, if *G* is instantiated at *w**, then *F* is instantiated at *w**.

So the idea behind (4) is this. Take the properties that are instantiated at a particular world, say the actual world. And now take the physical properties that are instantiated at that world. According to the Necessity View, if physicalism is true at the actual world, then for any property at all in the first class there is some property in the second class such that the first is necessitated—in the sense of metaphysical necessitation—by the second. To put it another way, if we call physicalism as defined by (4) 'necessitation physicalism' (following a suggestion in Leuenberger 2008) then the idea behind the Necessity View is that physicalism is necessitation physicalism.

6.3 Some variations on the basic theme

The Necessity View says that physicalism is necessitation physicalism, i.e. physicalism as defined in (4). But at this stage we should take note of a number of variations on the basic theme. The variations I have in mind are at least in two cases related to points made in the Commentary section of Chapter 2 above.

One of the points we made in that section was that, while it is not good enough for purposes of formulating physicalism to focus on particulars, it doesn't follow that one must concentrate on properties as such. Perhaps instead we should focus on truths or states of affairs? We may accommodate this suggestion by noting that we can adjust (4) so that it concerns states of affairs (we could make a similar adjustment for truths but I will ignore that here). This adjustment would result in the following version of the Necessity View:

(5) Physicalism is true at w if and only if for every state of affairs S that obtains at w, there is some physical state of affairs S^* obtaining at w such that, for all possible worlds w^*, if S^* obtains at w^*, then S obtains at w^*.

So on this view, physicalism tells us not simply that the instantiation of being in pain is necessitated by a physical property, but that states of affairs consisting in people's being in pain are necessitated by an entire (perhaps hugely complex) physical state of affairs.

Another point made in the Commentary section of Chapter 2 was that the Necessity View seems not to take particulars into account. We may deal with this by adjusting (4) so that it includes particulars. This would result in the following version of the Necessity View:

(6) Physicalism is true at w if and only if for everything x which exists at w, and every property F which is such that x has F at w, there is some physical thing y and some physical property G such that y has G at w, and for all possible worlds w^*, if y has G at w^*, then x has F at w^*.

So on this view, physicalism tells us not simply that the instantiation of being in pain is necessitated by a physical property but in addition that my being in pain is necessitated by a physical thing's (presumably a very complex physical thing) having a physical property.

Finally, one might think it is a mistake to concentrate, as the Necessity View does, solely on whether or not a property is instantiated. What is important for physicalism—one might think—is not simply whether a property is instantiated at a world but rather what the whole pattern of instantiation is of that property at that world. We may deal with this by adjusting (4) so that it concerns not whether or not a property is instantiated but what the overall pattern of distribution of a property is. This would result in the following version of the Necessity View:

(7) Physicalism is true at w if and only if for every property F exhibiting a pattern P of instantiation at w, there is some physical property G exhibiting a pattern P^* of instantiation at w such that, for all possible worlds w^*, if G exhibits P^* at w^*, then F exhibits P at w^*.

So on this view, physicalism tells us not simply that physical properties necessitate the property of being in pain but rather that they necessitate the whole pattern of instantiation of the property of being in pain.

What exactly is the relation among (4), on the one hand, and (5) to (7) on the other? For our purposes it suffices to make two points. First, I am going to operate in what follows with (4). While the versions of the Necessity View we have distinguished might well be different from each other, these differences will not matter to our discussion. Second, all four definitions—that is, (4), (5), (6), and (7)—have in common the fact that they are *modal* definitions of what physicalism is, i.e. a definition in terms of notions like possibility, necessity, possible worlds, and so on. There are also, however, various *non-modal* definitions of what physicalism is, where a 'non-modal' definition of physicalism is not couched in explicitly modal terms. As we will see as we proceed, whether to adopt a modal or a non-modal definition of physicalism is one of the key issues that we face in formulating physicalism of any sort.

6.4 Supervenience

In formulating physicalism as necessitation physicalism we have been taking our lead from Kripke. But there is a slightly different way of thinking about physicalism that takes its lead from Donald Davidson. In 'Mental Events,' Davidson wrote:

> Although the position I describe denies there are psychophysical laws, it is consistent with the view that mental characteristics are in some sense dependent, or supervenient, on physical characteristics. Such supervenience might be taken to mean that there cannot be two events alike in all physical respects but differing in some mental respects or that an object cannot alter in some mental respects without altering in some physical respects. Dependence or supervenience of this kind does not entail reducibility through law or definition; if it did, we could reduce moral properties to descriptive, and this there is good reason to believe cannot be done. (1970: 214)

Later on we will take up the other aspect of Davidson's position mentioned in this passage: the idea that there are no psychophysical laws. But for the moment let's focus on Davidson's apparent assertion that physicalism may be spelled out in terms of a supervenience thesis. What is supervenience and what is its relation to necessitation?

The idea of supervenience is often introduced with examples involving artworks or buildings. For example, suppose one says of a particular Brancusi sculpture that it has some aesthetic property—it is elegant, say. To be elegant is a somewhat elusive property. What is it for a sculpture to be elegant? And how do elegant sculptures differ from inelegant ones? One way to approach these questions might be to note that any sculpture, including those by Brancusi, instantiates various natural properties and relations, where by 'natural properties' I mean something like the ordinary physical properties of the sculpture, including its setting and context, and the psychological reaction that the sculpture provokes or tends to provoke. It seems natural to say that, whatever elegance is, it bears a certain kind of important relation to these natural properties, as follows: a sculpture that is identical to the original sculpture in terms of natural properties would be identical to it in terms of aesthetic properties. Contrariwise, any difference between this sculpture and another in terms of elegance will have to be a difference between them in terms of natural properties. The notion of supervenience can be used to express this relation. If the relation between the elegance of a sculpture and its natural properties is as I just described it, then elegance, and aesthetic properties more generally, supervene on natural properties.

The notion of supervenience that is introduced by examples like this has turned out to be a useful one in all sorts of philosophical contexts. Philosophers appeal to this notion to capture the relation between moral and natural properties (as Davidson notes in the passage above), between phenomenal and intentional properties, and in many other cases. On the other hand, perhaps because of its widespread use, supervenience has tended to be spelled out in a number of very different ways in the philosophical literature. As David Lewis once remarked about it, "in recent discussions, we get an unlovely proliferation of non-equivalent definitions" (1986a: 14).

While supervenience can be spelled out in various different ways, in the specific context of physicalism, it has become standard to formulate it in terms of the idea of duplication of possible worlds (cf. Lewis 1983; Horgan 1983; Jackson 1998). Suppose we say that one possible world is a physical duplicate of another just in case every physical property instantiated at the first is instantiated at the second; and suppose we say also that one possible world is a duplicate simpliciter of another just in case every property at all that is instantiated at the first is instantiated at the second. It then becomes possible to formulate physicalism as follows:

(8) Physicalism is true at w if and only if for any possible world w^* if w^* is a physical duplicate of w, then w^* is a duplicate of w simpliciter.

The Supervenience View, as I will call it, says that (8) is the correct definition of physicalism. To put it differently, if we say that physicalism as defined by (8) is 'supervenience physicalism,' then we can say that the Supervenience View says that physicalism is supervenience physicalism.

What is the relation between the Necessity View and the Supervenience View? As above, for our purposes it suffices to make two points. First, it will do no harm to assume in what follows that the two definitions are equivalent, or more cautiously, to assume that they are equivalent, so long as we assume that the class of properties at issue here is closed under negation, i.e. so long as we assume that if F is a property, then not-F is likewise a property. While there may be differences here, these differences will not matter to our discussion. Second, an important point about both the Necessity View and the Supervenience View is that they are modal definitions of what physicalism is, i.e. a definition in terms of notions like possibility, necessity, possible worlds and so on.

6.5 The Semantic View

We have so far introduced the Necessity View, noted various variations on its basic idea, and noted its relation to supervenience. In the remainder of the chapter I want to compare it with various alternative suggestions about what the relation is that the physical properties must bear to every property if physicalism is true. These alternative suggestions all spell physicalism out in non-modal terms.

The first alternative is the semantic version of physicalism associated with Carnap and Neurath, which we examined briefly in Chapter 1—the Semantic View, as we may call it here. On this view, physicalism is a thesis about meaning rather than about the nature of the world: it says that every statement or predicate is synonymous with some physical statement or predicate.

Now, stating this view in a way that mirrors the structure of the Necessity View is challenging, in part because we have been talking about properties and not predicates, and properties are not synonymous with anything. However, perhaps we can make progress here by supposing, perhaps implausibly, that each property is associated with a predicate that canonically or properly express it. The rough idea is that, for physical properties, there are predicates of a physical language which canonically express them; for psychological properties, there are predicates of a psychological language that canonically express them; and so on. If we do adopt this idea, the Semantic View may be expressed as follows:

(9) Physicalism is true at w if and only if for every property F instantiated at w there is some physical property G instantiated at w such that the canonical predicate expressing F is synonymous with the canonical physical predicate expressing G.

One problem with this proposal is whether we can make sense of the idea of canonical expression. Another problem is, as we noticed before, that neither Carnap nor Neurath makes it completely clear what a physical statement or predicate is; in particular, it looks like (9) inherits the unclarity in the notion of the physical that we looked at in Chapters 3 to 5. But, even if we waive both of these issues, there are still many reasons to deny the Semantic View.

First, there seem to be some perfectly meaningful predicates that are not synonymous with a physical predicate, and this is true on *any* reasonable understanding of 'physical predicate.' Consider, for example, 'has no soul,' as it occurs in sentences such as 'Otto has no soul.' This sentence is perfectly meaningful. Yet according to (9) it would have to be equivalent in meaning to a physical statement if physicalism were true. But this is extremely unlikely. Second, some philosophers, such as Quine (e.g. 1960), hold that the idea of synonymy or equivalence in meaning does not meet minimal standards of clarity. So Quine would reject (9) on this ground. Third, for some philosophers, the place of semantic notions in a physical world is a general philosophical question on a par with the questions about the place of consciousness or morality. But on this account, semantic notions are required in the very formulation of physicalism. Finally, there is the simple-minded objection that translation is a singularly difficult business. Translating Proust into English is something that people are still arguing about it, and while Proust might be a special case, it remains advisable that one should not associate physicalism with translation too closely.

6.6 The Identity View

It was for these and similar reasons that many philosophers in the 1950s and 1960s turned from a semantic to a non-semantic formulation of physicalism (e.g. Smart 1959). The most obvious candidate for such an account defines physicalism in terms of identity. We may formulate this Identity View as follows:

(10) Physicalism is true at world w if and only if every property instantiated at w is identical to some physical property instantiated at w.

This view is an improvement on the semantic formulation of physicalism because property identity is a matter, not of the meanings of the predicates that express those properties, but of the properties themselves. Nevertheless, it seems plain that (10) won't do either. One objection, as we noted in Chapter 2, is that some instantiated properties of social objects like the US Supreme Court do not look like physical properties on any definition.

A different, and historically more important, objection is the multiple realization objection (see Fodor 1974; for discussion see Bickle 2008). Take some psychological property, such as wondering whether it will rain soon. At the moment I am wondering whether it will rain soon so there is no doubt that this property is instantiated. But it seems clear that many creatures quite different from me might also wonder whether it will rain soon. Humans remote from me in physical and historical terms might wonder whether it will rain soon. Non-human creatures like dogs or yaks, frightened by the thunder, might also. So too might imaginary animals, like Ratty or Mole from The Wind in the Willows. So too might the Vulcans of Star Trek. So too might (non-actual) angels or devils. On the other hand, is it really plausible that all of these creatures instantiate the same physical property? Of course the answer to this question depends in part on what a physical property is—a difficult question as we have seen. But it is hard to imagine that, on any reasonable account of what a physical property is, it will turn out that all of these creatures instantiate the same one. On the other hand, that is what the physicalist is committed to if the Identity View is true. If (10) is true, physicalism entails that wondering whether it will rain soon is identical to a physical property, and this in turn entails that every creature who wonders this must instantiate the property in question. But since that is implausible either physicalism or the Identity View must go.

At this point, it becomes extremely attractive to replace the Identity View with the Necessity View, or something like it. On the Necessity View physicalism says that there is some physical property which is such that if I instantiate it, then I am wondering whether it will rain soon. But necessitation physicalism does not require the identity of wondering whether it will rain soon with that property. Indeed, it permits any number of other properties to be metaphysically sufficient for wondering whether it will rain soon. So the Necessity View provides an attractive account of multiple realization.

6.7 Maneuvers in defense of the Identity View

While it is natural to appeal to the Necessity View in the face of the multiple realization objection, this is not the only way to deal with that objection. In fact, there are a number of maneuvers that philosophers have employed to try to square the Identity View with the possibility of multiple realization.

One strategy that has been pursued here is to argue that the empirical credentials of multiple realization are not quite as strong as is sometimes thought (cf. Shapiro 2000; Bickle 2008). Proponents of multiple realization sometimes assume that it is a rather ubiquitous empirical phenomenon; what these critics argue is that it is not completely clear that it is, and that when we look closely at alleged cases of multiple realization—that is, cases in which two creatures share a mental property without sharing a physical property—it turns out either that the physical make-up of the creatures is not so different after all, or else that their psychology is not so similar. However, while this point might be true, it is not clear that it undermines the philosophical importance of the multiple realizability objection. After all, the Identity View commits a physicalist to the identity of (e.g.) psychological properties with physical properties. Since these identities are necessary, a physicalist must deny not only that psychological properties are in fact multiply realized but that they could be—and this commitment goes beyond the empirical issues.

A different strategy has been to assume that multiple realization is a possibility (whether or not it is an empirical fact), and to argue that even then it does not quite follow that an identity version of physicalism will need to be given up. To my knowledge, there are the following suggestions in the literature about how to do this:

(a) Some argue that while multiple realization shows that the property of (e.g.) being in pain is not identical to a single physical property, it does not show that particulars—people, events, processes—are not identical to physical particulars—'the token physicalism maneuver'(cf. Fodor 1974).

(b) Some argue that while multiple realization shows that the property of being in pain is not identical to a physical property, it does not show that the concept of being in pain might not apply to a creature only if they instantiate a physical property—'the concept/property maneuver' (cf. Kim 1998).

(c) Some argue that while multiple realization shows that the property of being in pain is not identical to a single physical property, it might yet be identical to a disjunction of physical properties—'the disjunctive property maneuver' (cf. Kim 1993).

(d) Some argue that while multiple realization shows that being in pain is not identical to a single physical property it may be that more specific properties, such as being in pain in humans or being in pain in Stoljar at 4.00 p.m. are identical to single physical properties—'the specific property maneuver' (cf. Lewis 1980).

(e) Some argue that while multiple realization shows that being in pain is not identical to a single first-order physical property, it might yet be identical to a single second-order physical property—'the second-order property maneuver' (cf. Melnyk 2003).

There is a considerable amount of philosophy lying underneath all of these suggestions. We will not be able to go through all of the ins and outs here. In what follows I will briefly indicate some problems with (a) to (d) before discussing (e) in further detail.

The problem with (a)—the token physicalism maneuver—is that if physicalism is merely the thesis that every particular is identical to some physical particular, then it is consistent with a standard form of dualism, viz. property dualism. (We saw this point in Chapter 2.)

The problem with (b)—the concept/property maneuver—is that it is no clearer than the distinction between concepts and properties on which it relies. In some sense there certainly is a distinction between concepts and properties. If concepts are anything like words, for example, then there are bound to be more properties than concepts; likewise, maybe concepts can be self-contradictory or incoherent in some way and nevertheless exist, but, on at least some views, it cannot be that properties are self-contradictory or incoherent and nevertheless exist. However, while there is a concept/property distinction, it is not clear that the appeal to it in this context is legitimate. In general, when we have a concept that seems non-self-contradictory, we assume there is a genuine (abundant) property that answers to it—why not here?

The problem with (c)—the disjunctive property maneuver—is that it looks as if it will not be able to say what is common to all the various realizations of mental states. All the different creatures who wonder whether it will rain soon have something in common. But on the disjunctive property maneuver, it is quite unclear that they do. On this view, all of them instantiate a disjunctive property, but since the disjuncts have nothing in common the idea that the property itself involves any commonality seems to have gone missing.

Finally, the problem with (d)—the specific property maneuver—is that it says, in effect, that there is no such property as pain simpliciter, and that there is only a more specific range of properties, such as pain-in-humans or pain-in-Martians; as such there is no sense to be made in any attempt to theorize about pain as such—there is no such thing. But is this really true? Isn't it the case that we can generalize across species in certain circumstances? To put it another way, even if there is such a property as pain-in-humans, and even if it is appropriate to focus on it for certain theoretical purposes, is there not also such a property as being in pain simpliciter?

6.8 The Realization View

The first four maneuvers in defense of the Identity View seem implausible; what of the fifth—the second-order property view? This idea requires separate treatment. For one thing it seems at first glance more plausible than any of the other ways of defending the Identity View. For another, defending the Identity View in this way naturally leads to a view which is of interest quite independently of its connection to the Identity View, which I will call 'the Realization View.'

In order to understand the second-order property maneuver and the Realization View, we need first to have the notion of a second-order property before us. In one reasonable sense, a second-order property is a property of a property. So, for example, the property of being physical is a second-order property if we can make sense of the idea of a property's being physical. However, in the context of the Realization View, a second-order property is not a property of a property but rather a property that involves (or perhaps whose canonical expression involves) quantification over other properties. So, to take a famous example due to J.L. Mackie (1973), consider the property of absorbency, i.e. being absorbent. This property is the (second-order) property of having some property that disposes an object (e.g. a cloth) to absorb water. This is not a property of a property, but rather a property of a cloth; it is second-order because to have that property means just to have some property that does such and such.

Now, the interest in second-order properties in the present context is that they are multiply realizable. To see this, consider two different cloths that are both absorbent. In the first, the property that disposes the cloth to absorb water is some feature of its weave; in the second, the property that disposes the cloth to absorb water is some feature of its thread. Both cloths are absorbent because both have the property of having some property that disposes them to absorb water. But the properties in question are different. We may put the point another way by saying that in cloth #1 absorbency is realized by the feature of the weave, while in cloth #2 absorbency is realized by the feature of the thread.

These ideas lead naturally to a proposal about what physicalism is, viz. the Realization View. Now, the simplest formulation of the Realization View would be to say that physicalism is true just in case every instantiated property is realized by some physical property. However, this simplest formulation has physicalism entailing that every instantiated property is a second-order property. And that can't be right. If an object has the property of having some property that does such and such, then presumably it also has the first-order property that does such and such. So a better way to formulate the Realization View is as follows:

(11) Physicalism is true at *w* if and only if every property instantiated at *w* is either identical to some physical property instantiated at *w* or is realized by some physical property instantiated at *w*.

On this view, what physicalism requires is that every property is either identical to or is realized by a physical property.

How plausible is the Realization View? As I said, it certainly is more attractive than the other descendants of the Identity View. But it also faces a serious problem. This arises from the observation that (11) as stated does *not* by itself formulate a sufficient condition for physicalism. In general, a property F realizes a property G if and only if F is the second-order property of having a property that satisfies certain conditions C, and G is the property that satisfies those conditions. However, this idea permits the possibility that the conditions C involve features that are inconsistent with physicalism on anyone's view. For example, C might involve being in a world that contains souls (cf. Melnyk 2003). But if that is so, the Realization View, far from providing an attractive definition of physicalism, does not provide a definition at all.

In order to respond to this objection, the realization physicalist will have to say something about C, the conditions in terms of which the second-order property is defined. But at this point a problem of principle emerges. For it would seem that C must *itself* be something for which physicalism is true. But how can it be guaranteed that physicalism is true for C? Well, at least given the material we have so far introduced, there would seem to be four options and none of them are very plausible:

1   It might be argued that C has a canonical formulation that is *synonymous* with some physical expression—but in that case the Realization View faces the problems of the Semantic View.
2   It might be argued that C is *identical* to something physical—but in that case the Realization View faces the problems of the Identity View, and in particular, a problem of multiple realization would emerge all over again.
3   It might be argued that C is *realized* by something physical—but in that case the Realization View faces an infinite regress, since the basic

problem will re-emerge when we spell out the relation of realization in this case.

4   It might be argued that C is *necessitated* by something physical—but in that case it is hard to see what the advantage is of the Realization View over the Necessity view, and in particular why necessitation (or perhaps some similar modal relation) should not be brought in from the very beginning.

If these options are exhaustive—and they are certainly the only ones we have looked at so far—it looks as if the Realization View is no advance on a modal definition of physicalism.

So far our focus has been on the version of the Realization View that spells out the background notion of realization in terms of second-order properties. However, it is worth noting briefly that there is a different notion of realization in the literature, which has been suggested by Sydney Shoemaker (2007). (Shoemaker himself says—2007: 14—that his proposal is a variant on the second-order property view; even so it is different enough to warrant separate treatment.) To put it roughly but well enough for present purposes, Shoemaker's suggestion is that a property F realizes another G just in case the causal profile of F is included in the causal profile of G, where (a) the 'causal profile' of a property F is, roughly, the set of causal powers that an object has if it has the property, and (b) the causal profile of one property is 'included' in another, just in case the set of causal powers that the first property bestows is a subset of the set of causal powers that the second property bestows. So to continue with our example borrowed from Mackie, consider the causal powers that a cloth has if its constituent threads have a certain microstructure—these might include the power to absorb water, the property to appear a certain way under a microscope, and the property of being resistant to tension. And now consider the causal powers that the cloth has if it is absorbent—these might include the property to absorb water. Since the causal powers associated with the second are included in the causal powers associated with the first, absorbency is, on Shoemaker's account, realized in this feature of the thread.

Shoemaker's proposal is an extremely interesting one, and raises a host of questions that we will not be able to take up here. For our purposes the important question is whether one can appeal to Shoemaker's account of realization to develop a more plausible version of the Realization View. The answer seems to be 'no'. For such a version of the Realization View faces the same sort of problem that we have just noted for the second-order property version, viz. on the Shoemaker-inspired version, the right-hand side of (11) does not provide a sufficient condition for physicalism either. The reason is that, on Shoemaker's account of realization, a property can be realized by another even if the properties in question are as distinct from one another as a dualist thinks of them. On Shoemaker's account, it is a contingent fact that the properties at issue here have the causal profiles that they do; it is therefore a contingent fact that the causal profiles of the physical properties include the causal profiles of the mental ones. But if that is so, realization in Shoemaker's sense is compatible with metaphysical dualism.

So far as I can see there are two ways in which a proponent of the Shoemaker-inspired version of the Realization View might respond to this. The first is to adopt a causal theory of properties, according to which—again, roughly, but sufficient for present purposes—the causal profile is not simply a contingent fact about a property but is exhaustive of its nature. However, while Shoemaker himself endorses the causal theory of properties, he makes clear this commitment is quite separate from his account of realization and is in any case a highly controversial view (2007: 142). So while we could develop the Realization View in this direction we do so at the cost of adopting a highly controversial view about properties. The second way to respond is to say that the fact that the physical properties have the causal profiles they do necessitates the fact that the mental properties have the causal profiles they do. However, to say this is in effect to admit that this version of the Realization View has to appeal to the Necessity View, and so is no advance on that view.

6.9 The Fundamental Properties View

We have been looking at three alternatives to the modal definition of physicalism offered by the Necessity View: the Semantic View, the Identity View and the Realization View. The last alternative I want to mention in this chapter is (what I will call) the Fundamental Properties View, which can be stated as follows:

(12) Physicalism is true at w if and only if every fundamental property instantiated at w is a physical property.

In fact we have already looked at the Fundamental Properties View, though not under that name, i.e. when we looked at Lewis's appeal to fundamental properties in Chapter 2; (12) is the same as the idea we considered there, but stated in a way that is continuous with the concerns of this chapter. As we saw, the notion of fundamental properties is somewhat controversial, and so it seems prudent to adopt the Necessity View rather than the Fundamental Properties View. However, as will emerge as we go on, the contrast between the Fundamental Property View and the Necessity View will need to be reconsidered.

Summary

In this chapter our focus has been on the Necessity View, which is one account of what relation must obtain between all properties and physical properties if physicalism is to be true. We saw that this view was one of a family of modal definitions of physicalism. We also contrasted the Necessity View with various non-modal accounts, such as Semantic, Identity, Realization and Fundamental Property Views. On the surface at least the Necessity View seems more plausible than these other views.

Recommended reading

For good summaries of the notion of supervenience and its use in stating physicalism, see Horgan 1993, the papers in Kim 1993, and Stalnaker 1996. Very good recent discussions are McLaughlin and Bennett 2005 and Wilson 2007. For the Identity View, see Smart 1959; and Kim 1993, 1998 and 2007. For a very good defense and discussion of the Realization View, see Melnyk 2003; see also Field 1992, and Shoemaker 2007. For multiple realization, see Fodor 1974; Kim 1993; Shapiro 2000; and Bickle 2008. For the Fundamental Properties View, see Lewis 1983 and 1994. Interestingly, Lewis defends a supervenience formulation of physicalism in 1983 and a fundamental properties formulation in 1994.

7

IS NECESSITATION
NECESSARY?

7.1 Introduction

In the formulation that we are concentrating on, the Necessity View is this:

(1) Physicalism is true at w if and only if for every property F instantiated at w, there is some physical property G instantiated at w such that, for all possible worlds w^* if G is instantiated at w^*, then F is instantiated at w^*.

So far we have focused on what (1) says, and on the relation between this view and various other views about what physicalism is. I want now to look more directly at substantive questions about the Necessity View, and in particular on the left-to-right direction of (1); that is, the claim that if physicalism is true, then every instantiated property is necessitated by some physical property. As we have seen, the notion of necessitation here is metaphysical or Kripkean necessity, and this in turn is defined in terms of all possible worlds. So in effect the left-to-right direction of (1) tells us that if physicalism is true, then something is true about all possible worlds. However, it is natural to raise an eyebrow at this. Must we define physicalism this way: that is, must it be the case that the right-hand side of (1) is a necessary condition for the left-hand side? It is this question, and various issues that follow on from this question, that I want to consider in this chapter.

7.2 Metaphysical v. nomological necessity

One obvious alternative to defining physicalism in terms of all possible worlds is to define it in terms of *some* worlds, i.e. in terms of some proper subset of all the possible worlds. The usual way of developing this point focuses on a subset of worlds in which a certain body of scientific laws is true—the 'nomologically possible worlds' as it is usually put. (The word *nomos* means 'law' in Greek.) If we restrict attention to the nomologically possible worlds, the following formulation of physicalism comes into view:

(2)   Physicalism is true at *w* if and only if for every property *F* instantiated at *w*, there is some physical property *G* instantiated at *w* such that, for all *nomologically* possible worlds *w** if *G* is instantiated at *w**, then *F* is instantiated at *w**.

The difference between (1) and (2) is that, according to (1), physicalism requires there to be a relation of metaphysical necessity between (e.g.) mental and physical properties, whereas, according to (2), physicalism requires only that a relation of nomological necessity obtain. In short, (2) permits the case in which mental and physical properties are connected but not as a matter of metaphysical necessity.

However, the problem with (2) is that, if it were defined this way, physicalism would be compatible with standard forms of dualism. As we have seen in Chapter 2, the standard dualist says that some mental properties are not necessitated by any physical property. But it is quite implausible to interpret this as the claim that mental properties are not *nomologically* necessitated by physical properties. On the contrary, it is quite common for a dualist to go on to say that physical properties and mental properties are related as a matter of scientific laws, in particular psychophysical laws, i.e. laws that relate the mental and physical. (Chalmers 1996, for example, defends and explores a position like this.) If so, dualism will permit that mental and physical properties are related as a matter of nomological necessity, but not as a matter of metaphysical necessity. To put the point differently, according to standard forms of dualism, the right-hand side of (2) will be true; but according to no form of dualism is the left-hand side of (2) true. So (2) will not do as a formulation of physicalism.

We seem, therefore, to have a straightforward answer to the question we started this chapter with, viz. must we define physicalism so that it entails something about all possible worlds? The answer is that we must do this, for otherwise we are not going to be able to discern a difference between physicalism and standard forms of dualism. Nevertheless, there are three important points to make in the light of this answer.

The first concerns the temptation when thinking about physicalism to refuse to talk about possible worlds at all. "Physicalism is a thesis about the nature of the actual world," one might say, "why then do we need to discuss such recherché objects as possible worlds?" This position sounds hard-headed at first, but on reflection it is confused. It is true that physicalism is a thesis about the nature of the actual world, but it is also true (as we have just seen) that it is a thesis with modal content, i.e. it entails various things about what is possible and what is not possible. In order to spell out this aspect of the thesis it is sensible to use the best tools available for us to do this. Possible worlds, possible worlds semantics, and related ideas are the best tools we have. So that is why we are using them in explicating what physicalism is. (Of course there are questions about what possible worlds are, but we will set them aside here. We certainly do not need to assume that possible worlds are worlds in the sense defended by David Lewis (1986a): concrete worlds of a piece with the actual world.)

The second important point concerns the contrast between the Necessity View and the rivals to that view which we set out in the previous chapter. These views disagree with each other in a number of respects. However, in light of the fact that any view about what physicalism is must distinguish it from standard versions of dualism, it would appear that all of the views discussed in the previous chapter must agree with something like the left-to-right direction of the Necessity View; that is, any thesis that has a chance of deserving the name 'physicalism' will at least have to entail (something like) the thesis that every property is metaphysically necessitated by a physical property. (I add the phrase 'something like' here because as we will see below, there are some qualifications that need to be made to this general statement.) This in turn implies that we can organize our discussion in this chapter around the Necessity View, and ignore the contrast between it and the other views; we will return to that issue in the next chapter.

The final important point to make is that, even if we agree that the left-to-right direction of the Necessity View is correct (or at any rate very nearly so), we should nevertheless *also* agree that this fact is in many ways a rather puzzling one, and indeed raises almost as many questions as it settles. What are these questions?

7.3 The contingency of physicalism

Well, one question concerns how physicalism, if it is a necessitation thesis, can be a contingent doctrine *at all*. As we have already seen, for most philosophers physicalism is not a necessary doctrine or a conceptual one, like a doctrine in mathematics or ethics. People who deny it are not making a conceptual mistake. On the other hand, if physicalism is contingent, how then can it be spelled out in terms of necessitation? If one property necessitates another, this is presumably a necessary truth; how then can physicalism be contingent?

The first thing to do when confronted with this question is to notice that it is similar in outline to questions that come up elsewhere in philosophy. For example, consider that extremely successful Australian children's music group, the Wiggles. One of the important facts about that group is that Anthony is, i.e. is identical to, the Blue Wiggle. But the statement, 'Anthony = the Blue Wiggle' is contingent, something that is true as a matter of fact rather than in all possible worlds. Greg *was* the Yellow Wiggle, after all, and now is not; so while it is true that Anthony is the Blue Wiggle, someone else might have been—Barack Obama, for example (at least in a very far off possible world!). On the other hand, the fact that someone besides Anthony might have been the Blue Wiggle presents us with a puzzle. For the relation between Anthony and the Blue Wiggle is the relation of identity, and surely identity is a necessary relation if anything else. Question: how can the statement 'Anthony = the Blue Wiggle' be contingent when the relation it asserts to obtain is identity?

Now, in *Naming and Necessity*, Kripke defended a straightforward and attractive answer to this question. The statement 'Anthony = The Blue Wiggle' is contingent because one of the expressions that flank the identity sign is what Kripke called a 'non-rigid designator.' An expression is a rigid designator just in case it denotes the same object in all possible worlds at which the object exists; and an expression is a non-rigid designator just in case it is not a rigid designator. To put it even more simply, what is contingent here is the identity *statement*, but the relation that obtains between the Blue Wiggle (i.e. Anthony) and himself is not contingent.

In the case of the necessitation we may say exactly the same, or at least a very similar, thing. For example, consider the statement 'my aunt's favorite property necessitates my uncle's favorite property.' This statement is a necessitation statement since the relation it asserts to obtain is necessitation. But it is nevertheless contingent, since it depends for its truth on the preferences of my aunt and uncle. If my aunt likes being red best, and my uncle likes being colored best, the statement is true; alternatively if my aunt likes being red best and my uncle likes being square, it is false. How is this possible? How is it possible that 'my aunt's favorite property necessitates my uncle's favorite property' can be contingent while the relation it reports is necessitation? The answer is the same as in the identity case. Necessitation statements may be contingent if their constituent expressions are non-rigid designators, or at least behave in relevant respects like non-rigid designators. And that is what is true in this case. In particular, the expressions 'my aunt's favorite property' and 'my uncle's favorite property' are expressions that denote (compatibly with their meaning) different properties in different possible worlds, and it is this that permits the statement to be contingent.

Once we accept the point that statements of necessitation in general can be contingent, it is an easy matter to see how physicalism in particular can be. Physicalism is the thesis that every instantiated property is necessitated by some physical property. This is a necessitation statement, but it is also contingent because the extension of the expressions 'every instantiated property' and 'some physical property' differs from world to world. At the world that Descartes imagines the actual world to be, for example, it is not true that every instantiated property is necessitated by some physical property; but at the world that Smart imagines the actual world to be, it is.

7.4 Physicalism and the physicalist conditional

Physicalism is a contingent necessitation thesis, but there is nevertheless a genuinely necessary thesis in the background here that it is important for our overall discussion to bring out.

Suppose that physicalism is in fact true and so that every instantiated property is necessitated by some instantiated physical property. Now imagine we had a sentence that reported exactly the distribution of every property instantiated in the world—call it 'S.' Let us stipulate that S uses only rigid designators for the properties it talks about. So S says that being square is instantiated here and here and here, being round is instantiated here and here, and so on for every instantiated property. (Of course, S is too complex for us to utter or understand, but let us ignore this.) Now imagine we also had a similar sentence that reported exactly the distribution of every *physical* property in the world—call it 'S*.' This sentence says that being mass is instantiated here, and being charge is instantiated there, and so on. And finally imagine we had the truth-functional conditional formed from these, i.e. the conditional 'If S* then S,' and call this conditional 'the physi-calist conditional.' Now, if, as we are supposing, physicalism is true, then the physicalist conditional is *necessarily* true, at least given the way we have defined it. The reason is this. If physicalism is true, then every instantiated property is necessitated by some physical property, and likewise the truth of S* necessitates the truth of S. But if the truth of S* necessitates S, then the sentence 'S necessitates S*' is necessarily true because it reports a necessary relation and involves only rigid designators. Finally if 'S necessitates S*' is necessarily true, the conditional 'if S then S*' is likewise necessary.

The basic point here has nothing to do with physicalism in particular; analogous comments apply to the aunt/uncle example. Suppose we had a sentence A that reported exactly the distribution of my aunt's favorite prop-erty. So, on the assumption that being red is my aunt's favorite property, A tells us that red is instantiated here, and here and here … and so on for every instantiation of red. And suppose we had a sentence B that reported exactly the distribution of my uncle's favorite property. So, on the assump-tion that being colored is my uncle's favorite property, B tells us that being colored is instantiated here, and here, and here … and so on for every instantiation of being colored. Finally, suppose we have the truth-functional conditional formed from these sentences: 'if A then B.' Now, if we assume that, as a contingent matter of fact my aunt's favorite property necessitates my uncle's favorite property, it follows that the conditional 'if A then B' is necessary. The reason it is necessary is that the sentences 'A' and 'B' do not contain any non-rigid designators or expressions that behave like non-rigid designators.

So it would seem that, while physicalism itself is contingent, it is also the case that, if it is true, there is a necessary statement which is also true, viz. the physicalist conditional. And this point is an important one for our discus-sion. One reason is that it permits us to formulate a distinction between a priori and a posteriori physicalism—I will come back to this at the end of the chapter. Another reason is that it helps answer a further puzzle about contingency that often confronts us when discussing physicalism. For, as we will see in Chapter 10, some key arguments in the philosophy of mind against physicalism are modal arguments in this sense: if sound they estab-lish the existence of a metaphysical possibility. But it is often asked how the existence of these possibilities could be so much as relevant to the truth of physicalism, i.e. since physicalism is a contingent doctrine. The answer is that, while physicalism is a contingent doctrine, it is also the case that if it is true, the physicalist conditional is necessarily true. And the truth of this conditional might well rule out the existence of the possibility that a modal argument claims to establish. So in a sense, the physicalist conditional is the bridge between the contingency of physicalism and the modal arguments in philosophy of mind.

7.5 The epiphenomenal ectoplasm problem

One might have hoped that the observation that a necessitation thesis can be contingent in just the same way that an identity statement can be contingent would be sufficient to deal with questions associated with the contingency of physicalism. But things are not so simple. For, in addition to the issues of rigid designation just discussed, there is a problem of a more technical nature that is *also* discussed under the heading of 'the contingency of physicalism.' This problem derives from the fact that, as so far stated, the Necessity View has physicalism being incompatible with various possibilities that no version of physicalism, precisely because of its contingency, should rule out.

To illustrate, suppose again that physicalism is true at the actual world. Of course, physicalism is not inconsistent with the existence of various psychological episodes or facts in the world; that is, various cases of pain, pangs of jealousy, feelings of melancholia, and so on. A physicalist, to put it differently, need not be an eliminativist about the mental (i.e. someone who holds that there are no psychological episodes or facts). So let us suppose (as is of course the case) that there are such psychological episodes. Now, how *many* are there? Well that is a difficult question, in part because it is difficult to know how to go about counting psychological episodes. But let us suppose, just to fix ideas, there is a definite number of such episodes, and that number is 17. (Of course this is absurd; but choosing this number is just a device to bring out the problem I want to discuss clearly.) Now, if there are 17 psychological episodes, then there is a particular property that is instantiated at the world, namely *being such that there are only 17 psychological episodes*. Indeed, everything that is instantiated in the world has this property; so for example if Barack Obama exists in the actual world (as of course he does) then he is such that there are only 17 psychological episodes. Moreover, if physicalism is true, there is some physical property that necessitates being such that there are only 17 psychological episodes.

All right so far; but now consider an alternative possible world, W^*. This world is identical to the actual world in respect of which physical properties are instantiated there, but with this difference: it contains some further mental particulars and properties. These particulars and properties are, let us stipulate, constituted by ectoplasm and so are clearly non-physical. And let us further stipulate that they are epiphenomenal in the sense that they make no causal contribution to anything. In short W^* is a world that is exactly like the actual world except that it contains some extra epiphenomenal ectoplasm. (Hence the name of the problem.)

Now, a physicalist should not deny that W^* is a *possible* world. Their claim is that physicalism is true at the actual world, which means that the actual world is certainly not W^*. But to say that W^* is not actual is not to say that it is not possible. Another way to put the point is this. Physicalism according to physicalists is a contingent fact. But if it is a contingent fact there is nothing to rule out the idea that there might be a world exactly like our world in physical respects but enriched in some way. W^*, however, is just an example of such a world, for it is a world that is exactly like the actual world in physical respects but with some additional epiphenomenal ectoplasm.

However, while W^* is a possible world, the problem for the Necessity View is that, according to it, if physicalism is true at the actual world then W^* is impossible. To see the problem, focus again on the property of being such that there are only 17 episodes. We agreed that this property is instantiated at the actual world. Is it likewise instantiated at W^*? It would seem not; for at W^* there is some further epiphenomenal ectoplasm, and this element constitutes some further psychological episodes. At W^*, in other words, it is not the case that there are only 17 psychological episodes. On the other hand, W^* and the actual world are identical with respect to the physical properties that are instantiated there. So we have found a property, viz. being such that there are only 17 psychological episodes, which is not necessitated by any physical property instantiated at the actual world, i.e. because W^* is precisely a counterexample to that necessitation claim. So if W^* is possible, physicalism is not true at the actual world. Contrariwise, if physicalism is true at the actual world, W^* is not possible. However, W^* seems perfectly possible and indeed is agreed to be possible by physicalists who emphasize the contingency of their doctrine. Conclusion: the Necessity View is false as a definition of physicalism.

There are two main ways to deal with the epiphenomenal ectoplasm objection in the literature. (Lewis 1983 suggests a third idea that involves the notion of an alien property; we will set this idea aside here.) The first, due to Frank Jackson (cf. Jackson 1998), is to introduce what is sometimes called a totality or a minimality condition (or a 'that's all' clause) into the

Necessity View. The basic idea is that physicalism should not say simply that physical properties necessitate all instantiated properties; it should rather say that physical properties *alone* necessitate all instantiated properties—the 'alone' bit indicates the implicit totality clause. A relatively clear way to state this idea is to replace (1) with (3)

(3) Physicalism is true at *w* if and only if for every property *F* instantiated at *w*, there is some physical property *G* instantiated at *w* such that, for all possible worlds *w** if *G* is instantiated at *w**, and *nothing else is instantiated at w**, then *F* is instantiated at *w**.

This version of the Necessity View avoids the epiphenomenal ectoplasm problem. If physicalism is true on this definition there is some physical property *G* that is such that if it is instantiated and nothing else is, then the property of being such that there are 17 psychological episodes is also instantiated. But *W** is no objection to this claim since while *G* is instantiated at *W** and there being 17 psychological episodes is not, it is not the case that *G and nothing else* is instantiated at *W**.

A feature of this proposal that is somewhat confusing on first hearing is what exactly 'and nothing else is instantiated' is supposed to mean. Taken literally, the phrase suggests that *nothing numerically distinct from G* is instantiated. But this can't be what is intended; for one thing, it is an assumption of the case that something else besides *G* is instantiated at the actual world, viz. the property of there being only 17 psychological episodes. Rather what it means is that *nothing that is not necessitated by G* is instantiated. This rules *W** out of consideration, since at this world something clearly not necessitated by *G* exists and is instantiated, viz. epiphenomenal ectoplasm and its properties.

The second suggestion about how to deal with the epiphenomenal ectoplasm problem is due to David Chalmers (cf. Chalmers 1996). Chalmers's suggestion is to restrict attention when formulating physicalism to properties of a certain sort, which he calls 'positive' properties. Now, a positive property can be understood in various ways. On one understanding, for example, a positive property is a property whose canonical expression does not involve negation. So if 'is red' canonically expresses the property being red, then being red is a positive property. However, this is not the notion Chalmers has in mind. Rather, for him a positive property is "one that if instantiated in a world *W*, is also instantiated by the corresponding individual in all worlds that contain *W* as a proper part" (1996: 40).

If we call this notion of a positive property a 'c-positive' property, we now have a second way to respond to the epiphenomenal ectoplasm, and this is to replace (1) with (4):

(4) Physicalism is true at *w* if and only if for every *c-positive* property F instantiated at *w*, there is some physical property G instantiated at *w* such that, for all possible worlds *w** if G is instantiated at *w**, then F is instantiated at *w**.

This version of the Necessity View avoids the epiphenomenal ectoplasm problem, since, on this definition, physicalism may be true at the actual world and yet *W** remains a possibility. The reason is that the property of being such that there are only 17 psychological episodes is clearly not a c-positive property, and so is not within the scope of the definition.

7.6 Epiphenomenal ectoplasm and supervenience

We have been looking at the epiphenomenal ectoplasm problem as an objection to necessitation physicalism, i.e. physicalism according to the Necessity View. However, in the literature on these matters, the objection is usually discussed in the context, not of the Necessity View, but the Supervenience View, which we considered in the previous chapter. At this point therefore, it may be helpful to note that the moves we just considered for necessitation physicalism have their counterparts when we focus on supervenience physicalism.

As we saw in the previous chapter, the Supervenience View defines physicalism as follows:

(5) Physicalism is true at *w* if and only if for any possible world *w** if *w** is a physical duplicate of *w*, then *w** is a duplicate of *w* simpliciter.

If we focus on this definition of physicalism, the epiphenomenal ectoplasm problem is that if (5) is true, the truth of physicalism excludes possible worlds that physicalism really ought not to exclude. In particular, suppose that physicalism is true and that *W** (as we defined it in the previous section) exists. Under that supposition the left-hand side of (5) is true while the right-hand side is false. That the left-hand side is true is a consequence of the suppositions just made—after all, we are supposing that physicalism is true. But why is the right-hand side false? Well, *W** is a physical duplicate of the actual world but is not a duplicate simpliciter of the actual world because it contains some epiphenomenal ectoplasm. In sum, if physicalism is true and W^* exists, (5) is false.

Once again there are two proposals about how to deal with this (bypassing, as before, Lewis's proposal). The Jackson proposal (1998) is to replace (5) with (6):

(6) Physicalism is true at a possible world w if and only if for any world w^* if w^* is a minimal physical duplicate of w, then w^* is a duplicate of w simpliciter.

By 'minimal physical duplicate of w,' Jackson means a possible world that is identical in all physical respects to w, but which does not contain anything else; in particular, it does not contain any epiphenomenal ectoplasm. Unlike (5), (6) does not have physicalism ruling out W^*, and so (6) is preferable to (5) as a statement of physicalism.

The Chalmers proposal (1996) is to replace (5) with (7):

(7) Physicalism is true at a possible world w if and only if for any world w^*, if w^* is a physical duplicate of w, then w^* is a c-positive duplicate of w.

By 'c-positive duplicate of w,' Chalmers means a possible world that instantiates all the c-positive properties of w where the notion of a c-positive property is defined as it was before. Unlike (5), and like (6), (7) does not have physicalism ruling out W^*, and so (7) is preferable to (5) as a statement of physicalism.

7.7 The blockers problem

The possibility of epiphenomenal ectoplasm presents a problem both for the Necessity View and for the Supervenience View, but as we have seen there seem to be at least two ways to respond to this problem. This is not the end of the story, however. For there is a further problem to consider, sometimes called the blockers problem, which focuses attention on Jackson's suggestion that (5) should be replaced by (6). (Cf. Hawthorne 2002 and Leuenberger 2008.)

Imagine a possible world exactly like ours with respect to the distribution of mental and physical properties, except for this difference: the relation between physical facts and mental facts is weaker than necessitation— mental facts are necessitated by physical facts so long as there are no facts which block that necessitation (blockers, as Hawthorne called them). For example, being in an overall physical condition P will necessitate being in pain so long as you do not also instantiate some further property B. If you are in both P and B you are not in pain; but if you are in P and not in B, you will be in pain.

The problem that this possibility raises for (6) is as follows. Let us suppose that the relation obtaining at a world W between the mental and the physical is one of weak necessity as just defined; that is, suppose that, at W, the mental is necessitated by the physical but only if certain blockers are absent. Intuitively it would seem that physicalism is false at W. On the other hand, if physicalism is defined in the way suggested by Jackson it would be true. After all, applied to W, Jackson's definition says that physicalism is true at W just in case any minimal physical duplicate of W is a duplicate simpliciter. But that seems to be true of W as we have imagined it. Conclusion: if blockers are possible, physicalism is false at W, and yet it should not be false on Jackson's definition.

Now, one response to the blockers problem is to say that it brings out the differences between various ways that physicalists have sought to respond to the epiphenomenal ectoplasm problem. In particular, if one adopts (7) rather than (6) as one's response to the epiphenomenal ectoplasm problem, this would have the advantage of not facing the blockers problem. For if the relation of the mental to the physical that obtains at W is one of weak necessity, then not only is physicalism false but it is also false that any world which is a physical duplicate of W is a c-positive duplicate of W—at some physical duplicate worlds, for example, there will be no psychological properties at all. So this suggests that, at least if blockers are possible, it is better to adopt (7) above rather than (6).

A difficulty for this response however is that (7) faces blocker-style problems of its own—a point brought out in Leuenberger (2008), as I read him. The problem is essentially that being in pain might not be a c-positive property in the sense mentioned in (7). For suppose it is possible that being in pain can be blocked. Then it is not true that if being in pain is instantiated in a world W, it is also instantiated by the corresponding individual in all worlds that contain W as a proper part—for in some of those worlds it will be blocked. On the other hand, if being in pain is not a c-positive property then (7) is silent on its status. Dualism might be true of being in pain, and physicalism could still be true if physicalism is defined as (7) suggests it should be.

A different response to the blockers problem for a proponent of (6) is to resist the intuition that physicalism is false at W in the circumstance described. But this seems a difficult position to sustain. It is true that the mere existence of a non-physical uninstantiated property does not compromise physicalism. But in the case imagined the existence of this property makes the relation between physical properties and mental properties look altogether too close to the relation that would obtain if dualism is true.

7.8 Necessitation and psychophysical laws

So it would seem that the epiphenomenal ectoplasm problem poses a very difficult problem for any attempt to formulate physicalism. To solve it in either of the two ways usually suggested is to lead directly to a further series of problems. On reflection, however, this is not that surprising. For at the heart of the epiphenomenal ectoplasm problem (and so at the heart of the blockers problem) are questions about negative properties, totality properties, generality, and so on. And these are notoriously difficult to deal with. Moreover, they are not problems that afflict physicalism in *particular*. Any theory that aspires for completeness, to say something about every instantiated property, is likely to run into them. Rather than trying to resolve them here, therefore, I want now to close our discussion of the necessity of necessitation by looking at two issues related to, but different from, those already discussed.

The first returns us to the famous passage from Davidson in which he said (in part): "Although the position I describe denies there are psychophysical laws, it is consistent with the view that mental characteristics are in some sense dependent, or supervenient, on physical characteristics" (1970: 214). We have discussed supervenience already; let's now focus on laws, and in particular on Davidson's denial that there are psychophysical laws. For the fact is that this denial is a somewhat remarkable one, given the issues we have just been considering. What is remarkable is not so much the denial that there are psychophysical laws, but the combination of that denial with the assertion of supervenience, or what we are assuming is the same thing, the assertion of necessitation. Let us examine why.

When philosophers talk about laws—and certainly when Davidson talks about laws—they usually have in mind a universally quantified statement that, as it is sometimes put, 'supports counterfactuals.' To take a classic example, consider the statement 'everything in my pocket is a gold coin.' This is a universally quantified statement—i.e. it has the form 'All Fs are Gs'—but it is not a scientific law on any definition. A major reason for this is that it is not true of an arbitrarily chosen object—my aunt, say—that if she were in my pocket she would be gold coin; in other words, it is not true of the statement that it supports counterfactuals. On the other hand, consider something that presumably is a law, e.g. the statement 'nothing travels faster then the speed of light,' or equivalently 'everything travels at a speed less than or equal to the speed of light.' Part of what makes this a law is that it supports counterfactuals, e.g. it is true of my aunt that if she were traveling it would be at a speed less than or equal to the speed of light.

If this or something like it is what is meant by a law, what Davidson is saying in the passage quoted is that there are no laws in this sense that connect the physical and the mental; that is what it means to say that there are no psychophysical laws. But this denial seems in conflict with the truth of necessitarian physicalism. Suppose (again) that physicalism as defined by the Necessity View is true, so that every instantiated property is necessitated by some physical property. And now suppose that the property of being in pain is one property that is instantiated in the actual world. Now, if physicalism is true, and being in pain is instantiated, it follows that there is some physical property, call it 'Phys,' which is such that if Phys is instantiated, then being in pain is instantiated. To put it differently, if physicalism is true, then the conditional 'If Phys is instantiated then being in pain is instantiated' is necessarily true. But if this conditional is a necessary truth it is very hard to see why it could not be converted into something that counts as a law. In the first place, it is a simple matter to transform it into the statement 'everything that is in Phys is in pain,' and this is a universally quantified statement. In the second place, it *does* seem to support counterfactuals: it is true of an arbitrarily chosen object—my aunt, say—that if she were in Phys then she would be in pain. Conclusion: Davidson's assertion of supervenience (and so, given our assumptions, of necessitation) is in contradiction with his denial of laws!

One way to respond to this is to accept the idea that Davidson's position is incoherent. But a better way is to notice that the property of supporting counterfactuals is a necessary condition, and not a sufficient condition, on something's being a law. The statement 'Everything which is Phys is in pain' might support counterfactuals, but something further is required if it is to count as a law. What more is required? Well this is a difficult question in the philosophy of laws, but one common idea is that the properties mentioned in the laws are somehow natural properties, where a natural property is a special sort of property that imposes a genuine naturalness on the things that have them. (The idea of a natural property is very closely related to the notion of a fundamental property we saw in the passage quoted from Lewis in Chapter 2. Lewis thought of fundamental properties as perfectly natural, and connects them to laws in his 1983 paper.)

If we agree that a statement must express natural properties in order to be a law, it is a simple matter to reconcile the assertion of necessitation and the denial of laws. If physicalism is true, the statement 'everything which is in Phys is in pain' is necessarily true and does support counterfactuals, but it would still fail to be a law if Phys is not a natural property. On the other hand, there is nothing in the assertion of necessitation to say that Phys is a natural property. Indeed, as far as the Necessity View is concerned, Phys might be a property the various instances of which have nothing at all in common with each other. If that is so, the Davidsonian denial of psychophysical laws is quite consistent with the assertion of necessitation (or in his case, of supervenience).

Of course that Davidson's position is consistent does not entail that it is true. Davidson argues for his denial of psychophysical laws in a complicated way that we will not be able to go into here. The important point for us is that there is no inconsistency between the Necessity View and the denial of psychophysical laws.

7.9 A priori and a posteriori physicalism

The final issue I want to consider in this chapter concerns the relation between the modal status of physicalism—whether it is contingent or not—and its epistemic status—whether it is a posteriori or not. As usually understood, physicalism is not only a contingent doctrine, it is also an a posteriori or empirical one. Now as we have seen there is no problem with the doctrine being contingent. Similar things might be said about its being a posteriori. So, in particular, the thesis that every instantiated property is necessitated by some physical property is an empirical and a posteriori doctrine, one that logically speaking is like the theory of evolution or of continental drift.

However, while it is not controversial that physicalism is an a posteriori doctrine, there is a question nearby that is controversial, namely the question of whether one should endorse what is usually called 'a posteriori physicalism' or 'a priori physicalism'.

Earlier we saw that if physicalism is true, the physicalist conditional is necessary. But now let us ask: is the physicalist conditional a priori or a posteriori? The answer to this is not determined by any assumption we have made so far. Physicalism itself is a posteriori certainly. But it does not follow that the physicalist conditional is a posteriori. After all, the modal status of physicalism might diverge from that of the physicalist conditional; why should the same not be true of its epistemic status? On the other hand, while our assumptions do not entail anything about the epistemic status of the conditional, they do make salient the possibility that it is a necessary a posteriori truth, and as such exhibits the same combination of modal and epistemic features that is exhibited by statements such as 'heat is motion of molecules.' Those who assert that this is the case are 'a posteriori physicalists'; those who assert this is not, i.e. that the physicalist conditional is a priori, are 'a priori physicalists'.

The distinction between a priori and a posteriori physicalism will re-emerge at a later stage in our discussion. For the moment, it is sufficient to make two points. First, the labels here are somewhat misleading. It is not physicalism that is a priori if a priori physicalism is true. Everybody thinks that physicalism is contingent and a posteriori. It is rather the physicalist conditional—i.e. something quite distinct from physicalism—that is a priori if a priori physicalism is true. Second, the question of whether the physicalist conditional is a priori is a very difficult one to resolve. To solve it one needs a theory of the necessity, a theory of the a priori and a theory of the relation between them. We will not be going into these theories in any detail in this book.

Summary

In this chapter, we have been considering the question of whether necessitation is necessary for physicalism. On the one hand, it would seem that necessitation is necessary for physicalism, for otherwise it is difficult to distinguish physicalism from various versions of dualism. On the other hand, this fact seems to create some challenges. Some of the challenges arise from the mere fact that phsyicalism is contingent. Others arise from the tension between necessitarian physicalism and the possibility of epiphenomenal ectoplasm and of blockers, the denial of psychophysical laws, and the empirical and a posteriori nature of physicalism.

Recommended reading

There is a very large literature on contingency and identity—the best place to start is probably Kripke 1980. For reasons I don't quite understand the contingency of materialism is not usually associated with the contingency of identity statements, but see Stoljar 2006 for a brief discussion. For the epiphenomenal ectoplasm problem, see Horgan 1983; Lewis 1983; Chalmers 1996; Jackson 1998; and Chalmers and Jackson 2001. For blockers, see Hawthorne 2002; and Leuenberger 2008. For psychophysical laws, see Davidson 1970; and the papers in part I of Heil and Mele 1995. In Davidson's chapter in the Heil and Mele volume (Davidson 1995), he seems to suggest that the notion of supervenience should be understood in such a way as to not entail metaphysical necessity; if so, this is a change of heart from his previous discussion. For the controversies surrounding a posteriori physicalism, see Byrne 1999, Block and Stalnaker 1999, Chalmers and Jackson 2001, and Soames 2007.

8

IS NECESSITATION SUFFICIENT?

8.1 Necessitation dualism

The character that we have mostly been subjecting to scrutiny over the last two chapters is the necessitation physicalist, i.e. the philosopher who believes physicalism according to the Necessity View. But it is now time to introduce a new character into the discussion, the necessitation dualist. We may think of the necessitation dualist as telling a story with two parts.

The first part is shared with a dualist of the standard sort. Dualists of the standard sort hold that psychological properties are distinct from physical properties in a certain important sense; for example, they hold that psychological and physical properties are as distinct from one another as shape properties and color properties. To give this relation a convenient name that for the moment neither prejudices nor explains its nature, let us say that according to the standard dualist, the psychological and the physical are *metaphysically distinct*. So too, according to the necessitation dualist, the psychological properties and the physical properties are metaphysically distinct.

The second part of the necessitation dualist story is not shared with a dualist of the standard sort; indeed, here things diverge dramatically. In this part of the story, the necessitation dualist adds that, while psychological and physical properties are metaphysically distinct, they are nevertheless necessarily connected: that is, in all possible worlds, if various physical properties are instantiated then so too are various psychological properties (and vice versa too on some versions of the view). This goes against the standard dualist view. The standard dualist, as we have seen, says that mental and physical properties are metaphysically distinct, but the standard dualist will go on to add that mental and physical properties are only contingently connected.

Indeed, the necessitation dualist goes against the standard dualist not only in holding that psychological properties are necessitated by physical properties but also in advancing a different account of what metaphysical distinctness is. As we will see in more detail in a moment, for the standard dualist, the notion of metaphysical distinctness is explained, at least in part, in modal terms; thus, mental properties and physical properties are metaphysically distinct precisely because it is possible for physical properties to be instantiated without mental properties and vice versa. What the necessitation dualist says, by contrast, is that a property F might be metaphysically distinct from another property G *even though* they are necessarily connected.

8.2 The problem

So that is the necessitation dualist—but what of it? Why is the necessitation dualist important for our discussion? The reason is that necessitation dualism presents a major problem for the Necessity View. To illustrate the problem, let us look (again!) at the Necessity View in the form that we have mainly been considering it:

(1) Physicalism is true at *w* if and only if for every property *F* instantiated at *w*, there is some physical property *G* instantiated at *w* such that, for all possible worlds *w**, if *G* is instantiated at *w**, then *F* is instantiated at *w**.

Suppose now that the actual world is indeed as the necessitation dualist imagines it to be; that is, suppose that at the actual world the psychological properties and the physical properties are as different from each other as the traditional dualist believes, and yet they are related to each other by necessitation. In that circumstance, the left-hand side of (1) is false. For, if the world is as the necessitation dualist imagines it to be, physicalism is clearly not true. On the other hand, in the circumstances imagined, the right-hand side of (1) is true., or at least could perfectly well be. For the necessitation dualist's position is precisely that the psychological properties *are* necessitated by physical properties. So it would seem that if necessitation dualism represents a way for the actual world to be, then it is possible that the left-hand-side of (1) is true while the right-hand side is false. But then (1) is false and so is the Necessity View.

A number of points of clarification are required in order to have this problem in focus. First, the issue here does not concern the truth of necessitation dualism so much as its *coherence* or (if this is different) its *possibility*. Suppose you think that as a matter of fact necessitation dualism is false. That is irrelevant to the present argument. Whether or not necessitation dualism is true, so long as it is coherent, we will have the materials for an argument that (1) is false.

Second, the problem has nothing to do with the issues arising from what a physical property is. As far as that is concerned, the necessitation dualist, the traditional dualist, and the physicalist are in agreement: for all three positions require a distinction between physical and other properties, they just offer different views about the relation between these kinds of properties. So in order to discuss necessitation dualism we can set those issues to one side.

Third, the problem has nothing to do with the various subtleties that, as we saw in the previous chapter, it is necessary, or might be necessary, to incorporate into the Necessity View in order to answer the epiphenomenal ectoplasm problem and the blockers problem. The problem of necessitation dualism has nothing to do with these issues either, and we may set them aside. More generally, in the previous chapter we considered various challenges to the left-to-right direction of the Necessity View; that is, to its claim that necessitation is necessary for physicalism. But in this chapter we are concerned with a challenge to the right-to-left direction of the view; that is, its claim that necessitation is sufficient.

Finally, I have presented the problem so far in the form of a straight counterexample to (1). But one might also present the issue by asking how, if the Necessity View is true, physicalism is to be distinguished from necessitation dualism. On the Necessity View, it is sufficient for physicalism that every instantiated property is necessitated by a physical property. But if necessitation dualism is true, that is the case. Why then is necessitation dualism not a form of physicalism as it palpably seems not to be? In what follows, I will move back and forth between this 'distinction' way of putting the basic problem, and the other, 'counterexample,' way.

8.3 Further examples of the problem

The problem for the Necessity View that we just introduced is generated by the example of the necessitation dualist. But it is not generated only by that example. On the contrary, an analogous problem will arise whenever there are clear examples of positions according to which there are instantiated properties that, on the one hand, constitute an intuitive objection to physicalism but that on the other hand are necessarily connected to the physical. The necessitation dualist is one example of a position of this general type, but there are certainly others.

The easiest way to generate examples like this is to consider theories that require for their truth various properties that are normally thought to falsify physicalism, and then to imagine a necessary connection between those properties and physical properties. So, for example, consider the vitalist about biological properties. The usual way to think of that position involves the suggestion that there is a contingent connection between élan vital and physical properties. But we can readily imagine a necessitation version of vitalism, and this will constitute a problem for the Necessity View in much the same way as necessitation dualism does. (It is possible to construct similar examples using primitive colors or emergent chemistry as well.)

A more controversial way to generate examples is by considering necessary beings (i.e. things that exist in all possible worlds), and the properties that they instantiate. Philosophers have suggested various examples of such beings, but perhaps the most obvious ones in this context are numbers and other mathematical objects, on the one hand, and God, on the other. It might be thought that both sorts of objects exist and instantiate properties that are inconsistent with physicalism. If so, physicalism is presumably false. On the other hand, it will still be true that physicalism is true on the Necessity View, because there is a trivial sense in which these things and their properties are necessitated by the physical, i.e. because they exist in all possible worlds.

There is a difference in plausibility here between the mathematical case and the theological case. It is certainly true that numbers and their properties are necessarily connected to the physical. But it is not at all clear that they are inconsistent with physicalism. Of course numbers and their properties are not physical in the sense of the starting point physical; whatever else they are numbers are not located or solid, for example. But as we have seen in Chapters 3 and 4, if physicalism is to be true we will need a significantly more relaxed account of being physical. And it is not at all clear that, according to this more relaxed account, numbers are not physical. In *Word and Object*, for example, Quine argues that the existence of numbers is not counter to physicalism precisely because the existence of numbers seemed to be required for physics (Quine 1960).

On the other hand, the theological example cannot be so easily dismissed. Of course there are different ways to conceive of God. But on one reasonable way, God is an object rather like the souls that would exist if substance dualism were true; it is just that he exists (if he exists) necessarily. Now, if that is so, physicalism is inconsistent with the existence and nature of God so conceived (though it might be consistent with the existence and nature of God conceived in some other way). But the trouble is that there is nothing in the Necessity View to explain this. Physicalism as the Necessity View construes it could perfectly well be true *even* if God in this sense exists. (It is important to notice that, as with the case of necessitation dualism, the issue here turns on the *coherence* of this theological position, not its truth: if it is coherent, we have a counterexample to the Necessity View.)

In sum, even if the mathematical example can in this context be set aside, it remains the case that the theological example presents a problem for the Necessity View somewhat in the way that the necessitation dualist example does. However, while acknowledging that this is the case, I will in what follows mainly concentrate on the necessitation dualist case rather than the God case (or indeed the vitalist and other cases mentioned earlier). The replies to the underlying problem we will discuss have a straightforward extension in these other cases, but I will leave this implicit in what follows.

How then are we to reply to this objection from necessitation dualism to the Necessity View? In the following two sections, I am going to look in detail at one response, which I call 'the incoherence reply'. After that I will examine three others more briefly.

8.4 The incoherence reply

According to the incoherence reply, the problem of distinguishing necessitation dualism from physicalism can be dealt with simply: necessitation dualism is incoherent, and so there is no problem at all of distinguishing it from physicalism. Put differently, the objection says that the world at which necessitation dualism is true is a world that provides a counterexample to (1) and so to the Necessity View. But of course if there is no such world, there is no counterexample.

But why think that necessitation dualism is incoherent? The main reason arises from what is called in contemporary philosophy 'Hume's dictum.' (The question of whether the real Hume, the eighteenth-century Scottish philosopher, held Hume's dictum will not be our concern here; what I have in mind is a thesis that a number of philosophers defend and develop and call 'Hume's dictum'; see Lewis 1986a, and Armstrong 1999.) In slogan form, Hume's dictum is that there are no necessary connections between metaphysically distinct existences. By 'existences' here, a proponent of Hume's dictum means 'things that exist,' and so if we assume that properties are things that exist—as I noted in Chapter 2 I am assuming—then Hume's dictum entails as a special case that there are no necessary connections between metaphysically distinct properties. For convenience we can here concentrate exclusively on properties, leaving other existences, i.e. items of other ontological categories, aside.

Now, necessitation dualism certainly is inconsistent with Hume's dictum, at least on the surface. As we saw, necessitation dualism is a doctrine with two parts. The dualist part is that mental properties are metaphysically distinct from physical properties. The necessitation part is that mental properties are necessarily connected to physical properties because physical properties necessitate mental properties. The conjunction of these two claims implies that there are necessary connections between metaphysically distinct properties. But of course Hume's dictum denies this. Hence, if Hume's dictum is true, necessitation dualism is false.

One might point out that this conclusion is not quite the conclusion that necessitation dualism is incoherent, and so does not quite get you to the main suggestion of the reply we are considering. There are two responses to this. First, Hume's dictum is often held to be not simply true, but analytically true, and so is a constraint on what can be said. If so, inconsistency with Hume's dictum means inconsistency with coherence. Second, even if the argument we just considered fails to show that necessitation dualism is incoherent, it would certainly show (if successful) that necessitation dualism is inconsistent with a necessary truth, i.e. Hume's dictum. And that would be enough to save the Necessity View.

But of course, even if necessitation dualism were inconsistent with Hume's dictum, this would only cause a problem if the dictum were true. And of course whether it is true depends on what it means, and this depends on what 'metaphysical distinctness' means. What then does 'metaphysically distinct' mean? Well, as we will see in a moment there are various things it *could* mean. But, at least as far as the proponent of the incoherence reply is concerned, what 'metaphysical distinctness' means is what 'modally distinct' means. In turn what this means is as follows:

> A property F is modally distinct from a property G if and only if it is possible that F is instantiated and G is not *and* it is possible that G is instantiated and F is not.

So for example, the property of being red is modally distinct from the property of being square because it is possible for something to be red and nothing to be square and vice versa. On the assumption that metaphysical distinctness just is modal distinctness, therefore, the property of being red is metaphysically distinct from the property of being square.

If metaphysical distinctness just is modal distinctness, the incoherence reply looks extremely persuasive. On the one hand, when a proponent of Hume's dictum says that there is no necessary connection between metaphysically distinct properties, what is meant, on the interpretation we are considering, is that there is no necessary connection between *modally distinct* properties. But this last claim is not merely true but analytically so: when one property is modally distinct from another *of course* there are no necessary connections between them. Similarly, when the necessitation dualist says that mental and physical properties are metaphysically distinct but necessarily connected, what is meant, on the interpretation we are considering, is that mental and physical properties are modally distinct but necessarily connected. But this claim is not merely false but analytically so: when one property is not necessarily connected to another *of course* they must be modally distinct as well. Hence the incoherence reply appears to have a straightforward response to the objection to the Necessity View that we have been considering. If necessitation dualism were coherent, the Necessity View would have trouble distinguishing it from physicalism. But if it is not, trouble is avoided.

8.5 Varieties of distinctness

What can be said about the incoherence reply to the necessitation dualist objection to the Necessity View? On the one hand, it is certainly right that Hume's dictum is analytic if 'metaphysically distinct' means 'modally distinct.' But, on the other, it is open, both to a necessitation dualist, and to a proponent of the objection from necessitation dualism, to insist that this is not what they intend by 'metaphysically distinct' and so the incoherence objection misses the point. The underlying issue here is important for our discussion so at this point it is worth pausing to discuss some other interpretations of what 'distinctness' could mean.

According to the first, 'metaphysically distinct' means 'numerically distinct', where:

F is numerically distinct from G if and only if F is not identical to G.

This is a very natural suggestion; after all, this is what 'distinctness' usually means. However, this cannot be what 'metaphysical distinctness' means either for the necessitation dualist or for the proponent of Hume's dictum. As regards the necessitation dualist, the whole point of that position is that mental and physical properties are not simply numerically distinct (any proponent of multiple realizability might agree to that) but are distinct in a more profound way as well; 'metaphysical distinctness' is a label for this more profound way. As regards Hume's dictum, if this were the thesis that there are no necessary connections between numerically distinct existences it would be trivially false. For consider being red and being colored— there is a necessary connection between these properties because being red necessitates being colored. And yet being red is numerically distinct from being colored because some things are colored but are not red (lemons, for example).

According to the second way of interpreting distinctness, 'metaphysical distinctness' means 'distinctness in essence or nature' where:

F is distinct in essence from G just in case the essence of F is wholly distinct from the essence of G.

The essence of a thing, as I understand it, is the totality of its essential properties. Correlatively, the essence of x is wholly distinct from the essence of y if and only if none of the essential properties of x are also essential properties of y. So what it means for one property to be distinct in essence from another is for the first to have no essential properties that the second one has. On this interpretation, what Hume's dictum means is that, between two properties that share no essential properties, there are no necessary connections either. Likewise, what the necessitation dualist is asserting is that, at least on occasion, there precisely are necessary connections between properties that share no essential properties.

However, the cogency of this response depends on what an essential property is. On some views, an essential property is simply a necessary property, i.e. a property had by a property in all worlds in which it is instantiated. However, if that is what is intended, then this interpretation is no advance and necessitation dualism remains incoherent. On other views, however, not all necessary properties are essential properties. For example, Kit Fine (1994) argues that it is necessary that Socrates is a member of his singleton set—i.e. the set that has only Socrates as a member—but it is not essential to Socrates that he is a member of this set, and, similarly, it is necessary that Socrates is such that $2 + 2 = 4$ but it is not essential to Socrates that he is. If Fine is right about these examples, it would be possible to defend the idea that there are essential properties which are not necessary properties. In turn, this would make it possible to articulate a version of Hume's dictum that may be reasonably denied by the necessitation dualist.

However, the question of whether there is a distinction between necessity and essence is a difficult one to adjudicate. It might be argued that the distinction that Fine is pointing too here is simply a distinction between necessary properties that we find interesting and necessary properties that we find boring. The property of being such that $2 + 2 = 4$ is certainly a fairly boring property since everything has it. So it is not one that people are likely to mention when they tell us what the essence or nature of Socrates is. But for all that it might be part of his essence or nature. If so, it is difficult to see how to draw the distinction between necessity and essence in the way that this interpretation of Hume's dictum requires.

According to a third interpretation, 'metaphysical distinctness' is not to be explained by pointing to some other relation, like numerical or modal distinctness. Rather it is interpreted as a primitive notion that one may introduce by reflecting on examples. (I am indebted here to a discussion with Jonathan Schaffer.) Suppose we look again at the examples we have considered: Fine's example of Socrates and his singleton set, mental and physical properties according to the necessitation dualist, God and the physical world. One might think that there is a pattern in such examples, a pattern we can somehow cotton on to just by thinking about them. We may capture the pattern by saying that in each case the relation of metaphysical distinctness is instantiated, and this seems a good way to introduce the notion of metaphysical distinctness. But one may introduce the notion of metaphysical distinctness in this way without having to hand an explanation of what metaphysical distinctness is in any other terms. To put it differently, one may introduce metaphysical distinctness in this way, and still say that it is a primitive notion. But, if it is a primitive notion, then there may be no contradiction in denying Hume's dictum nor in asserting that necessitation dualism is true.

However, there are two problems with this suggestion. First, the suggestion seems to assume that in all of these cases just mentioned there is a single relation of metaphysical distinctness that is instantiated. But is this really true? For example, take the relation that holds between Socrates and his singleton set. Is this the same relation (or even the same sort of relation) as that which would hold between the mental and the physical if necessitation dualism were true? It is certainly not clear that this is so. But if not, then it is not clear that the procedure adopted by primitivists about metaphysical distinctness will be successful.

Second, and this point is related to the first, the suggestion that metaphysical distinctness is a primitive notion appears dialectically weak against the philosopher who thinks that necessitation dualism is incoherent. For such a philosopher is very likely to think that a primitivist notion of metaphysical distinctness is incoherent as well! Of course, the primitivist will say in response that there is no reason to suppose the notion is incoherent, and that everybody must take something as a primitive. But at this point the issue is likely to degenerate into a squabble about standards of clarity. Indeed, a squabble of this sort was always on the cards the moment the incoherence reply suggested that necessitation dualism is incoherent. In general, when philosopher A accuses philosopher B of being incoherent, it is always open to philosopher B to insist that philosopher A has the wrong standards of clarity or coherence. And the trouble is that it is difficult to adjudicate this sort of dispute.

8.6 Three further replies

We will come back to the idea of taking metaphysical distinctness as a primitive later on in this chapter. Meanwhile, let me briefly discuss three further replies to the objection from necessitation dualism against the Necessity View.

8.6.1 The realization reply

According to the realization reply, the objection demonstrates that the Necessity View is false, and the proper response to the problem is to reject the Necessity View in favor of the Realization View. As we saw in Chapter 6 the Realization View assumes something like the following form:

(2) Physicalism is true at w if and only if every property instantiated at w is either identical to some physical property instantiated at w or is realized by some physical property instantiated at w.

This account of what physicalism is does not face the problem of distinguishing itself from necessitation dualism, the proponent of the realization reply says, for the necessitation dualist precisely denies that mental properties, say, are realized in physical properties.

Why does the necessitation dualist deny that mental properties are realized by physical properties? A good way to see the plausibility in this idea is to recall that the Realization View is a descendant of the Identity View, for which physicalism is the thesis that every instantiated property is identical to a physical property. It should be clear that the Identity View is inconsistent with necessitation dualism since the necessitation dualist is denying that mental properties are identical to physical properties. But the Identity View of course has problems of its own, in particular, the objection from multiple realizability. So, while the Identity View does not face the problem of distinguishing physicalism from necessitation dualism, its other problems are sufficient to think that there is no point adopting it.

It is at this juncture that the Realization View enters the picture. The Realization View does much better than the Identity View on the issue of multiple realization, but one might think it preserves enough of the spirit of the Identity View to be in a good position to avoid the objection from necessitation dualism. In summary, the Realization View looks as if it avoids both Scylla and Charybdis: it avoids the multiple realization objection to the Identity View ('Scylla'), and the necessarian dualist objection to the Necessity view ('Charybdis'). It is no wonder then that many philosophers have suggested that the Realization View is the right way to spell out physicalism (cf. Melnyk 2003; Poland 1994)

However, while it is true that the Realization View is attractive in these ways, it remains the case that the Realization View faces some serious problems of its own. As we noted at the end of Chapter 6, the Realization View does not articulate a sufficient condition for physicalism either in its standard development or in the development suggested by Shoemaker's work. The problem was that it is consistent with realization physicalism that some version of dualism is true. Moreover, once we have necessitation dualism firmly before our minds this problem looks worse rather than better. To make the point with the Shoemaker-inspired version of the Realization View, Shoemaker says that a property F realizes a property G

just in case the causal role associated with F is included in the causal role associated with property G. But it is consistent with this that F and G are metaphysically distinct and yet necessarily connected. As before, one might avoid this problem by adopting a causal theory of properties, but this theory is very controversial.

8.6.2 The explanation reply

According to the explanation reply, the objection from necessitation dualism is a good one, i.e. it refutes the Necessity View in the form we have been considering it. However, says the proponent of the explanation reply, to meet it you must adjust (1) so that it contains a commitment to explanation on the part of the physicalist. The key idea is that a physicalist is not someone who says merely that every instantiated property is necessitated by a physical property, but he or she also imposes some explanatory or epistemological condition on what the necessitation can come to. If we impose this further condition on what physicalism is we no longer face the problem of distinguishing physicalism from necessitation dualism, the proponent of the explanation reply says, for while the necessitation dualist thinks that mental properties are necessitated by physical properties, he or she does not think that this necessitation is explained or is explanatory.

However, the main problem with this suggestion is that it is unclear what this further explanation condition could amount to. On the most straightforward development of this idea, it is simply the suggestion that there must be some explanation for the idea that the necessitation relation obtains. But this idea faces two serious problems. First, it is unclear why the necessitation dualist cannot seek to explain the necessitation relation as well. In general there seems nothing in necessitation dualism to suggest that the position is somehow opposed with the idea of explanation. Terrence Horgan (1993), who defends something like the explanation reply in a famous paper, responds in part to this point by saying that while both the necessitation dualist and the physicalist might demand an explanation of necessitation, only the physicalist will demand an explanation that is, as he puts it, 'materialistically adequate.' However, while this is true it is also quite un-illuminating. Of course necessitation dualists are not seeking an explanation of the necessitation relation that is *materialistically* adequate—they are seeking one, if at all, that is *necessitation dualistically* adequate. But this does not improve our understanding of the distinction between physicalism and necessitation dualism.

The second problem with this development of the explanation reply is that it is quite unclear that the physicalist must, of necessity, require that there is an explanation of why the necessitation relation obtains. Suppose a physicalist insists what while the necessitation thesis obtains, there is no further explanation for this fact. No doubt this would offend the sensibilities of various philosophers, including some physicalists; nevertheless, it is unclear why it would be a problem for physicalism as such.

One might try to develop the explanatory reply in a different way by connecting it with themes that have already emerged in our discussion. For example, one might suggest that when the proponent of this reply insists that the connection between the mental and physical be adequately explained, what they are insisting on is something like a priori physicalism of the kind mentioned in the previous chapter. It is easy to distinguish necessitation dualism from a priori physicalism, the proponent of this reply says, for while the necessitation dualist thinks that mental properties are necessitated by physical ones, he does not think that they are a priori necessitated by the physical properties.

However, the problem for this suggestion is that it conflates the distinction between a priori and a posteriori physicalism with the distinction between necessitation dualism and physicalism. In effect, what this proposal says is that the a posteriori physicalist holds a position indistinguishable from the necessitation dualist. But this does not seem to be so. A posteriori physicalism is an interesting version of physicalism, and one that might well be appealed to so as to respond to various famous arguments against physicalism. Nevertheless, it is a version of physicalism—and necessitation dualism is not supposed to be a version of physicalism.

A different possible response has been put forward in a recent paper by Frank Jackson (2006). According to this response, physicalists do not say simply that the physical facts necessitate the mental facts, they say in addition that they do so *de re a priori*. But the problem in Jackson's proposal is that it is unclear what the notion of the de re a priori amounts to. On the usual understanding, a proposition is a priori or not just in case we can come to know that it is true without relying in an epistemically important way on experience. But then the property of being a priori is de dicto rather than de re, i.e. it attaches to propositions rather than objects or properties. What Jackson wants to say is that one may understand the idea of the a priori in such a way that it attaches to objects or properties, and not merely to propositions. But it is highly controversial whether this can be so. In consequence, it is highly controversial whether Jackson's suggestion about how to distinguish physicalism from necessitation dualism can be made to work.

8.6.3 The fundamental properties reply

According to the fundamental properties reply, the objection from necessitation dualism demonstrates that the Necessity View is false, and the proper response to the problem is to reject the Necessity View in favor of the Fundamental Properties View. As we saw in Chapter 6, that Fundamental Properties View assumes something like this form:

(3) Physicalism is true at *w* if and only if every fundamental property instantiated at *w* is a physical property.

The Fundamental Properties View has the resources to drive a wedge between physicalism and necessitation dualism, the proponent of this reply says, because, while the physicalist says that every fundamental property is physical, the necessitation dualist says that some fundamental properties are non-physical, it is just that these fundamental properties bear a necessary connection to other physical fundamental properties.

Now one problem with this response is, as we mentioned in Chapter 2 and then again in Chapter 6, that the notion of a fundamental property is speculative in various ways. But another problem is that it is natural to interpret Lewis in the passage I quoted in Chapter 2 (cf. Lewis 1994) as supposing that every fundamental property is modally distinct from every other fundamental property. But if that is so, it is no good interpreting a necessitation dualist as saying that mental and physical properties are necessarily connected and yet are fundamental. That possibility is something that Lewis's account of fundamental properties denies.

Could it be that we could somehow detach the idea of a fundamental property from the idea of modal distinctness? That is the suggestion of a number of recent philosophers (for example, Schaffer forthcoming and Rosen 2010). These suggestions take up issues we cannot go into in this book. However, it is possible to state a related idea using materials we have already introduced. It is natural to read Lewis as saying that every fundamental property is modally distinct from every other. But it is also natural to break this idea up into two separate ideas. The first connects fundamental properties with metaphysical distinctness as follows: a fundamental property is metaphysically distinct from every other fundamental property. The second explains metaphysical distinctness in terms of modal distinctness. Putting these two ideas together we obtain the suggestion that fundamental properties are modally distinct from each other.

But suppose that we adopted instead a different account of metaphysical distinctness; for example, suppose we adopt instead the primitivist account I sketched above. Then it would be possible to accept the first of the two claims just distinguished and reject the second. In particular, it becomes possible to say that a fundamental property is metaphysically distinct from every other fundamental property, and yet deny that this entails that every fundamental property is modally distinct from every other.

If something like this idea can be made to work, one might appeal to the Fundamental Properties View to distinguish the physicalist from the necessitation dualist. The physicalist says that every fundamental property is physical; whereas according to the necessitation dualist both mental and physical properties are fundamental (even though they are necessarily connected). Moreover, we would have arrived at a major reason to abandon the Necessity View in favor of the Fundamental Properties View, viz. that the Necessity View can, while the Fundamental Properties View cannot, distinguish physicalism and necessitation dualism.

However, can the idea be made to work? Well that depends on how plausible the primitivist account of metaphysical distinctness is. As we have already seen, however, at least for a proponent of the incoherence reply above, it is not plausible. And in addition, there are two further sources of concern about this development of the Fundamental Properties View. First, it is not clear that with this suggestion we have moved much beyond the initial statement of our problem. Our starting point was that the necessitation dualist says that mental properties are metaphysically distinct from each other even though they are necessarily connected. The suggestion we are now considering is that the necessitation dualist says that mental properties are metaphysically distinct from physical properties even though they are necessarily connected. But on the face of it, that just looks like the point that a necessitation dualist is a necessitation dualist, while a physicalist is not.

Second, there is an issue here for the philosophical significance of physicalism. As we saw in Chapter 1, physicalism is of interest in part because, if it is true, it articulates a necessary condition on something being a fact, i.e. something is a fact if either it is a physical fact or else it bears a certain relation to the physical facts. The interest in this idea derives precisely from the idea that putative facts, such as mental or moral facts do not meet this necessary condition, and that, as a consequence a certain kind of philosophical project—to show that they do meet the necessary condition or why it does not matter that they do not—comes into view. Now if we interpret this account of what it is to be a fact in modal or logical terms, it is possible to see how to carry about the program in philosophy associated with physicalism. But what we are considering now is the idea that physicalism is to be spelled out in part in terms of a primitive relation of metaphysical distinctness. This means that the necessary condition on being a fact is somewhat unclear, and this threatens to undermine the philosophical significance of the thesis of physicalism.

8.7 Negotiating the impasse

To this point I have set out the problem that necessitation dualism presents for the necessitation physicalist, and have considered some responses to this objection. The upshot of the discussion is somewhat inconclusive. Some proposals, such as the explanation reply and the realization reply, seem clearly inadequate, at any rate as developed here. Other proposals seem more promising or at any rate harder to adjudicate. But no proposal carries the day.

Is there a way to move forward? I think so. For if we set aside the realization and explanation replies, it seems reasonable to say that our discussion has resolved itself into a dispute between the philosopher who thinks that 'metaphysical distinctness' just means 'modal distinctness' and therefore dismisses necessitation dualism as incoherent, and the philosopher who thinks that metaphysical distinctness is a primitive not explained in terms of anything else. Neither philosopher holds a position that is particularly appealing. The first is open to the charge that they have an undefended theory of clarity; the second is open to the charge that they have pointed at rather too many relations.

On the other hand, perhaps we can split the difference here. To see how, notice that, while we were talking about fundamental properties in the previous section, the basic point there could be formulated in a way that bypasses the idea of fundamental properties entirely. The point there was that one might appeal to the notion of metaphysical distinctness to formulate physicalism in such a way that it is distinct from necessitation dualism. But one does not have to depart from the basic shape of the Necessity View in order to do this. In particular, consider this variation on the Necessity View:

(4) Physicalism is true at *w* if and only if for every property *F* instantiated at *w*, there is some physical property *G* instantiated at *w* such that

    (a) for all possible worlds *w** if *G* is instantiated at *w**, then *F* is instantiated at *w**, and

    (b) *F* is not metaphysically distinct from *G*.

In form this is different from the Necessity View because it contains an extra clause; but is it different in content? Well, from the point of view of the philosopher who thinks metaphysical distinctness just is modal distinctness, the second clause here is redundant—clause (a) entails clause (b) and so, while you can add it if you want, it adds nothing to the content of the Necessity View. By contrast, from the point of view of the philosopher who thinks that metaphysical distinctness is a primitive notion distinct from modal distinctness, the second clause is not redundant and involves a significant departure from the Necessity View. Hence, whether or not (4) differs much from the Necessity View depends on one's background theory of metaphysical distinctness.

On the other hand, both sorts of philosopher will agree that (4) is able to respond to the objection from necessitation dualism. The philosopher who supposes that metaphysical distinctness is modal distinctness will also suppose that necessitation dualism is incoherent—such a philosopher thinks that the Necessity View has nothing to fear from the objection anyway. But since (4) is, from this point of view, identical in content to the Necessity View, it too has nothing to fear. The philosopher who supposes that metaphysical distinctness is not modal distinctness will not suppose that necessitation dualism is incoherent—such a philosopher thinks that the objection from necessitation dualism refutes the Necessity View. But since (4) is, from this point of view, different in content from the Necessity View, and indeed is different in exactly the way that meets the objection, such a philosopher will think that (4) does not face the objection. As far as the objection from necessitation dualism goes, therefore, both sorts of philosophers can accept (4), it is just that they will hear it in their own way.

8.8 Reductionism v. non-reductionism

I don't mean to suggest that this diplomatic way forward is anything more than that; obviously it leaves the substantive issues for the Necessity View unresolved. Rather than attempting to discuss these matters further, I will close this chapter, and indeed the discussion of the Necessity View and its rivals that we have been having over the last three chapters, by considering briefly a question that I think is illuminated by what we have said: the question of whether a non-reductive form of physicalism is possible.

We saw in Chapter 6 that necessitation physicalism is attractive because it exempts a physicalist from saying both that the mental is semantically equivalent to, and identical to, the physical. Many think it is attractive for another reason too, viz. it permits what is sometimes called 'non-reductive physicalism.' Indeed, when supervenience or necessitation versions of physicalism first began to make an appearance in the 1970s it was precisely their connection to a 'non-reductive' form of physicalism that for many people explained their attractiveness. In the 1990s there was a significant reaction against this, with many philosophers saying that attachment to non-reductive physicalism is a piece of bad faith: the 'non-reductive' part here registers commitment on the part of non-reductive physicalists to a kind of dualism, while the 'physicalist' part registers commitment to a kind of physicalism—but since these two commitments are inconsistent, the non-reductive physicalist position is a myth.

It seems to me, however, that what is mythical here is not so much non-reductive physicalism but the idea that there is a clearly defined question about whether non-reductive physicalism is mythical. The problem with the debate over non-reductive physicalism is that too many things are meant or could be meant by 'reductive' and, in consequence, by 'non-reductive'. Moreover, once these various things are made clear, it becomes apparent that, in all but one case, there is no real question of whether non-reductive physicalism is possible. In all but one case, that is, on some readings of the question, the answer is "clearly yes"; while on others the answer is "clearly no."

To illustrate this, let us draw out from the discussion that we have been having over the last three chapters various proposals about what 'non-reductive physicalism' could reasonably mean:

- It could reasonably mean a version of physicalism that rejects the idea that there is any synonymy or analytic equivalence between physical statements and every other statement—if so non-reductive physicalism is possible, because physicalism is not a semantic thesis.
- It could reasonably mean a version of physicalism that rejects the idea that every instantiated property is identical to a physical property—if so, non-reductive physicalism is possible, because necessitation physicalism does not entail property identity.

- It could reasonably mean a version of physicalism that rejects the idea that there are psychophysical laws linking, e.g. the psychological and the physical—if so, non-reductive physicalism is possible because necessitation physicalism is consistent with the denial of laws.

- It could reasonably mean a version of physicalism that rejects the idea that mental properties and physical properties are metaphysically distinct—if so, non-reductive physicalism is impossible, for if mental properties and physical properties are metaphysically distinct then dualism is true (even if the form of dualism in question is necessitation dualism).

- It could reasonably mean a version of physicalism that rejects the idea that the physicalist conditional (which we introduced in Chapter 6) is a priori—if so, it is a bit unclear whether reductive physicalism is possible, i.e. it depends on unresolved issues in philosophy of language and epistemology about the relation between the a priori and the necessary. (This is the exceptional case mentioned above.)

So far as I am aware there are no other meanings of the term 'reductionism'; it follows that, with the possible exception of the issue of a priori and a posteriori physicalism, the controversy over reductive physicalism is misguided.

Summary

In this chapter, we have been considering whether necessitation is sufficient for physicalism. As we have seen, the claim that it is sufficient is that it seems open to counterexamples—the one I have been concentrating on arises mainly because of necessitation dualism. There are various ways to try to meet the counterexample, though we have been mostly interested in two: the first denies the coherence of the alleged counterexamples; the second adds a further condition to the Necessity View that I called metaphysical non-distinctness, where this is a primitive non-modal notion. In the end we did not decide between those two proposals, and instead devised a form of words that both sides could agree to. We also briefly considered the much-discussed question of whether physicalism can assume a non-reductive form or not.

Recommended reading

The necessitation dualist position is often read into Broad 1925; for discussion see McLaughlin 1992. For the theological objection, see Jackson 1998. For a discussion of the various notions of distinctness, see Stoljar 2008 and Wilson forthcoming. For the realization reply, see Melnyk 2003. For the explanation reply, see Horgan 1993. For classic versions of non-reductive physicalism see Davidson 1970 and Fodor 1974. For some classic papers arguing that non-reductive physicalism is a myth, see Kim 1993. A good early discussion of non-reductive physicalism is Boyd 1980.

9

SKEPTICS AND
TRUE BELIEVERS

9.1 Recapitulation

Where are we? Well, we said in the introduction we would focus on three sets of questions: the interpretation, truth and significance of physicalism. In Chapter 1, we saw that the significance of physicalism was best explained by its role in what we called 'the standard picture,' a picture that may be expressed in terms of five theses:

1 Physicalism is true—the basic thesis.
2 Physicalism summarizes the picture of the world implicit in the natural sciences—the interpretative thesis.
3 It is most rational to believe the picture of the world implicit in the natural sciences, whatever that picture happens to be—the epistemological thesis.
4 Physicalism is, prima facie, in conflict with many presuppositions of everyday life—the conflict thesis.
5 The way to resolve these conflicts is to propose views about how to interpret the presuppositions of everyday life so that they are compatible with physicalism—the resolution thesis.

We then noted that in order to evaluate these theses, we would need to become much clearer about what physicalism is; in other words, we would need to discuss the interpretation of physicalism. In Chapters 2 to 8, we pursued this question by dividing it into two sub-questions. First, what is it for something to be a physical property? Second, what is it for one property to necessitate another?

As regards the first sub-question, we saw in Chapters 3 to 5 that, while there are certainly different legitimate accounts of what it is for a property to be physical, none of these easily permit a true formulation of physicalism. The matter came to a head at the end of Chapter 4, where we formulated an argument whose conclusion was a metathesis about physicalism, according to which there is no version of it that is (a) true and (b) deserves the name. The argument for this metathesis, to repeat, went as follows:

P1   In formulating physicalism, we must operate either with the Starting Point View or some liberalized version of the Starting Point View.

P2   If we operate with the Starting Point View, it is possible to articulate a version of physicalism that deserves the name, but that version is false.

P3   If we operate with a liberalized version of the Starting Point View, it is possible to articulate a version of physicalism that is true, but that version does not deserve the name, because either
(a)   it is true at possible worlds where no version of physicalism should be true; or   Possibilist
(b)   it is false at possible worlds where no version of physicalism should be false.   Actualist

C   There is no version of physicalism that is both true and deserving of the name.

In Chapters 3 and 4 we saw that the premises of this argument are plausible, and then in Chapter 5 we distinguished the argument from a better known but more controversial argument, Hempel's dilemma. In particular, while the argument of Chapters 3 and 4 is a dilemma that concerns the formulation of physicalism, it is distinct from Hempel's dilemma (or, anyway, from Hempel's dilemma as usually understood) because it places the entire issue in a modal or conceptual context rather than a temporal or historical one.

As regards the second sub-question, we saw in Chapters 6 to 8 that what the physicalist means by necessitation is at least metaphysical or Kripkean necessitation. But we also saw that in order to explicate physicalism correctly one is obliged to appeal to metaphysical notions, not only metaphysical necessity itself but also less well understood notions such as metaphysical distinctness and the lack of it.

In the final two chapters (Chapters 10 and 11) I will turn from the interpretation and significance of physicalism to questions of its truth. Before being in a position to do that, however, we need in this chapter to return to the standard picture, and to focus, in particular, on the consequences for this picture of the argument for the metathesis formulated in Chapter 4.

9.2 The metathesis and the standard picture

On the face of it, this metathesis is in serious conflict with the standard picture. For suppose that the metathesis is true and there is no version of physicalism that is both true and genuine. Then the basic thesis, the very first thesis of the standard picture, is false. The basic thesis says that physicalism is true. If there is no version of physicalism that is both true and deserving of the name, the basic thesis is false.

Consider next the interpretative and epistemological theses. One of the interesting features of the standard picture is that these two theses together form premises of an argument for the basic thesis. If the metathesis is true, however, then this argument fails because its conclusion is false. To put it differently, if the metathesis is true, either physicalism does not summarize the picture implicit in the natural sciences or it is not most rational to believe that picture. If we set aside, as I am doing throughout this book, the question of whether it is in fact rational to believe the picture of the world implicit in the sciences, we arrive at the view that the interpretive thesis is false. Whatever the world-view of modern science is, it couldn't possibly be physicalism, for there is no version of that thesis that is both true and genuine.

Finally, consider the conflict thesis and the resolution thesis. A further interesting feature of the standard picture is that these two theses not only provide us with an account of what a large class of philosophical problems consist in, they also articulate a strategy for how to solve them. Many philosophical problems have their origin in the incompatibility of the presuppositions of everyday life and physicalism, and the way to solve these problems is by interpreting those presuppositions so that they are consistent with physicalism. If there is no true genuine thesis of physicalism, however, then while it might be right to say that the existence of (e.g.) color is incompatible with physicalism, it is hard to see how this should be a good way to spell out a philosophical problem about color. Nor is it easy to see what would be the point of interpreting color so that colors are compatible with physicalism. Hence if physicalism is false we lose any motivation for the resolution thesis: if the existence of colors is inconsistent with something that is false, there is no motivation at all to rethink our conceptions of color.

Not only does the metathesis have serious consequences for the standard picture, it has serious consequences for philosophy in general. As we saw in Chapter 1, the standard picture is extremely attractive for at least two reasons: first, it clearly articulates a role for philosophy that escapes the dilemma mentioned by Rorty in the passage I quoted (see p. 18); second, it represents a large class of philosophical problems as being highly unified. If one wants to pursue an appropriately scientific form of philosophy that does not collapse into science, the philosophy of philosophy implicit in the standard picture looks not simply attractive but obligatory. So the metathesis puts significant pressure on the very enterprise of philosophy.

We seem therefore to have arrived at an important juncture in our general project of interpreting physicalism. Reflection on what it is leads us to the conclusion that it couldn't possibly play the role assigned to it in the standard picture. In a nutshell: reflection on its meaning undermines its truth: if there is nothing it could mean that is true, it is not true.

How should one respond to this state of affairs? In my experience, the literature on these matters is dominated by two very different and extreme reactions—that of (what I call) the skeptic, and that of (what I call) the true believer. In the next two sections I am going to set out these two positions. I will not try to attribute them to any particular philosopher but will state them in my own way.

9.3 The skeptic

The skeptic endorses the argument for the metathesis and agrees with its conclusion. According to the skeptic, there is no version of physicalism that is both true and deserving of the name. The skeptic then goes on to draw consequences for the nature of philosophy. As we have seen, the metathesis is on a collision course with the standard picture. So the skeptic about physicalism will also be a skeptic about the standard picture. Likewise, if the standard picture is central to a lot of philosophy, the skeptic about physicalism becomes a skeptic about a lot of philosophy.

Not only does the skeptic hold the metathesis, and accept its apparent consequences, he or she also goes on to offer a diagnosis of why the argument is successful. The diagnosis is that contemporary physicalists are trying to combine two things that should never be combined. On the one hand, they do not want to disown their intellectual ancestors—to borrow a phrase from Lewis in the passage I quoted at the end of the Introduction (see p. 11). That is, they want to insist that their theory of the world bears a very deep relation to the traditional form of physicalism—what I have here called starting point physicalism. On the other hand, they want to be thoroughly modern materialists—to adopt a subtitle from Melnyk 2003 (Melnyk in turn is adopting a phrase of Jerry Fodor's). That is, they want to insist that their theory of the world is a piece—though of course a highly abstract piece—of thoroughly up-to-date science. But, says the skeptic, you cannot have it both ways. For starting point physicalism is in an important sense a commonsensical picture of the world: it entails that everything is necessitated by something of a commonsensical nature since ordinary physical objects and their distinctive properties are commonsensical. On the other hand, a crucial feature of contemporary science is its divorce from common sense; to the extent that it has a world-view, it would be more natural to say that it entails that everything is necessitated by something not of a commonsensical nature. Contemporary physicalism is therefore in the impossible position of trying to combine something commonsensical with something not. Small wonder, thinks the skeptic, that there is no way to formulate the doctrine.

Suppose that the skeptic is right that there is no potentially true thesis of physicalism at all, or at any rate none of the kind that philosophers have traditionally intended. Then the interesting question becomes why it is that philosophers have clung to this thesis through thick and thin; that is, what explains the persistence of the thesis beyond what you would expect? The answer, the skeptic thinks, has roughly to do with factors internal to philosophy. Given the way that philosophers think about metaphysical problems about the presuppositions of everyday life it is crucial that we have available to us a set of facts which in a sense are 'the facts on the ground,' i.e. are the facts that we can take for granted, facts which for philosophical purposes are unobjectionable. The concept of the physical is often brought in, in a confused sort of way, for that set of facts. This explains why the concept is used in the way that it is. But—says the skeptic—this raison d'être for the concept has nothing to do with its latching on to anything in the world. Of course, this is a very negative view of the concept. It says that the appeal of the concept is sustained not because of an underlying unity either in the things to which it applies or in the concept itself but rather because of highly contingent circumstances, in particular, aspects of the cultural history of philosophy.

The skeptic's position on the concept of the physical and of physicalism may usefully be contrasted with a range of skeptical positions that might be more familiar. For example, take the concept of race (cf. Appiah 1991). The concept of race seems to be founded in part at least on an empirical claim that might have been true. It might have been true that there were various sub-groupings in human beings, and that these sub-groupings themselves explained certain cultural and social factors (though, of course, even if that were the case various moral or ethical claims based on those alleged 'facts' would still have been unjustified). But, the skeptic about the concept of race continues, those empirical facts are mistaken, and so the concept of race has lost its place in our understanding of biological or social reality. Like the skeptic about the concept of race, the skeptic about the thesis of physicalism says that, while there are empirical claims associated with that thesis that might have been true, as things turned out they are not true.

Another example, which in fact presents a closer analogy to the concept of the physical, is skepticism about the philosophical concept of givenness, in particular that expressed by Wilfred Sellars, in his famous paper 'Empiricism and the philosophy of mind' (1956). Sellars argued—to put it roughly but well enough for our purposes—that the idea of the given was, as he put it, a 'hybrid' or 'mongrel' concept, in that it combines together two ideas that have very little to do with each other: the idea of that on which a belief is justified, and the idea of sensation. Sellars thought that philosophers who formulated various philosophical questions on the basis of the notion of givenness were confused and that the thing to do was to reject both it and the philosophy erected on it. The skeptic's position on the concept of the physical and of phsycialism is very similar. Just as Sellars took himself to be rejecting, as he put it, the "whole framework of givenness" so too the skeptic about physicalism takes him- or herself to be rejecting the whole framework of the physical.

The skeptic's position on the concept of the physical is analogous to skepticism in other domains, but the skeptic is not committed logically to a number of other claims that might be thought to go along with it. In particular, as I am describing this position:

• The skeptic isn't (or needn't be) a skeptic about physics: physics is an ongoing theory about the world; the skeptic need not deny that physics as it is currently constituted, or as it will be constituted in some ideal limit, is the complete and literal truth about the world.

- The skeptic isn't (or needn't be) saying that the concept of the physical in the ordinary sense is in any way problematic: the skeptic needn't be denying that, in the ordinary sense of the term, there are physical objects.
- The skeptic isn't (or needn't be) a kind of coherentist: as we saw in Chapter 2 a coherentist is often someone who holds a coherence theory of truth; but there is no connection at all between skepticism about physicalism and a coherence theory of truth.
- The skeptic isn't (or needn't be) a kind of dualist: a dualist (at least of the standard sort) holds that physicalism is true of most of the world, but not all; this kind of view is as committed to the coherence of physicalism as the physicalist is.
- The skeptic isn't (or needn't be) a kind of idealist: a skeptic could perfectly well hold the sort of position which in Chapter 2 I called 'naturalistic platonism' and this is incompatible with idealism (and with dualism for that matter).

If the skeptic about the physical is not any of these things, what is the consequence of being a skeptic? Well, as we have seen, the main thing that follows, or seems to follow, is skepticism about the kind of philosophy articulated in the standard picture, for example, the kind of philosophy articulated by Price in the passage we quoted in Chapter 1. That is why a skeptic about the physical is usually a skeptic about large parts of philosophy too.

9.4 The true believer

So much then for the skeptical position on the thesis of physicalism—what of the other extreme response to the argument I have been considering, that of the true believer?

The true believer starts at the opposite end of the argument from the skeptic, and in particular starts by rejecting the metathesis that there is no true genuine version of physicalism. Why reject the thesis? The reason has to do with the practice of philosophy. Anyone who has discussed seriously the key arguments in philosophy of mind or language or free will or ethics knows how seductive these can be. It is simply a fact that these arguments have enormous intuitive appeal. Moreover, we have an established practice of talking about these things in great detail, and there is considerable convergence on what counts as a contribution to the topics, let alone a good or bad contribution. In the light of these facts, says the true believer, it is impossible or at least it is extremely unlikely that there is nothing at all going on here. Our practice of debating physicalism presupposes, if it is legitimate, that there is a thesis to be debated. But our practice surely is legitimate. Hence there is a thesis here, contrary to the metathesis.

If we accept the point that the metathesis is false because it is inconsistent with our practice, the interesting question becomes what is wrong with the argument for it, i.e. the argument I set out at the end of Chapter 4 and repeated at the beginning of this chapter. Since the argument is valid, the issue for the true believer becomes one of which premise or premises to reject; the true believer rejects the conclusion of a valid argument, so he or she obviously is committed to the falsity of one or more of the premises.

There are a number of options at this point, but the most likely one for the true believer to deny is the third premise, viz. the claim that:

P3   If we operate with some liberalized version of the Starting Point View, it is possible to articulate a version of physicalism that is true, but that version does not deserve the name, because either
(a)   it is true at possible worlds where no version of physicalism should be true or
(b)   it is false at possible worlds where no version of physicalism should be false.

Against this premise, the true believer will say there is a definition of physicalism which deserves the name, and this is what I called in Chapter 4 'actual theory physicalism,' that is, that one according to which physical properties are those expressed by the true physical theory of the actual world, whatever that happens to be. The true believer will also say that, as a matter of fact, actual theory physicalism bears a very close resemblance to current theory physicalism, though as David Lewis (1983: 33–4) once put it "presumably somewhat improved." The true believer will agree that this thesis is not a thesis that was held by the great materialists of the past. And they will probably also agree that this thesis is not held by philosophers who inhabit the twin-physics world. But (they will say) so what? Just because physicalism is not quite the same as traditional physicalism that does not mean it is not deserving of the name. The general idea is that while this may not be physicalism in a traditional sense, it is still deserving of the name because it is possible to formulate various questions about physicalism in terms of it.

The skeptics will be unmoved by this. "True," they will say, "you can define any thesis you like and call it 'physicalism,' but if you do that you are mis-describing your own practice since philosophical problems stated in terms of physicalism do not concern anything that specific." The true believers will be likewise unmoved: "True," they will say, "the philosophical context of contemporary physicalism is different from the philosophical context of traditional materialism, but it is still close enough to deserve the name."

Skeptic: "No it isn't!"
True believer: "Yes it is!"

9.5 A false presupposition?

In one form or another, this debate has gone on a long time. Skeptics hold their position, and believers hold theirs, and neither side seems willing to budge. One might be tempted at this point to throw up one's hands. Isn't this just another instance of a stalemate in philosophy?

It certainly seems that way. But let us look closer. To start with, there is much that is plausible in both the position of the skeptic and that of the true believer. For their part, the true believers seem right about the practice of philosophy. It certainly is difficult to argue, once one is in the swim of philosophical problems, that there is nothing to them or that they are ill founded. What is the theory of ill-foundedness that could generate this result? At the very least, the skeptic seems to shoulder a considerable burden of explaining what is going on in these discussions, and why it is that they seem legitimate when they are in fact not. On the other side of the ledger, the skeptics seem right about the thesis of physicalism. Once that concept loses its moorings from ordinary modes of thinking about the physical it is very difficult to see how it is going to be able to recover a reasonable pattern of judgments about cases.

If there is plausibility in both sides of this debate, it is natural to wonder whether there might be a way to reconcile them. The key idea is to identify a false presupposition shared by both skeptics and true believers. If there is a presupposition that they both share, and if that presupposition is false, we might be able to formulate a position that is a synthesis of both.

For the remainder of this chapter I am going to consider three ways in which this synthesis might be achieved. According to the first, the skeptic and the true believer share a mistaken philosophical methodology. According to the second, the skeptic and the true believer share the idea that physicalism is a thesis, when in fact physicalism is not a thesis but is instead a kind of attitude. According to the third, the skeptic and the true believer accept a false conditional thesis about the nature of the philosophical problems associated with the standard picture. As we will see, it is the third suggestion here that I think has most to recommend it.

9.6 Rejecting conceptual analysis?

As we saw in Chapter 3, there are two methodological ideas lying behind the argument for the metathesis: the first was the idea that the concept of a physical property is a cluster concept, and the second was the idea that we might use the method of cases to test which elements in the cluster should be included in any proposal about how to explain what a physical property is. For many philosophers, however, these ideas are associated with a discredited picture of what philosophy is, a picture whose demise owes quite a lot to the criticisms of positivism given by Quine, Smart and others, mentioned in Chapter 1. The discredited ideas are usually lumped together under the label, 'conceptual analysis,' i.e. the project of trying to give necessary and sufficient conditions for concepts like knowledge, causation or personal identity. So we might put the point in slogan form by saying that the argument for the metathesis mistakenly presupposes conceptual analysis.

To spell out this idea in more detail, let us look again at the first premise of the argument for the metathesis:

P1   In formulating physicalism, we must operate either with the Starting Point View or with some liberalized version of the Starting Point View.

As I have presented them, both the skeptic and the true believer accept this premise. The skeptic accepts it, for the skeptics accept that the argument of which it is a premise is sound. The true believer accepts it, for while the true believer rejects the argument, as we have seen, the premise he attacks is P3 not P1.

On the other hand, it is easy to suspect that an attachment to conceptual analysis is what makes this premise plausible. What can be meant after all by 'formulating physicalism' except the project of providing logically necessary and sufficient conditions for physicalism? However, if that is what is meant, the suggestion that in formulating physicalism you 'must' operate with one or another conception seems at bottom to be the suggestion that one must define physicalism in one or another of these ways.

If what makes P1 plausible is an attachment to conceptual analysis, and if conceptual analysis is a discredited approach to philosophy, we are now in a position to make two related points. The first point is that the argument for the metathesis can be rejected because its first premise is false, i.e. because it presupposes conceptual analysis. The second point is that the debate between the skeptic and the true believer should be rejected because each side agrees that conceptual analysis is the appropriate method of figuring out what physicalism is. Their disagreement is precisely about whether we can use conceptual analysis to arrive at a reasonable statement of what physicalism is. But since this disagreement presupposes conceptual analysis, it should be rejected.

9.7 Evaluating the rejection of conceptual analysis

How successful is this attempt to reject the dispute between the skeptic and the true believer? Well, the question of whether and in what sense conceptual analysis is mistaken is an extremely large issue, and one that we will not be able to go into in detail in this book. However, even if we do not go into it in detail, I think it can be shown that the rejection of conceptual analysis of the kind we have just been looking at does not have much of an impact on the arguments we have been considering. There are two points to make.

First, when people reject the idea of providing necessary and sufficient conditions for philosophically important concepts what they mean to reject is not the project of providing necessary and sufficient conditions *as such*, but rather the project of providing necessary and sufficient conditions *of a certain sort*. For example, there was a period in 1970s epistemology when philosophers were devoted to the task of providing necessary and sufficient conditions for knowledge—i.e. completing something of the form 'S knows that p if and only if ... .' Opponents of conceptual analysis often criticize this period of philosophy as being concerned with something that was both fruitless and pointless. However, what was fruitless and pointless here (if anything) was not the project of providing necessary and sufficient conditions for knowledge but rather the attempt to provide reductive and quite general necessary and sufficient conditions, i.e. conditions which are spelled out in concepts quite distinct from the concept of knowledge. To put it differently, what is controversial here is the project of providing an *analysis* of knowledge in a traditional sense, not the project of providing necessary and sufficient conditions that illuminate the concept.

However, while it might be that the project of providing analyses of important philosophical concepts is fruitless and pointless—we need not take a stand on that issue here—this has no impact on the argument for the metathesis or, related to that, the dispute between the skeptic and the true believer about the standard picture. The reason is that it is implausible to interpret the metathesis argument as demanding an analysis of either the notion of a physical property or of physicalism in this sense. In particular, in setting out the argument for the metathesis we never once imposed the requirement that physicalism or physical property be analyzed in this sense. Admittedly, I have said that it would be no good if the circles of definition were too tight; for example, in Chapter 3 I said that defining a physical property in terms of the notion of a purely physical object represents too small a definitional circle. But this rejects a proposal on the ground that it is un-illuminating, not on the ground that it is circular.

So the first point to make about the suggestion that the dispute between the skeptic and the true believer presupposes conceptual analysis is that it does not presuppose it, at any rate, it does not presuppose it in a philosophically objectionable form. The second point to make is that when people reject the method of cases as a component of the project of conceptual analysis, what they mean to reject is not reflection on cases *as such* but reflection on cases of an *extremely unusual sort*. For example, in discussions of personal identity (i.e. in discussions of what makes a person the same through various changes) one often encounters some quite bizarre cases—brain swapping, tele-transportation, and the like. The critics of conceptual analysis often say that, while it is unsurprising that a smart philosopher can dream up such recherché cases, it is inappropriate to think that anything about our concept or what it denotes could be illuminated by reflection on them. For—the critics will say—our ordinary concept of personal identity was in place well before anybody came up with such examples, and presumably was not designed to apply to them. This in turn suggests that, even if we obtained agreement on how to respond to these cases (something which is in itself unlikely), nothing about how we are disposed to respond to such cases is going to shed light on the concept. To put it differently, what is controversial here is the project of *unrestricted* reflection on cases, not the project of reflecting on cases that are (in an admittedly hard to define sense) appropriate to the concept being discussed.

However, while it might be that reflecting on unrestricted cases is a mistake—again, this is something we need not decide here—this will once again have little or no impact on the argument for the metathesis and related considerations. The reason is that it is implausible that a proponent of this argument requires the idea that one should reflect on an unrestricted class of cases. On the contrary, none of the cases we considered in Chapters 3 and 4 are far-fetched, and in fact have been discussed at some length by physicalists themselves. Admittedly for people not already involved in philosophy, some of these are pretty far-fetched; it is pretty far-fetched for example to consider worlds at which dualism or vitalism or color primitivism is true, not to mention worlds such as the twin-physics world. But on the other hand, these examples are not far-fetched relative to the way in which the concept is used. The concept of a physical property or physicalism is, as we have been discussing it, a specifically philosophical concept. What is at issue here is not an ordinary concept but rather a philosophical invention, though one with a long history. So it is not at all clear then that the cases we have been considering are in any way inappropriate to the concept.

For these two reasons, therefore, I think it is doubtful that a rejection of conceptual analysis is going to resolve the dispute between the skeptic and the true believer. Accordingly, the next suggestion I want to consider focuses on a quite different aspect of that dispute.

9.8 Van Fraassen on empiricism and physicalism

The question of how to formulate physicalism has counterparts when we widen our gaze from physicalism to other philosophical doctrines. For example, many philosophers have been called (and have called themselves) 'empiricists,' 'rationalists,' 'realists,' and so on. Sometimes we take ourselves to know in our bones what it is to be one of these things. But relying on your bones isn't a good way to do philosophy, and so the question arises 'What is an empiricist (or a rationalist, or a realist ...) *exactly*?'

One philosopher who has confronted this question head on in the case of empiricism is Bas van Fraassen. In *The Empirical Stance* (2002), he considers at some length the idea that empiricism is some sort of belief or proposition or thesis which empiricist philosophers have held—for example, the thesis that any philosophically legitimate belief must bear a certain sort of relation to experience. On this proposal, the sense in which both Locke, say, and Quine are empiricists (both are usually called empiricists in textbook discussions) is captured because both believe that philosophically legitimate beliefs bear a certain sort of relation to sensory experience.

As van Fraassen points out, however, any serious attempt to spell out what this thesis might be runs into a rather major roadblock. Does the empiricist thesis apply to itself? Notice that as formulated the thesis says something about *every* belief, i.e. every belief is such that it bears a certain relation to sensory experience. But then if empiricism itself is legitimate, as the empiricist presumably thinks it is, then it *itself* must bear the relation at issue to experience. But what sort of relationship could this be? On the face of it the thesis of empiricism (unlike, for example, the thesis that there are pumpkins) is very remote from any sort of confirming experience.

One might respond to this problem by interpreting the required relation to experience very loosely. But if one does that one threatens to permit many proposals about the world that the empiricist hoped to rule out. As van Fraassen emphasizes, empiricists have typically been opposed to (something they call) metaphysics. (It doesn't matter for present purposes what this is.) If one construes the relation to experience that is involved in empiricism liberally enough, then both it and metaphysics will be included; but if you construe it too tightly, then while metaphysics is ruled out, so too is empiricism itself. The overall conclusion of this line of thought is that empiricism is either too restrictive, in which case it would entail that empiricism itself is illegitimate; or it is very liberal, in which case it loses its philosophical point.

In order to solve this problem, van Fraassen suggests that empiricism should be thought of, not as a belief or proposition, but rather as a stance. He writes:

> A philosophical position can consist in something other than a belief about what the world is like. We can, for example, take the empiricist attitude toward science rather than his or her belief about it as the most fundamental characteristic. Then we are led to the following suggestion ... A philosophical position can consist in a stance (attitude, commitment, approach, a cluster of such—possibly including some propositional attitudes such as belief as well). Such a stance can of course be expressed, and may involve or presuppose some beliefs as well, but cannot be simply equated with having beliefs or making assertions about what there is. (2002: 47–8).

If commitment to empiricism is a stance in the way that van Fraassen suggests, the problems of formulation that beset empiricism might be overcome. Certainly if empiricism is not a thesis, then the self-reference worry at least as stated goes away. Empiricism will not apply to itself if it is explicitly concerned with propositions and it itself is not a proposition.

Now, physicalism does not face a self-reference worry in quite the way that empiricism does, but the general idea that philosophical positions ought to be construed as stances or attitudes rather than beliefs is nevertheless suggestive for our own discussion. Could the idea be applied to the problem of formulating physicalism? Van Fraassen is explicit that it can. Physicalism, he says,

> is not identifiable with a theory about what there is but only with an attitude or cluster of attitudes. These attitudes include strong deference to the current content of science in matters of opinion about what there is. They include also an inclination (and perhaps a commitment, at least an intention) to accept (approximative) completeness claims for science as actually constituted at a given time. (2002: 59)

Transposing this idea into the framework we have been using, van Fraassen's suggestion is that in the debate between the skeptic and the true believer both are wrong. The skeptic is arguing that there is no genuine thesis of physicalism that is plausibly true; the true believer is arguing that there is. Both are wrong, van Fraassen would say, for both assume that if physicalism is anything it is a thesis. Van Fraassen's proposal is precisely that it is not. If there is no thesis of physicalism in the first place, it is no wonder that the skeptic cannot find a true or genuine version of the thesis. Likewise, it is no wonder that the true believer is on shaky ground insisting that he has found one.

What is van Fraassen's motivation for supposing that commitment to physicalism, or perhaps physicalism itself, is a stance? His key observation is that physicalists are able to constantly readjust their position in the light of new scientific discoveries. This observation he thinks, shows that commitment to physicalism cannot be a matter of belief:

> How shall we identify what is really involved in materialism? Our great clue is the apparent ability of materialists to revise the content of their main thesis as science changes. If we took literally the claim of a materialist that his position is a simple belief, we would be faced with an insoluble mystery, for that belief would then consist in the claim that all is matter, as currently construed. If that were all there was to it, how would such a materialist know how to retrench when his favorite scientific hypothesis fail? (2002: 58)

Van Fraassen's position in this passage and elsewhere clearly has much in common with the skeptical view. His negative views about the thesis of physicalism are largely similar. But his positive proposal about how to make sense of the situation is quite different. As we saw, the skeptic generally thinks that there is no coherent position in the vicinity at all. But van Fraassen's view, on the contrary, is that there is a coherent position, it is simply that adopting that position involves adopting a stance rather than holding a particular thesis.

9.9 Evaluating the stance idea

What should we make of van Fraassen's view? Like the rejection of conceptual analysis we considered above, it is attractive because it suggests a way of moving beyond the debate between the skeptic and the true believer. However—and here too van Fraassen's proposal is like the rejection of conceptual analysis—I think it is unlikely that the reconciliation we are achieving is going to be found in this direction. The problem this time is that it is quite unclear that being a physicalist is helpfully analyzed as adopting a stance. Once again there are two points to make.

The first point is that the stance that van Fraassen identifies could not possibly be the one taken by the physicalist, for it is possible to be a physicalist and not adopt that stance. When van Fraassen tells us what the stance is that is involved in physicalism, he makes an explicit reference to physics and physical theory. But it is perfectly possible to be a physicalist and have no views at all about physics. Take the ancient Greek philosopher Democritus. It is not true that he took any stance at all toward the physics of his day, i.e. because the idea that there *was* any physics in Democritus' day is preposterous. There was simply no institution of science in those days, and so nothing that could count as physics in this sense. So Democritus could not have taken a stance toward it. But Democritus *was* a physicalist—indeed, he was one of the first. Hence commitment to physicalism need not be a stance, or at any rate, need not be a stance in the way intended by van Fraassen.

One might reply to this objection that it would, if successful, prove too much. For as we saw in Chapters 3 to 5, almost any reasonable version of physicalism will appeal to a physical theory of some sort. Wouldn't the Democritus problem I just mentioned apply to any of these proposals just as much as it does to van Fraassen's? The answer to this is that, while these proposals certainly appeal to the idea of a physical theory, that idea needs to be distinguished from the idea of physics as an institution. What they appeal to is physical theory construed in the abstract as an account of the nature, behavior, and constitution of ordinary physical objects. In that very general sense Democritus can be said to have had a physics too. What he did not have, obviously, is the institution of science, and in particular the institution of physics.

One might reply now that what is good enough for other formulations is good enough for van Fraassen. In particular, just as various other formulations of physicalism might employ a rather abstract notion of physics (physical theory and so forth), so too could van Fraassen's. However, while it is true that van Fraassen's account could certainly be developed in this direction, it is unclear that doing so leaves anything of the original proposal. For now it looks as if one is taking a stance toward a particular theory, i.e. something that is true or false. But if that is so, then it is hard to see what is left of the distinction between taking a stance and believing a proposition.

So the first point to make about van Fraassen is that adopting a stance toward physics is not necessary for holding physicalism. The second point is that it is not sufficient either. Suppose, just to fix ideas, we interpret 'taking a stance' in the relevant sense as meaning something like 'having a disposition to believe various things, e.g. that current physics tells you the complete truth about the world.' Perhaps we might think of it as a habit of thought or a tendency or policy to form certain beliefs. It seems reasonable to say, to a first approximation, that both Hobbes and Smart have this disposition. So now we have something that they both had in common, which is good because it shows that people who call themselves 'materialists' but are separated by 300 years of science have something in common. Moreover, they have something in common which it is inappropriate to assess for truth, for, while beliefs are truth-assessable, dispositions to believe are not. (If someone has a certain habit of thought, you can't ask 'is that true or false?', whereas if someone has a certain belief, you can.) So, on that interpretation of what van Fraassen says, it looks like we have made progress.

But appearances can be deceptive. For once we have said that Hobbes and Smart share this disposition to believe, it is easy to see that various other people might share that disposition too, and that these others are not physicalists in any ordinary sense. Consider again the counterpart of Smart in the dualist world, dualist Smart. (The counterpart of Hobbes would have done just as well.) Dualist Smart might also have the disposition to believe that current (or, at any rate, actual) physics tells you the complete truth about the world. But dualist Smart is no physicalist. So the stance that van Fraassen identifies is not sufficient for being a physicalist.

9.10 Physicalism as inessential in discussions of physicalism

Our interest both in van Fraassen's proposal that 'physicalism is a stance' and in the rejection of conceptual analysis has been driven by a desire to move beyond the debate between the skeptic and the true believer we reviewed a few sections ago. If either suggestion is correct, there is a false presupposition that is shared by both sides of this debate. However, van Fraassen's proposal is not correct, and while the rejection of conceptual analysis may or may not be correct, it is hard to see why it has any impact on the issues.

There is, however, a third way here. Both the skeptic and the true believer presuppose that physicalism is a thesis, and there is also something else they both presuppose. This is a conditional claim that if the nature of the physicalism is as the skeptic says, then the philosophical use of the physicalism is illegitimate. The skeptical position rather obviously makes use of this presupposition. Skeptics argue from claims about the nature of the thesis to the idea that philosophical use of the thesis is illegitimate. But true believers also make use of this presupposition, using it to argue in the reverse direction. True believers argue from the idea that philosophical use of the thesis is legitimate to a claim about the nature of the thesis.

We may bring out this point by looking once again at the underlying argument that distinguishes the skeptic and the truth believer. That argument, once again, was:

P1 In formulating physicalism, we must operate either with the Starting Point View with some liberalized version of the Starting Point View.

P2 If we operate with the Starting Point View, it is possible to articulate a version of physicalism that deserves the name, but that version is false.

P3 If we operate with a liberalized version of the Starting Point View, it is possible to articulate a version of physicalism that is true, but that version does not deserve the name, because either (a) it is true at possible worlds where no version of physicalism should be true or (b) it is false at possible worlds where no version of physicalism should be false.

C   There is no version of physicalism that is both true and deserving of the name.

In their approach to this argument, the skeptic and the true believer both endorse a further premise along the following lines:

P4 If there is no version of physicalism that is both true and deserving of the name, then philosophical problems and arguments that are stated in terms of physicalism ought rationally to be rejected rather than taken up and discussed seriously, i.e. the standard picture ought rationally to be rejected rather than taken up and discussed seriously.

From P4 and C, we may derive a further conclusion, namely:

C# Philosophical problems and arguments that are stated in terms of physicalism ought rationally to be rejected rather than taken up and discussed seriously.

The skeptic agrees with C#; indeed it is C# that lends the skeptic's position most of its interest. The true believer denies C#; indeed their point about the practice of philosophy is precisely designed to deny C#. But both sides agree that P4 is true. The skeptic thinks that P4 is true because otherwise there would be no way to move from the metathesis (C) to C#. The true believer thinks that P4 is true because otherwise there would be no way to infer from the falsity of C# to the falsity of C and so to the denial of P3. (Remember that the true believer denies P3, as we saw earlier.)

Once it is appreciated that both the skeptic and the true believer agree to P4, however, it is clear how we might negotiate our way past their debate, viz. argue that the P4 is false. P4 says that skepticism about the thesis of physicalism entails skepticism about philosophical uses of the thesis of physicalism. But it is not at all clear that this is true. For it is possible that a philosophical thesis plays only an inessential role in the formulation of a philosophical problem. In particular, it is possible that physicalism plays only an inessential role in the pieces of reasoning in which it occurs; that is, in the various arguments apparently for and against physicalism, what really matters is not physicalism but something else. If so, we can partly agree with both the skeptic and the true believer: on the one hand, true believers are (largely) right that the use of the thesis is legitimate; on the other hand, the skeptics are (largely) right that the thesis itself is not.

But of course, that physicalism plays an inessential role in the pieces of reasoning in which it occurs is so far only a conjecture. Is the conjecture true? To answer that question we must turn to the third of the three topics

I said in the introduction we were going to consider: the truth and falsity of physicalism, and in particular the arguments for and against its true and falsity. It is with these arguments that we will be occupied in the final two chapters.

Summary

In this chapter, we returned to the dilemma for the formulation of physicalism that we arrived at in Chapter 4. We have examined two extreme reactions to that dilemma, that of the skeptic and that of the true believer. We saw that, while neither of these extreme positions is attractive, they nevertheless both contain an element of truth. We then considered three ways of attempting to overcome the debate between the skeptic and the truth believer: rejecting conceptual analysis, rejecting the idea that physicalism is a thesis, and distinguishing between the thesis of physicalism and various uses of that thesis. It was the third of these ways that held most promise.

Recommended reading

Skeptical positions are suggested (a bit obliquely) in Chomsky 2000 and van Fraassen 2002; see also Mellor 1973 and Crane and Mellor 1990. The position of the true believer is on show in Jackson 1998 and Papineau 2001. If you read them carefully, you will see that both Jackson and Papineau use the same sentence in responding to these concerns, 'the problem is more apparent than real'—but what problem is it precisely that is more apparent than real? For a recent discussion of conceptual analysis see Williamson 2008; for van Fraassen's expressivist view, see van Fraassen 2002. For a slightly longer discussion of the idea that physicalism is inessential in discussions of physicalism, see Stoljar 2006.

10

ARGUMENTS AGAINST PHYSICALISM

10.1 The super-tasters

Imagine a race of creatures called 'super-tasters.' Super-tasters are exactly like you and me in every physical respect. The world they inhabit is exactly like the world we inhabit in every physical respect. Just as there is a grand scientific story (the big bang, continental drift, evolution by natural selection, etc.) about how our world works, so too there is a grand scientific story (the same story, in fact) about how their world works. The world of the super-tasters is exactly the same as our world right down to the last atom, or whatever it is that modern physics says fundamentally exists in place of atoms. Is the world of the super-tasters therefore *exactly* the same as our world? No, there is one small difference: for the super-tasters, bitter things taste more bitter, and sweet things more sweet.

For example, when we taste ginseng tea, it is sweeter than green tea; the same is true for the super-tasters. But when the super-tasters taste ginseng tea—something physically the same as our ginseng tea—it is sweeter than our ginseng tea, i.e. the taste they have is sweeter by some degree than the taste we get in the same circumstances. If you had an experience that was phenomenally just like the one that your super-taster counterpart had when he or she tastes ginseng tea, you would think it was sweeter than the taste you have when you taste ginseng tea. If your super-taster counterpart had an experience that was phenomenally just like the one that you have when you taste ginseng tea, he or she would think the taste was not as sweet.

Of course, this difference between the super-tasters and us does not show up in any bit of their (or our) overt behavior or cognitive processing. The world of the super-tasters is physically exactly the same as ours, and so their cognitive and neurological systems are physically exactly like ours, and this means in part that super-tasters behave, and are disposed to behave, exactly like us. If we sipped some ginseng tea and it was sweeter than we expected, we would say so; that is true of the super-tasters too. Nevertheless the taste that the super-tasters get from ginseng tea is sweeter (maybe only marginally so) than the taste that we get from ginseng tea. In sum, the world of the super-tasters is exactly like ours down to the last detail, it is just that some of their experiences are, as we might say, increased on a phenomenological dimension.

Are the super-tasters possible? Offhand it would seem so. They are imaginable or conceivable after all. (At any rate they seem offhand to be imaginable or conceivable; did we not just imagine or conceive them?) And we often suppose that what is imaginable or conceivable is, thereby, possible. However, if the super-tasters are indeed possible, physicalism is false. For physicalism says that every property instantiated in the actual world is necessitated by a physical property, and the world of the super-tasters is a counterexample to this claim. On the one hand, there is no difference in physical properties between our world and the world of the super-tasters, at both worlds the same grand scientific story is true. On the other hand, there is a difference in what properties are instantiated; in particular, there is a difference in the properties associated with the taste of ginseng tea. So the possibility of the super-tasters is inconsistent with physicalism. Hence, if they are possible—as they seem to be—physicalism is false.

10.2 The conceivability argument

The argument that I have just given is a version of what is usually called a conceivability or modal argument against physicalism. (I will use the phrase 'conceivability argument' here.) What are we to make of this argument? In this chapter, I am going to look at this argument and at some other arguments against physicalism. One question we will be interested in, of course, is whether such arguments are sound. But another question, and in fact for us the more important question, is what the role of physicalism in these arguments is. At the end of the previous chapter, we formulated a conjecture about physicalism, viz. that physicalism plays an inessential role in any reasonable piece of reasoning in which it occurs. We will be interested in the plausibility of this conjecture when it comes to the conceivability argument and other arguments against physicalism.

We may begin by making a number of points about the basic nature and plausibility of the argument.

10.2.1 Formulation

The conceivability argument (CA) can be formulated in various ways, but a relatively clear formulation, and one we will adopt, is as follows:

C1 It is conceivable that there is someone identical to me in respect of all physical truths but different with respect to some psychological truth (e.g. it is conceivable that there is a super-taster, who is physically the same as me, and yet to whom ginseng tea tastes sweeter than it does to me).

C2 If it is conceivable that there is someone identical to me in respect of all physical truths but different with respect to some psychological truth, it is possible that there is.

C3 Ergo, it is possible that there is someone identical to me in respect of all physical truths but different with respect to some psychological truth.

C4 If it is possible that there is someone identical to me in respect of all physical truths but different with respect to some psychological truth, physicalism is false.

C5 Ergo, physicalism is false.

So understood, CA is a valid argument for the falsity of physicalism. It also naturally breaks into two halves. The first half of the argument (C1–C3) establishes, if sound, the existence of a possibility on the basis of imagination or conceivability; that is why the argument is called a conceivability argument. The second half of the argument (C4–C5) goes on to connect that possibility with the falsity of physicalism.

10.2.2 *The background modal epistemology*

There are a number of controversial points about CA, and indeed about conceivability arguments in general. One set of questions concerns the modal epistemology that is in the background of the argument, i.e. what possibility is, what conceivability is, and what the epistemic relation is between the two, or at any rate what a proponent of the argument must assume is the epistemic relation between the two. On the surface, the argument seems to assume that conceivability is evidence of possibility, just as perception might be thought of as evidence for claims about what is in fact the case. To illustrate, suppose I know that there is a cup of ginseng tea on the table. How do I know this? The natural answer is I see the cup, or perhaps that I see that there is a cup. But now suppose I know that, while there isn't in fact a cup of green tea on the table, there nevertheless could be; that is, suppose I know that it is *possible* that there is a cup of green tea on the table. How do I know this? Obviously, it can't be that I see the cup; by hypothesis, there is no cup there to see. But a natural alternative answer is that I know that it is possible that there is a cup of green tea on the table because I can imagine or conceive that there is. It is this simple idea that lies behind the thought that conceivability is a guide to possibility.

However, while this idea is simple, it is also controversial (see, e.g. the papers in Gendler and Hawthorne 2004). Some doubt that there is any such state as conceiving or imagining, at least if that is thought of as a state that involves some sort of special faculty (e.g. Williamson 2008). Some object that there are altogether too many notions of conceiving or imagining, and that the suggestion that conceivability is evidence of possibility is only plausible because it blends them together. Others think that the argument assumes that conceivability is epistemically more secure than possibility when in fact this is not so; the claim that something is conceivable, they say, is no more secure than the claim that it is possible—indeed, perhaps it is the same claim differently expressed. These questions about conceivability and possibility are interesting and prove tricky to deal with. But with a small exception to be noted below, we will not be required to discuss them here. For these questions do not call into doubt the idea that there is something to conceivability arguments; what they call into doubt are various *theories* about what conceivability arguments in general consist in. And theories of what conceivability arguments consist in are not our topic here.

10.2.3 *Questions of scope and contingency*

CA is potentially ambiguous in the sense that it might (*might*) employ different notions of 'conceivability' but it is also ambiguous in terms of what philosophers usually call 'scope.' For example, consider the third premise of the argument, C3. When we make the quantificational structure of this premise explicit it is clear that it has at least two readings. On the first, which we may call the *wide-scope reading*, it comes out as:

C3w For all physical truths *t* and some psychological truths *t**, it is possible that there is someone identical to me in respect of *t* but different with respect to *t**.

Here the quantifiers 'all physical truths' and 'some psychological truths' take wide scope with respect to the 'it is possible that' operator. By contrast, on what we may call the *narrow-scope reading*, it comes out as:

C3n It is possible that for all physical truths *t* and some psychological truths *t**, there is someone identical to me in respect of *t* but different with respect to *t**.

Here the quantifiers 'all physical truths' and 'some psychological truths' take narrow scope with respect to the 'it is possible that' operator.

The distinction between the two readings of C3 is closely related to another controversial feature of CA, its relation to the contingency of physicalism. Suppose, with C3, that it is possible that there is someone identical to me in all physical respects but different in some psychological respects. Why should that in any way threaten physicalism? For isn't physicalism a contingent truth? If so, why should it not be perfectly possible for there to be super-tasters so long as they are not actual? To put the point differently, physicalists are interested in what is going on in this world; why then do they need to be concerned with what is going on at some other worlds?

We have come across this idea—that physicalists do not need to worry about non-actual possible worlds—before (in Chapter 7). It is indeed a common one. Physicalists often say, and often thump the table while they say it, "Look, I am interested in the real world. What then do I care about these possible cases!" However, while the idea is common, it is also mistaken. As we have seen, if physicalism is true, then every instantiated property is necessitated by some physical property. This thesis is contingent because it is contingent which properties (including which physical properties) are instantiated. However, as we saw in Chapter 7, if physicalism is true, it is nevertheless the case that the physicalist conditional ('if S then S^*') is necessarily true, where S is a sentence which summarizes all the properties which are instantiated in the actual world, and S^* is a sentence that summarizes all the physical properties which are instantiated in the actual world. On the other hand, if C3 is true on its wide-scope reading—i.e. if C3w is true—then it is clear that the psychophysical conditional is contingent. For on its wide-scope reading, C3 says precisely that there is a situation in which the antecedent of the physicalist conditional is true and the consequent is false.

We may bring out this point in a different way by focusing not on C3 but on C4. Since the antecedent of C4 just is C3, it too may be given a wide-scope or a narrow-scope reading, just as C3 can. On its wide-scope reading, which is what the proponent of the argument intends, C4 comes out as:

C4w If, for all physical truths t and some psychological truth t^*, it is possible that there is someone identical to me with respect to t and different with respect to t^*, then physicalism is false.

But given what we have said it is clear that C4w, and so C4, is true. If the antecedent of C4w is true, then the physicalist conditional is not necessary; but if the physicalist conditional is not necessary, then the consequent of C4w is true. As I remarked in Chapter 7, the physicalist conditional acts as a bridge between the conceivability argument and the contingency of physicalism.

10.2.4 The plausibility of the background examples

The sources of controversy that we have so far mentioned are focused on very general questions about CA. But there are more specific questions too. In particular, there is in fact not one argument here but many depending on which example is in play. I have used here the example of the super-tasters. But other writers use the idea of a zombie world, in which zombies are people who are physically like us but lack experiences or phenomenal consciousness altogether (e.g. Chalmers 1996). Others use the example of the inverted spectrum, in which the experiences that two people have might be 'inverted' in the sense that the color experience that one has when he looks at grass is identical to the color experience that the other has when he looks at blood (cf. e.g. Shoemaker 1982). In these cases the structure of the argument is the same, it is simply that the possible world that is claimed to be imagined (and so the possible world that is claimed to exist) is different. I have used the super-tasters here in part because it is less controversial than these others. It is controversial that there could be someone physically exactly the same as me and yet who lacks any experiences altogether. Similarly, it is controversial that there could be someone who is physically the same as me and yet who has the experience of seeing red where I have the experience of seeing green—the reason is that the asymmetries in the color system make this kind of switch hard to countenance (cf. e.g. Byrne 2004). But the super-tasters seem much less controversial because they only involve a minimal increase along a phenomenological dimension.

10.2.5 CA and the knowledge argument

Finally, there is an argument closely related to CA that requires special mention: the knowledge argument against physicalism (KA). As usually presented, KA says that it is possible to know all the physical facts without knowing the psychological facts, and that in consequence physicalism is false. KA can be thought of as a conceivability argument or modal argument too, it is simply that here we are interested not in whether it is possible for someone to be physically identical to me without being psychologically identical, we are rather interested in whether it is possible for a person to know all the physical facts without knowing all the facts. For example, one might imagine someone who knows all the physical facts about me, and yet does not know if when I taste ginseng tea it is sweet to degree n and no more or rather sweet to degree m and no more. There are a number of differences between KA and CA; in particular, there is a way KA is less controversial and a way it is more. The way in which it is less controversial is that the possibility on which it is based is not controversial; it is not controversial that in some sense or other it is possible for someone to know all the physical truths without knowing all the psychological truths. But it is more controversial in that the step from the existence of this possibility to the falsity of physicalism is questionable. However, while there are certainly these differences between CA and KA, I will concentrate here on the former; what I say about CA can be extended to KA, but I will leave that implicit.

10.3 Catalogue of responses

So that is the conceivability argument against physicalism, in at least one standard version. How to respond? Well, as I noted in the introduction, there are two broad strategies here. One is to provide an account of tastes and other experiences according to which their existence is compatible with physicalism—a functionalist or behaviorist account, for example. The other, which has dominated recent discussion, is to argue that CA is mistaken *even* if there is no such account to hand. Discussing either of these strategies in detail is something that we will not be able to do in this book; these issues are among the most discussed in philosophy of mind today. Instead, in this section, I will briefly set out three answers to the argument that are instances of the second strategy. The point is not to so much to go through all of them in detail, but to convey a sense of what the possibilities are for the physicalist.

10.3.1 A posteriori physicalism

The first answer—perhaps this is the dominant strategy in the recent literature—has been to appeal to some version of what we called in Chapter 7 'a posteriori physicalism.' As we have seen a number of times, if physicalism is true, then there is a conditional, which I call the physicalist conditional, which is necessarily true. According to a posteriori physicalism, this conditional is necessary and a posteriori, and if that is so—says the proponent of this answer to CA—the argument collapses.

Why should CA collapse if the physicalist conditional is necessary and a posteriori? There might be a number of ways of connecting the idea of the necessary a posteriori with CA, but perhaps the most straightforward one is via a certain way of thinking of what conceivability is. On this view, what 'it is conceivable that p' means is 'it is not a priori that not p.' So in particular, what 'it is conceivable that water is not H_2O' means is that 'it is not a priori that water is not H_2O.' Now in the argument we are considering we are in effect already talking about the negation of the proposition that physicalists are attached to. Factoring this into the argument, we obtain the suggestion that C1 and C2 *properly understood* are as follows:

C1* It is not a priori that there is someone identical to me in respect of all physical truths but different with respect to some psychological truth.

C2* If it is not a priori that there is someone identical to me in respect of all physical truths but different with respect to some psychological truth, then it is possible that there is.

Once we face the argument in this form, however, the proponent of the necessary a posteriori response will say that it is unsound because C2* is false. We know that there are examples of the necessary a posteriori which falsify C2*, and why could not physicalism be precisely such a one?

However, there are two main challenges to this idea. First, it is not clear that, in the context of the argument 'it is conceivable that p' *does* mean 'it is not a priori that not p.' (This is the place in our discussion I mentioned above in which we need to go a little into the question of what conceivability is.) Presumably this is one way to interpret what 'it is conceivable that p' means. But there are also other ways. For example, someone might think that 'it is conceivable that p' means something like 'it is imaginable that p' or 'it appears possible that p' or something of the kind. If that is so, then even if the second premise of the argument is false when 'it is conceivable that p' is read one way, it is not false when read another way.

Second, it is not clear that C2* is false, even if we read 'it is conceivable that p' as 'it is not a priori that p.' For this depends on how one thinks of the relation between the necessary and the a priori. According to some philosophers, while it is not always legitimate to infer from 'it is not a priori that not p' to 'it is possible that p', there are certain cases in which this is appropriate, and CA is one of those cases (cf. Chalmers and Jackson 2002). Of course these claims are extremely controversial, and are heavily criticized by other philosophers; as I noted in Chapter 7, we will not be going into them in this book. But controversial or not, they do at least show that the mere existence of the necessary a posteriori is not enough by itself to respond to the CA.

10.3.2 The phenomenal concept strategy

The second answer to CA is 'the phenomenal concept strategy' (as I have called it elsewhere; see Stoljar 2005). The general idea of the phenomenal concept strategy is to say that, instead of thinking about experiences, we should think instead about how experiences are represented in speech and thought. More particularly, the phenomenal concept strategy begins with the point that any attempt to expound CA will involve the employment and possession of phenomenal concepts, such as the concepts of pain, itch, and so forth. But these concepts, it is alleged, have some special features, and when these special features are sufficiently attended to it will become apparent that the argument is a failure.

Now, different exponents of the phenomenal concept strategy have different features or alleged features of phenomenal concepts in mind. Some say they have special epistemological features. Others say they are a special kind of indexical. Some say they have a special possession condition, e.g. they constitutively involve having the relevant experiences. As such, the phenomenal concept strategy raises a number of different concerns (for further discussion and references see Stoljar 2005, and the papers in Alter and Walter 2007).

However, while there are various versions of the phenomenal concept strategy, most of the criticisms of the strategy abstract away from the precise ways in which it is implemented. There are at least three such criticisms. First, it has been argued that the strategy both over-generates and under-generates in that if successful it would defeat conceivability arguments which we know, or at least have excellent reason to believe, are sound—the perfect actor argument against behaviorism is one such argument (see Stoljar 2005). Second, it has been argued that there are really no phenomenal concepts of the sort required by the strategy (e.g. Tye 2009; Stalnaker 2008). Third, it has been argued that the fact of having a phenomenal concept bears the same sort of relation to physical facts as facts about sensations already do. If so, the phenomenal concept strategy answers the first CA only to face another one (see, e.g. Chalmers 2007 and Levine 2007).

10.3.3 *The epistemic view*

The third and final answer to CA that I will mention is what is sometimes called the 'epistemic' view or the 'incomplete knowledge' view. According to this view, the best (i.e. the most reasonable) response to the problem is to suppose that we are ignorant of a certain type of physical or non-experiential truth. In particular, this supposition explains (a) why CA and similar arguments have such a grip on our imagination and (b) why it is mistaken to follow them to their conclusion.

How does the hypothesis of ignorance answer CA? Again, there are a number of ways of spelling out the connections here, but a particularly straightforward one focuses attention on its first premise:

C1 It is conceivable that there is someone identical to me in respect of all physical truths but different with respect to some psychological truth (e.g.

it is conceivable that there is a super-taster, who is physically the same as me, and yet to whom ginseng tea tastes sweeter than it does to me).

According to the epistemic view, we are not entitled to this premise. All we are entitled to is a weaker premise, which we might formulate as C1^:

C1^ It is conceivable that there is someone identical to me in respect of all *known* physical truths but different with respect to some psychological truth (e.g. it is conceivable that there is a super-taster, who is the same as me in respect of known physical truths, and yet to whom ginseng tea tastes sweeter than it does to me).

The difference between C1 and C1^ is that C1^ quantifies over known physical truths while C1 quantifies over all physical truths. If there are unknown physical truths that are relevant (as a proponent of the epistemic view says it is reasonable to believe there are) then the two premises are quite different. It is one thing to imagine phenomenal truths coming apart from the known physical truths; quite another to imagine them coming apart from all the physical truths.

Suppose then that there is a difference between C1 and C1^—what follows? Well, if we try to run the argument using C1^ in place of C1, the conclusion we will inevitably arrive at is not that phenomenal truths are contingently connected to all physical truths but only that they are contingently connected to the epistemically available ones. But this conclusion, because it shows only the incompleteness of our knowledge, a physicalist might well be able to live with.

The initial attractiveness of the epistemic view isn't hard to see. That we are ignorant about the nature of phenomenal consciousness is a scientific truism, though of course reasoning about our own ignorance raises problems; for one thing, it is quite impossible to say in any detail what fact or facts we are ignorant of. And that such ignorance has an impact on arguments founded on imaginary cases (which is the type of argument CA is) is likewise very compelling on the surface. Surely what we can and cannot imagine is constrained by our knowledge or lack of it.

However, while the epistemic view is attractive on the surface, it is also controversial. Many philosophers operate under the assumption—in Wittgenstein's famous phrase—that, at least for philosophical purposes, 'all the facts ... lie open before us.' This rules out the epistemic view, since it assumes (again: for philosophical purposes) that all the facts are in. And even those who do hold the epistemic view hold it in a form that is unlikely to attract converts. For example, Colin McGinn (1989) defends a position like the epistemic view, but the focus of his discussion is on the idea that we are cognitively closed (as he puts it) with respect to certain physical truths, i.e. that coming to know such truths is inconsistent with our biological nature. Once again, I won't be able to go into the pros and cons of the epistemic view here. (Though for the record I should say it is my own preferred solution to the problem; see Stoljar 2006.)

10.4 The role of physicalism in the conceivability argument

So far we have been concerned with setting out CA and with the question of whether it is sound. I turn now to the second of two questions distinguished earlier about the conceivability argument, viz. what the role of physicalism is in it.

We can begin with the observation that as stated CA is clearly an argument *about* physicalism; its conclusion is that physicalism is false. And if that is so, the metathesis that we have discussed both in Chapter 4 and Chapter 9 looks like a disaster for the argument. The metathesis is that there is no thesis of physicalism that is (a) true and (b) deserves the name. On the face of it that thesis robs the CA of its interest. After all, if there is no genuine thesis of physicalism that is true, there is scarcely much point in developing the CA against it.

However, while the metathesis looks in conflict with CA, it is important here to recall the strategy for avoiding this conflict that we formulated at the end of Chapter 9. The strategy is to ask what role physicalism plays in the pieces of reasoning in which it occurs. If physicalism plays an inessential role, then the nature and plausibility of these pieces of reasoning should be unaffected by the fact—assuming it to be a fact—that there is no version of physicalism that is both genuine and plausibly true.

So let us ask in accordance with this strategy what the role of physicalism is in CA. The answer is that physicalism does indeed play an inessential role in CA, and so the interpretative difficulty for physicalism should not affect CA itself. There are two key points to make. The first is that CA (or arguments analogous to CA) would refute if successful not only all of the versions of physicalism that we have discussed but a good many further theses as well. The second is that if we consider all the theses that CA (or arguments analogous to CA) would refute if successful, it emerges that these theses have a property in common, viz. according to all of them the distinctive properties of experience are not necessitated by, and are metaphysically distinct from, all other properties. But what this suggests is that physicalism conceived of as a thesis of the world drops out of the picture: what is important for CA is not the suggestion that consciousness isn't physical, what is important is that it is distinct from everything else. Let me amplify on these two points in turn.

10.4.1 CA, if successful, would refute more than physicalism.

Suppose we are faced with a person who, perhaps for good reasons, thinks that starting point physicalism is a true description of the world. One way in which we might try to argue them out of their position is by discussing various developments in the history of science. But setting that aside, another way would be to advance a version of CA. Clearly if CA were successful, it would refute starting point physicalism.

Not only would CA refute (if successful) starting point physicalism; it would also refute other versions of physicalism that we have considered previously: actual theory physicalism, current theory physicalism, twin-physicalism and so on. Take, for example, current theory physicalism. Someone who holds that present physics is a complete theory of the world holds a philosophy of nature that is quite remote from starting point physicalism, but they are nevertheless squarely in the target range of CA; mutatis mutandis for the other theories.

Of course the fact that if successful CA would refute any of the various versions of physicalism we have discussed isn't that surprising; one might even think that lying in the target range of CA is part of what makes these theses versions of physicalism. But in fact things don't stop there. Suppose we are faced with a person who (again for good reasons) supposes that physics plus vitalist biology provides a complete description of the world. Such a person is not a physicalist in any sense. And yet at least to a first approximation it looks as if CA (or a counterpart of CA) could now be used to argue that this kind of vitalism-cum-physicalism is not true. So the argument could be used to refute a person who believes various positions not normally thought of as versions of physicalism.

Indeed, it is not even clear that the point we have made is limited to this style of anti-physicalism. For suppose we are faced with a person who holds a certain traditional kind of dualism. Such a person might hold that each human being is a complex of a body and soul, and that various properties of the soul need to be taken into account to explain aspects of the nature and behavior of humans. It might well be that CA (suitably adjusted) could be used to refute such a position too. It is not obvious that we could not imagine someone exactly the same as us in terms of physical and spiritual states, and yet whose experience is increased on a certain phenomenological dimension. But if that is so then this version of dualism lies in the target range of CA just as much as these other theories.

10.4.2 CA and fundamental properties.

So, if it were successful CA would not simply refute various forms of physicalism, it would also refute many traditional versions of non-physicalism as well. But at this point, the question we need to ask ourselves is whether there is a pattern in any of the things we have just noticed. In particular, is there something in common that all of the theses that lie in the target range of CA possess? On the face of it all of the proposals we have just considered have in common that experiences must be necessitated by something else. This is fairly clearly true on all of the versions of physicalism we have considered, and on the versions of anti-physicalism that appeal to vitalism. But it is also true on the version of dualism I sketched. On that view, experiences are necessitated by various theoretical entities such as various features of the soul. To borrow Lewis's notion of a fundamental property, but in a way that does not decide how exactly to spell out that notion, we might say what all of these theories have in common is that they entail that the distinctive properties of experiences are not fundamental. Likewise, we might say that what the CA is pushing us toward—if you like, this is the objectionable conclusion that the argument forces you to accept—is that the distinctive properties of experiences *are* fundamental. If that is so, the proper formulation of the argument has nothing to do with physicalism construed as a thesis about the world.

10.5 Does this strategy generalize?

In the previous chapter we formulated a conjecture about physicalism, viz. that physicalism plays an inessential role in any reasonable piece of reasoning in which it occurs. What we have just been doing is showing how this conjecture plays out in the case of one piece of reasoning that involves physicalism, i.e. CA.

But of course, as we saw in Chapter 1, according to the standard picture all sorts of philosophical questions may be understood as questions about how to place or fit the presuppositions of everyday life in a physical world, i.e. a world in which physicalism is true. The presuppositions we had on the table were:

- that people perceive things and have sensations of various kinds, e.g. taste sensations, cramps, itches, nausea;
- that people speak and think about the world and about each other;
- that at least some words have meaning;
- that people's bodies, and physical objects in general, are colored, textured, have various tastes, and emit sounds and smells;
- that people's bodies, and physical objects in general, are solid or have bulk or fill in space;
- that people have reasons for thinking and acting as they do, and that those reasons may be subjected to normative (including moral) scrutiny;
- that people sometimes act and think freely;
- that people participate in group decisions and actions, and in turn the actions of these groups impact on the individuals who constitute them;
- that there are mathematical and logical truths (e.g. "$5 + 7 = 12$"), and that people can come to know these mathematical and logical truths.

We have concentrated so far only on the sensation case; can what we said about this case be replicated in these other cases?

In fact there are two quite separate questions here, one general and one specific. The general question is whether some version of the strategy mentioned at the end of Chapter 9 applies in these other cases. According to the standard picture, there are a number of philosophical problems about the presuppositions of everyday life that are stated in terms of physicalism: is the reference to physicalism (the physical and so forth) essential in the formulation of these problems? The more specific question is whether the particular implementation of the strategy we have just seen in the case of CA applies in these other cases. In the case of CA it seems reasonable to view the underlying problem as concerning not whether consciousness is physical, but whether it is fundamental; is something similar true in these other cases?

Now, as regards this second, more specific, question, there is a line of thought that suggests the answer to it is yes. On the face of it, we do seem to confront a range of philosophical problems about the distinctive properties introduced by the presuppositions of everyday life: freedom, morality, meaning, and so on. The standard picture interprets these problems as concerning the compatibility of freedom, morality, and so forth, on the

one hand, with physicalism on the other, an interpretation that is on a collision course with the skeptical view that there is no genuinely true thesis of
physicalism. But suppose instead we interpret all these problems as being
about whether freedom, morality, and so forth are fundamental. If so, the
skeptical position about physicalism would call for only a very minimal
adjustment to the standard picture. In each case we face an argument that
the crucial feature involved is a fundamental feature, be it a moral fact or
a fact about freedom or whatever. Since it seems reasonable to assume that
these features are not fundamental, we have in each case a philosophical
problem on our hands.

I think this proposal certainly is tempting, and it is one we should take
seriously. But in the end I doubt it provides a reasonable account of the philosophical problems that confront us. The problem is not that it is mistaken
to deny that the features associated with these presuppositions are fundamental. Denying this is very much in the spirit of the position I sketched in
Chapter 2, naturalistic platonism, and my own view is that it is preferable
to adopt this view in place of the traditional options of dualism, idealism,
and physicalism. (Though one might of course question whether it is a
world-view in the traditional sense.) The problem is rather that the generalization—that many philosophical problems are about whether presuppositions of everyday life involve fundamental properties—is not a useful one
in the sense that it does not reveal very much about the basic nature of the
problems at issue. If we begin to look closely enough at the philosophical
problem of consciousness we realize that it is not, as it is usually advertised
as being, a problem about how to place consciousness in a physical world.
But we also realize, or so I will argue, the features that generate the problem
of consciousness are not present in these other cases. Indeed, what emerges
is that the metaphors of placing or fitting or finding various items in a
physical world mask a good deal of disunity among various philosophical
problems. Once we realize that, any pithy generalization is bound to seem
inadequate to the complexity of the issues.

In saying that the particular strategy that we have outlined in the case of
the consciousness problem is unlikely to be repeated in the case of other
problems, I don't mean that these other problems should be rejected rather
than taken up seriously. So even if the *specific* question of the two distinguished a moment ago is answered in the negative, this does not mean that
the *general* question is. On the contrary, it seems to me quite plausible that
the strategy we mentioned in the previous chapter can indeed be followed
in the case of these other problems. The suggestion rather is that the precise

implementation of the strategy that we just looked at in the case of CA seems unlikely to me to be repeated. The basic point is that the standard picture interprets a lot of philosophical problems as being all of a piece. This is not that surprising given the historical origins of the picture—the positivist picture from which it developed likewise views a lot of philosophical problems as all of a piece. But when we look at philosophical problems in detail what seems most striking is not the similarities among them but the differences.

Of course charting out the differences and similarities between different philosophical problems is not something that can be undertaken lightly. Rather than attempting that, however, I will in what remains of this chapter look briefly at three problems that are often thought of as similar to the consciousness problem. The take-home message will be that they are all rather different both from it and from one another.

10.6 Intentionality

The first piece of reasoning to be considered involves an aspect of mental states different from consciousness, namely, what contemporary philosophers—roughly following the nineteenth-century philosopher, Brentano—call their *intentionality*. The intentionality of a mental state is its aboutness. When I think of Vienna or believe that the computer is on the desk or fear that the planet will get hotter, I instantiate mental states which are in a hard to define sense about Vienna, or the computer on the desk or planet Earth. The idea is that mental states (and speech acts) have a property rather like signs, sentences, and gestures; that is, they are about or represent things other than themselves.

Now, as I understand it, the traditional philosophical problem about intentionality derives from the fact that while aboutness looks offhand like a relation that, e.g., I bear to something else, it becomes clear when you think about it that it could not be such a relation. There are at least three separate considerations here:

1   In general, if I bear a relation R to a thing o, then o must exist. But the relation of thinking about, were it to exist, is not like this. I can think about Valhalla, but Valhalla does not exist; likewise while I can think about Vienna and Vienna does exist, it does not follow that Vienna exists merely from the fact that I think about it.

2   In general, if I bear a relation R to a thing o, then there is some particular thing, viz. o, to which I bear that relation. But the relation of thinking

about, were it to exist, is not like this. I can think about a man, but no
man in particular.
3   In general, if I bear a relation R to a thing o, and o = o*, then I bear that
same relation to o*. But the relation of thinking about, were it to exist,
is not like this. I can think about Vienna, and Vienna is the birthplace of
Schubert, without its being true that I am thinking about the birthplace
of Schubert (e.g. perhaps I have never heard of Schubert).

Following a suggestion of Michael Thau (2002) we summarize these facts
by saying that they are the 'paradoxes of intentionality.'
There are various proposals about how to deal with these paradoxes. We
will not go into them here. The important point for us is that there is no
internal connection between the paradoxes of intentionality and physicalism.
It is sometimes said that, in light of the paradoxes, intentionality could not
be instantiated in a physical world, i.e. a world in which physicalism is true.
Maybe so, but of course the same thing is true of non-physical worlds as
well. Suppose I am a physicalist who is worried by the paradoxes of intentionality. Giving up physicalism in an attempt to try to solve these paradoxes
is a pointless exercise, since the paradoxes will remain even if physicalism
were false. Again, suppose classical dualism is true and I am some sort of
complex of an ordinary physical object and soul; it is still impossible for me
to stand in a relation to things that don't exist! In sum, the paradoxes of
intentionality will remain whether physicalism is true or not, hence they do
not concern physicalism. So here we have further evidence for the conjecture formulated in the previous chapter: physicalism plays an inessential
role in the philosophical problem of intentionality.
But this is not to deny that philosophers often take the opposite view.
Here is Jerry Fodor in a famous passage:

> I suppose that sooner or later the physicists will complete the catalogue
> they've been compiling of the ultimate and irreducible properties of things.
> When they do, the likes of spin, charm, and charge will perhaps appear
> upon their list. But aboutness surely won't; intentionality simply doesn't
> go that deep. It's hard to see, in face of this consideration, how one can be
> a Realist about intentionality without also being, to some extent or other,
> a Reductionist. If the semantic and the intentional are real properties, it
> must be in virtue of their identity with (or maybe of their supervenience
> on?) properties that are themselves neither intentional nor semantic. If
> aboutness is real, it must be really something else.

> And indeed ... the deepest motivation for intentional antirealism derives
> not from such relatively technical worries about individualism and holism
> as we've been considering, but rather from a certain ontological intuition:
> that there is no place for intentional categories in a physicalistic view of the
> world; that the intentional can't be naturalized. It is time that we should
> face this issue. What is it, then, for a physical system to have intentional
> states? (1987: 97)

The language that Fodor uses in the last part of this passage is clearly
suggestive of the standard picture. The key motivation for the intentionality problem ("the deepest motivation for intentional antirealism"), he
says, is the idea that there "is no place for intentional categories in a physicalistic view of the world." What then does Fodor mean by "a physicalistic view of the world"? Like most adherents of the standard picture, he
doesn't say. (In another place, he writes, "these days we are all materialists
for much the reason Churchill gave for being a democrat: the alternatives
seem even worse"; Fodor 1994: 292). Moreover, if we ask what he means,
it is very plausible that there is no version of physicalism that makes sense
of what he means. And this makes it doubtful that the deepest motivation
for the problem can really be as Fodor says.

Can we find a way to interpret the issue that Fodor is getting at in
such a way that physicalism has no role in it? Well, we have already in
effect done so. The key motivation for the intentionality problem, we
might say, is the paradoxes of intentionality, and these bear no internal
connection to physicalism. Hence, even if the skeptic about physicalism
is right, this will have no impact on any philosophical problem about
intentionality.

It might be replied that a better way to take what Fodor is saying in this
passage brings the intentionality issue closer to the consciousness issue.
What he is saying there is that whatever the ultimate and irreducible things
are exactly, it would seem that intentional properties are not among them.
To put this point in the Lewisian vocabulary that we have been adopting so
far, Fodor seems to be saying that intentionality is not a fundamental property and as such we face a problem about the place of intentional categories
in a world that is fundamentally not intentional.

Now, it is certainly true that it is unlikely that intentionality is a
fundamental property; to that extent there is truth in what Fodor says.
However, it is much less clear that this is a good way to spell out a philosophical problem about intentionality. First, in the case of sensations, the

ARGUMENTS AGAINST PHYSICALISM   203

problem is generated not simply by the observation that the distinctive properties of experience are not fundamental but by the combination of that observation with a positive argument that they must be fundamental, i.e. CA. But in the case of intentionality we don't seem to have any such positive argument. Second, while it is true that intentionality is not fundamental, the same thing can be said about mountains, and so to the extent that Fodor has identified a key philosophical problem about intentionality he would also have identified a philosophical problem about mountains! But surely, if there is a philosophical problem about intentionality it should have something specific to do with intentionality! Finally, if the problem is primarily about whether intentionality is fundamental, it doesn't seem to have anything to do with the paradoxes of intentionality, but this seems quite implausible. Hence, while it is plausible that intentionality is not a fundamental property of the world, this observation itself does not seem to be what generates the philosophical problem.

Finally, it might be said that there are other problems that concern intentionality and what I have said has not taken them into account; for example, there are arguments such as Ned Block's (1981) Blockhead Argument or John Searle's (1980) Chinese Room Argument. That is perfectly true, but it seems to me that the pattern that we have focused on will repeat itself in all of these cases. These are arguments not against physicalism but against something else (computational theories of mind, in Searle's case; and behaviorism and neo-behaviorism in Block's case). However, while I believe that is so, what I have just said is merely an expression of that belief; I will not attempt to establish it here.

10.7 Meaning

In the passage we quoted in Chapter 1, Huw Price talks of the fate of the M-worlds: meaning, mentality, morality, and modality. We have so far focused on the second of these, the mental (indeed, on two aspects of the mental, consciousness and intentionality). The fourth, modality, is, it seems to me, something of an interloper. Physicalism is stated partly in modal terms, and so while there are no doubt philosophical problems about modality, it is difficult to see that they could usefully be stated in terms of the place of the modal in a world in which physicalism is true. But what of the other two M-worlds he mentions, meaning and morality? I will close this chapter by looking (*exceedingly* briefly) at these.

In recent philosophy, the problem of meaning is often discussed in the light of Kripke's (1982) discussion of Wittgenstein on rule following. As I understand it, the problem arises because of the connection between facts about what words mean—e.g. that the word 'dog' means dog—and facts about word usage. Kripke suggests that, according to the ordinary conception of meaning, we must in principle be able to "read-off" (26) the semantic truths from these truths about dispositions to use a word in various ways. I take this to mean that it is a conceptual truth that if there are semantic truths, then every such truth is entailed by some relevant dispositional truth. On the other hand, it is central to Kripke's discussion that there are examples which show that we cannot read-off the meaning of a word from any fact about dispositions to use that word. The upshot is that there can be no facts about semantic meaning, i.e. because such facts if they existed would bear a contradictory relation to facts about use.

Now if the problem of meaning is generated in this way, then like the other problems we have considered, it seems to bear no essential connection to physicalism and so is untouched by any interpretative problem that we might raise about physicalism. This is not say that it is often presented as involving this connection; often, for example, the problem is treated as being simply a variation on the intentionality problem as interpreted by Fodor (see, e.g. Boghossian 1989, and for related discussion see Field 1972). It is rather to say that this way of thinking about the philosophical problem of meaning (or at least this philosophical problem of meaning) does not get to heart of matter. The heart of the matter is that meaning seems on the one hand essentially connected to use, and on the other is not essentially connected to use.. But this fact—if it is a fact—does not concern physicalism.

10.8 Morality

Finally, what of the placement problem for moral properties such as an action's being right or a state of affairs' being valuable? In recent philosophy, problems of this sort are often discussed in the light of examples such as Harman's famous (1977) case in which we observe a case of cat burning. As I understand it, the problem here concerns how we might come to know (if we do) that acts of this kind are morally wrong. On the one hand, we are endowed with no moral faculty that operates in any way like perception; hence it seems natural to say that we come to know that such actions are morally wrong, if we do, by inference from knowledge of the non-moral facts of the situation. On the other hand, if we come to know about morality by inference, then it is unclear why moral judgment should be motivating in the way that it seems to be; after all, knowledge of non-moral facts is apparently not motivating on its own, and reasoning does not seem to take us from a non-motivating state to a motivating one.

Now, if the problem of morality is generated in this way, it too seems to bear no essential connection to physicalism and so is untouched by any interpretative problem that we might raise about physicalism. (Becoming a dualist, for example, is not to the point.) This is not say that it is often presented as involving a connection to physicalism; it is after all natural to read the passage from Price as suggesting something like this. It is rather to say that this way of thinking about the philosophical problem of morality (or at least this philosophical problem of morality) does not get to heart of matter. The heart of the matter is that our knowledge of morality on the one hand seems to be a function of more standard forms of inquiry, and yet on the other hand seems not to be. But this fact—if it is a fact—is independent of physicalism.

Summary

In this chapter, we have considered some of the main arguments against physicalism or at least some of the main arguments that physicalism is inconsistent with the presuppositions of everyday life. We focused on the conceivability argument against physicalism, but we also considered (extremely briefly) arguments about intentionality, linguistic meaning, and morality. Of course these are not the only possible arguments. Nevertheless, they seem good test cases for the conjecture that we formulated at the end of the previous chapter, namely that physicalism plays an inessential role in any piece of reasoning in which it occurs. As we have seen, there is considerable reason for favoring that conjecture.

Recommended reading

For extensive discussion on the conceivability argument, see Chalmers 1996 as well as the papers in Chalmers 2002. See also Nagel 1974 and 1986. For my own views see Stoljar 2006. For extensive discussion of the knowledge argument see Nagasawa, Ludlow, and Stoljar 2004 and Stoljar 2006. For the phenomenal concept strategy see the papers in Alter and Walter 2007 as well as Stoljar 2005, Loar 1990 and Sturgeon 2000. For a nice discussion of the idea that physicalism plays an inessential role in the knowledge argument see Lewis 1988, in particular the 'curiouser and curiouser' section. The argument I gave in section 10.4 is simply an adaptation of what Lewis says there to CA, though Lewis does not draw the conclusion mentioned here as I understand him. For issues of intentionality, meaning, and morality the best places to look are those already mentioned in the text.

11

ARGUMENTS FOR PHYSICALISM

11.1 Introduction

One of the more remarkable documents in the history of attempts to formulate physicalism is V.I. Lenin's *Materialism and Empirio-Criticism*, which was written while the communist activist (and later first president of the Soviet Union) was in exile in Vienna in 1908. Lenin was responding to the suggestion of a number of philosophers and physicists at the time that developments of a technical kind in physics suggested or entailed that idealism was true—a conclusion that was anathema to Lenin's political views which presupposed a materialistic outlook. Lenin seemed to have believed that workers in the shipyards and on farms would be less likely to be communists if they believed that its foundations were inconsistent with physics, a view that at the very least seriously underestimates how busy such people are. However, even if Lenin's motivation for discussing the formulation of physicalism is open to question, what he said—in part at least—is sensible, at any rate as I read him. What Lenin says, to put it rather roughly, is that there are two conceptions of matter or, equivalently, two conceptions of the physical. In one sense—and this is the sense at issue in discussions of idealism—matter is something which is not spiritual in nature. In another sense, matter is what is discussed by contemporary physics.

The strategy we considered in the previous chapter has a certain affinity with Lenin's. We did not discuss idealism there (though I will come back to it briefly in the conclusion of this book). And, while it is not clear to me that Lenin is really suggesting this, we certainly did not *define* the physical as the non-mental or non-spiritual. As we saw when we discussed the so-called 'via negativa' in Chapter 4, to define the physical as the non-mental is quite implausible. On the one hand, there may be properties that are both mental and physical, e.g. being in pain if the mind–brain identity theory is true. For another there may be properties that are neither mental nor physical, e.g. élan vital. But both possibilities are ruled out by the via negativa (at least in its simplest form); hence this proposed definition should be rejected.

However, rather than attributing to Lenin this implausible definition of 'physical,' one might instead read him as suggesting something weaker and more interesting, viz. that in philosophical discussions putatively about physicalism, what is really at issue is something different, e.g. whether consciousness is fundamental, or whether intentionality is a relation, or whether meaning is constitutively connected to use, or whether we can come to know about moral properties using established systems of inquiry. Obviously, this suggestion is very close to the spirit of our discussion.

But of course, the arguments we have looked at so far have all been arguments against physicalism, or at any rate arguments that physicalism is inconsistent with a number of the presuppositions of everyday life—what then of the arguments for physicalism? It is these that are my topic in this final chapter before concluding.

11.2 The impressionistic argument

As I have already noted a number of times, one rather impressionistic argument in favor of physicalism is present in the standard picture. The epistemological thesis, the second constituent thesis of the standard picture, says that we should believe the world-view of science whatever that view happens to be; and the interpretative thesis, the third constituent thesis, says that physicalism is somehow implicit in the world-view of modern science. Now, there is much to say about the epistemological thesis. However, since it has no particular connection to physicalism, we shall set it aside in this book. So, when thinking about the impressionistic argument, the key question for us is whether the interpretative thesis is true, i.e. whether physicalism is implicit in the world-view of contemporary science.

Actually this question is much harder to answer than it sometimes seems. For one thing it assumes something quite unobvious, viz. that modern science—a hugely complicated thing, after all—has a world-view in the first place. Does it? Well, in the first of the two passages that I use as an epigraph to this book, Carl Gillett and Barry Loewer come close to saying that it does: "Every era has its Weltanschauung and in much contemporary philosophy the doctrine of 'physicalism' plays this role." But why think that every era, construed as a period of history, has its Weltanschauung or world-view? Of course it may be that Gillett and Loewer are tacitly assuming that 'era' and 'world-view' are inter-defined, so that an era is by definition a period of history characterized by a world-view. Then what they say is perhaps true, but it is also uninteresting. For now it is unclear that every period of history is an era; a fortiori, it is unclear that our period of history is an era.

Moreover, even if we assume that contemporary science has a world-view, it is far from clear that physicalism is the world-view in question. Of course that depends on what physicalism is. Suppose, for example, physicalism were the thesis defended by Carnap, that any statement is translatable into a physical statement, where a physical statement is a statement that concerns ordinary physical objects. That semantic thesis could hardly be the world-view of modern science. Or suppose that physicalism were the thesis held by classical materialists, such as Lucretius or Gassendi, i.e. that every instantiated property is entailed by some property characteristic of classical atoms. Then physicalism might fairly be said to be Lucretius's world-view, but not ours.

What about the thesis that physicalism is the thesis that everything is necessitated by physical facts, where this means something like 'the facts described by contemporary or near contemporary physics.' That is the thesis that Smart and other contemporary physicalists believe. Is that our world-view? Well that is certainly a better candidate than the other two we just considered. But there is nevertheless considerable reason to doubt that this thesis—current theory physicalism, as we called it in Chapter 5—is our world-view. First, there are problems about whether this thesis is true, problems of the sort discussed in the previous chapter. Second, this kind of physicalism is an extremely specific thesis—a point that comes out clearly both in our discussion of the twin-earth example in Chapter 4 and of Hempel's dilemma in Chapter 5. One would have thought that a world-view is a very general thesis, and one that could persist through various changes. But there is no chance of this thesis persisting through changes. Third, it is extremely optimistic about our epistemic powers (cf. Jackson 1982). If it is true, we know in broad outline what the nature of the world is. But in fact, one might think it is an obvious fact about our world-view, if we have one, that we are ignorant in certain important and deep ways. It seems part of our world-view, to put it differently, that we inquirers have merely a partial knowledge of the world we inhabit. If so, it is difficult to credit the kind of physicalism advanced by Smart and others as our world-view.

One might suggest that physicalism is our world-view simply by default; that is, since idealism or dualism is not our world-view, physicalism is. (Cf. Fodor's reference to Churchill that I quoted in the previous chapter.) But of course this is a non sequitur. From the fact—assuming it to be a fact—that dualism or idealism is not our world-view it does not follow that physicalism is. It remains a possibility that we have no world-view at all, or that something else, e.g. naturalistic platonism, is our world-view. Indeed, it is quite plausible to think that when some physicalists insist that physicalism is true, what they really mean is that naturalistic platonism is true.

There is also a quite general problem with saying that physicalism of any sort is the world-view of modern science. For to say this is in effect to assimilate the world-view of modern science (assuming of course it has one) to one of the great world-views of the past, i.e. classical materialism. But it is quite unclear that classical materialism, with its connotations of perceptual availability and epistemic optimism, is an appropriate model for contemporary science. And in any case, why think that contemporary thought should be interpreted in the light of ancient categories? On the face of it, a better way to proceed would be to look at contemporary science and attempt to give a good faith statement of what its world-view, if any, is.

11.3 From the impressionistic argument to the causal argument

If the arguments for physicalism were limited to this impressionistic argument, therefore, the case for it, while not without force, would nevertheless be less persuasive than it is sometimes presented as being. Perhaps because of this, however, in recent years philosophers have paid considerable attention to a different argument. This argument uses principles about causal reasoning—for this reason we may call it 'the causal argument'. The causal argument is not inconsistent with the impressionistic argument; it might rather be construed as saying in much more explicit terms what the impressionistic argument is gesturing at.

In the remainder of this chapter, I want to set out and consider the causal argument in some detail. There are two slightly different ways of formulating the argument depending on whether we focus on the notion of an event, or on the notion of a property. In the next section I will discuss the argument in its event version; in the section after that I will look at the argument in its property version. (It is the property version that we will mainly discuss.) After setting out the argument in both versions, we will turn to its evaluation. As in the case of the arguments considered in the previous chapter, we will be concerned in the chapter not only with the evaluation of the argument but with the question of to what extent our ruminations on the formulation of physicalism bear on its evaluation.

11.4 The event version

The first premise of the causal argument in its event version is a thesis that is sometimes called the 'causal closure of the physical' or the 'completeness of physics'—'causal closure,' as I will call it. The general idea of causal closure is that the system of physical causes and effects in the world is causally closed in the sense that every effect in that system has a cause from within that system. This idea can be expressed in various ways. Here is one way that is relatively straightforward:

(1) For all physical events e, if there is an event e^* such that e^* causes e, then e^* is a physical event.

So, for example, suppose I throw a brick and break a window. This event, the breaking of the window, clearly has a cause, viz. my throwing the brick. What causal closure tells us in addition is that this cause, my throwing of the brick, is a *physical* event, for the event it caused, the breaking of the window, is clearly a physical event. Notice that (1) does not rule out the idea that some events are uncaused; for example, perhaps the beginning of the universe itself has no cause, or perhaps there are random uncaused events. All it says is that, among the physical events which have causes, all of them have physical causes.

The second premise of the argument is the idea that mental events cause physical effects—the causal efficacy of the mental, as it is sometimes called. According to the causal efficacy of the mental:

(2) For any mental event e, there is a physical event e^* such that e causes e^*.

The idea here may again be brought out with an example. Suppose I touch a hot stove and move my arm away quickly. My arm moving is a physical event in a natural sense, and my being in pain—or, better, my going into a state of pain—is a mental event. So here we have one example of a mental event having a physical effect. Of course, this is just one example. The causal efficacy of the mental goes further than this; it says that every mental event has a physical effect, and so what is true of pains is true of mental events in general.

One might object that the causal efficacy of the mental is too bold to be plausible. Surely all that is true is *some* mental events cause physical events; might there not be mental events which either cause no other events, or which only cause mental events? However, there are two responses to this. First, what is being claimed here is only that every mental event has some physical effect or other; it is not being ruled out that the effects in question might be extremely remote or indirect. And it is not so bold to say that every mental state has at least some remote physical effects. Second, the boldness of the claim here does not affect the assessment of the causal argument, and makes its presentation somewhat easier, so we may let it stand.

The third premise of the argument is a principle about causation that is sometimes called the 'no-over-determination' principle or the 'exclusion' principle. A natural way initially to state this thesis is as follows:

(3) For all events e and e^*, if e causes e^*, then there is no event e^{**} such that
   (a) e^{**} is distinct from e and
   (b) e^{**} causes e^*.

Later we will see that there are various ways to interpret this principle. But for the moment, the thing to notice is that the three premises (1)–(3) entail that any mental event is identical to a physical event. To illustrate, take some mental event, say the onset of a pain. By the causal efficacy of the mental, this event causes a physical event, say the movement of a foot. By causal closure we know that this physical event, the movement of the foot, has a physical cause if it has a cause. But since we know (i.e. because it is obvious) that it has a cause, we may infer that it has a physical cause. Now what is the relation between the pain that caused the movement and this physical cause? By the exclusion principle, these events must not be distinct. Hence they are identical, and we have the conclusion that the physical cause of the movement of the foot must be identical to its mental cause. But then the onset of a pain is identical to a physical event.

11.5 The property version

The suggestion that (1)–(3) entail that every mental event is a physical event seems reasonable on the surface, but one might nevertheless wonder how, even if it is right, it is supposed to bear on *physicalism* in the sense we have been discussing it. For, as we have noted a number of times, physicalism is a thesis about properties, and not simply a thesis about particulars. But events are often thought of as a certain kind of particular. On the face of it the onset of my pain is an event that occurs at a particular time and place just as the French Revolution is an event that occurs at a particular time and place. On the other hand, if events are particulars, then even a property dualist might agree that every mental event is identical to some physical event. Since no property dualism can agree with physicalism, however, it is hard to see how the conclusion of the causal argument in its event version bears on physicalism at all.

The sense in which the causal argument in its event version does not tell us anything about physicalism may be brought out in a different way as well, a way which speaks to the specific concerns of the argument, and does not rely on the general point that physicalism is inconsistent with property dualism. We often think not simply of one *event's* causing another but of a *property's* being causally efficacious in the production of one event by another. When I throw the brick through the window, the *weight* of the brick is causally relevant to the window's breaking while the *color* of the brick (presumably) is not. But the causal argument in its event version says nothing at all about properties. It leaves open, in particular, whether the properties that are efficacious in one event's causing another are necessitated by the physical or not. In that sense too, it leaves the main concerns of physicalism untouched.

It is these weaknesses in the event version of the argument (or at any rate, weaknesses when it is construed as an argument for physicalism) that the property version of the argument is designed to overcome. (And it is for these reasons that we will concentrate on the property version of the argument here.) To obtain a property version of the argument, we need to adjust the premises of the event version of the causal argument. Causal closure becomes:

(4) For all physical events e, if there is an event e^* such that e^* causes e, then
  (a) e^* is a physical event and
  (b) there is a physical property F such that F is causally efficacious in e^*'s causing e.

The causal efficacy of the mental becomes:

(5) For all mental events e, there is a physical event e^* such that e causes e^* and there is a mental property F such that F is causally efficacious in e's causing e^*.

Finally, exclusion becomes:

(6) For all events e and e^*, if e causes e^*, and if there is a property F which is causally efficacious in e's causing e^*, then there is no property G such that
  (a) G is distinct from F and
  (b) G is causally efficacious in e's causing e^*.

With these three premises in place we have an argument, not just for the conclusion that every mental event is a physical property but that every mental property (or anyway every causally efficacious mental property, but let us set this aside) is a physical property. For suppose I begin to feel pain. By (5) this feeling of pain causes a physical event, say movement of the foot, and there is a property of the feeling, e.g. its hurting like bally-o, which is causally relevant in the pain's causing the movement of the foot. But the movement of the foot is a physical event, and so by (4) there is a physical property, say my being in neural state N, which is causally relevant to production of this event. What is the relation between the mental property, hurting like bally-o, and the physical property, being in a neural state? By (6), these properties are identical, and more generally mental properties are identical to physical properties. So the property version of the causal argument is an argument to the conclusion that mental properties are identical to physical properties.

11.6 The causal argument and the varieties of dualism

An important feature of the causal argument that is worth bringing out straightaway is its connection to the varieties of dualism. As we noted in Chapter 2, while dualism comes in different forms, one important distinction is that among the interactionist, the epiphenomenalist, and the over-determinationist forms of dualism. In effect, each of these different versions of dualism denies one of the three premises of the causal argument.

The interactionist dualist says that mental properties and events play a causal role that is quite distinct from but analogous to, the role that physical properties and events play. The interactionist position is therefore a denial of closure: it says that it is not the case that whenever one event causes a physical event, there is a causally efficacious property of the first event that is physical; sometimes this property is a non-physical property, and moreover, is a property not necessitated by a physical property. The epiphenomenalist says that some mental properties are not causally efficacious in the production of any physical event (or that no mental properties are causally efficacious, on some developments of the view). The epiphenomenalist position is therefore a denial of the causal efficacy of the mental: it says that it is not the case that every mental event has a physical cause and that a mental property is efficacious in the production of that cause. The over-determinationist says that mental properties might be causally efficacious, but only if quite distinct properties are also efficacious at the same time and in the same way. The over-determinationist position therefore denies the exclusion principle: it says that sometimes if a property is causally efficacious in the production of some event then a distinct property may also be causally efficacious.

11.7 Problems with exclusion

We have so far set out the causal argument, focused on its property version (as opposed to its event version), and noted its connection with the forms of dualism. But how successful is the causal argument? Well, to begin with there are a number of different problems with the exclusion thesis, a thesis on which the causal argument crucially relies.

To see the first problem, let us look again at that thesis in its property version:

(6) For all events e and e^*, if e causes e^*, and if there is a property F which is causally efficacious in e's causing e^*, then there is no property G such that
   (a) G is distinct from F and
   (b) G is causally efficacious in e's causing e^*.

It is easy to see that (6) is false. Consider a case in which the movement of a white ball causes the movement of a red ball, which in turn causes the movement of a black ball. Here we have three events in sequence—call them 'white,' 'red' and 'black'— the first causing the second, which then causes the third. In such a case, red causes black, and it is presumably the case that there is a property of red, e.g. its involving a particular collision, that is causally efficacious in red's causing black. But it is also the case here that white causes black, for white causes red, which in turn causes black; moreover, it is presumably also the case that there is a property of white, e.g. its involving a *different* collision, which is causally efficacious in its causing black. But since the causally efficacious property of white is distinct from the causally efficacious property of red, we have a violation of (6) as stated.

To avoid this result one would need to amend (6) so that it is limited to *direct* causation rather than causation of any sort. It is true that white causes black, but it does so only indirectly, i.e. it does so only because it causes something else (red) that then causes black. On the other hand, red causes black directly, i.e. red causes black but not via anything else. This suggests that (6) should be replaced with:

(6*) For all events *e* and *e**, if *e* directly causes *e**, and if there is a property *F* which is causally efficacious in *e*'s directly causing *e**, then there is no property *G* such that
    (a) *G* is distinct from *F* and
    (b) *G* is causally efficacious in *e*'s directly causing *e**.

(6*) avoids the problem of indirect causation. But, of course, if (6) is replaced by (6*), then so too will all the other theses need to be replaced. I will leave it as an exercise for the reader to see whether this affects the plausibility of the reasoning.

The second problem for exclusion is that over-determination seems a perfectly possible, even if an unlikely, thing to happen. The classic example is the firing squad case. In this case, a prisoner is killed by firing squad and yet the death is over-determined, i.e. it was caused both by Soldier A's firing *and* by Soldier B's firing. If such a case is possible, which offhand it seems to be, then (6)—and (6*) for that matter—is false. Both theses rule out the firing squad case, and so rule out over-determination. But, since the case is possible, both are false.

There are two ways in which one might seek to defend the exclusion principle against this second objection. First, it might be argued that when you look closely at examples like that of the firing squad it turns out that you do not have genuine violation of exclusion here. Perhaps, for example,

A's bullet hit a microsecond earlier than B's, and so B's didn't really cause the death, even though of course it would have done if A's somehow didn't. Or perhaps A's bullet causes the prisoner to die *in a certain way* that B's does not, even though both cause the prisoner to die. A difficulty with this response is that while it is true that one might try to describe any apparent example of over-determination so that it is not the genuine article, it is hard to shake the feeling that over-determination is nevertheless empirically possible. (There is no contradiction in it, for example.) And the problem with exclusion in any of the versions we have been considering is that it rules it out a priori, or at least seems to rule it out a priori.

The other way to respond to the objection is to focus on the idea that over-determination might sometimes happen, but not as a matter of course. One way (not the only way) to incorporate that idea into the exclusion principle is to interpret it so that it applies, not to any events but simply to the vast majority:

(6**) For *almost* all events e and e^*, if e directly causes e^*, and if there is a property F which is causally efficacious in e's causing e^*, then there is no property G such that
(a) G is distinct from F and
(b) G is causally efficacious in e's directly causing e^*.

What this principle says or implies is that while over-determination might happen, it does not happen as a general rule. If it does not happen as a general rule, one might think, it is safe to conclude that in any particular case in which a mental event causes a physical event, there is no other event that does so—for the presence of some other cause is very unlikely. To put the point another way, unless we assume that something analogous to the firing squad case goes on in a person every time they move their hand because they feel hot—something that seems unlikely—we can assume that over-determination does not happen in the case of the mental.

11.8 Exclusion and distinctness

Even if the friend of exclusion can avoid the two problems just mentioned, however, there is a third problem that is much more serious. To see the problem, let us look again at the exclusion principle, this time focusing on the simple version we noted before. (Strictly speaking, we should be limiting ourselves to direct causation and almost all events rather than all events, but we can ignore these complications in this section.) That simple version was:

(6) For all events e and e*, if e causes e*, and if there is a property F which is causally efficacious in e's causing e*, then there is no property G such that
   (a) G is distinct from F and
   (b) G is causally efficacious in e's causing e*.

What this principle tells us is that if some property F is causally efficacious in bringing about some effect then no *other* property is causally efficacious as well. But in fact such a principle looks too strong to be plausible.

Here is an example from Stephen Yablo (1992) that brings this out. (Yablo provides analogous examples that apply to the event version of the principle.) Suppose we say that an earthquake is violent if it is such as to register over 5 on the Richter scale. It will seem natural in many circumstances to say that the earthquake's being violent is causally efficacious in a building's falling over. But being violent is numerically distinct from being barely violent, where 'being barely violent' means only just getting past 5 on the Richter scale. (These properties are numerically distinct because, while being barely violent entails being violent, one can be violent without being barely so.) Now the problem is that, if it turns out that the earthquake's being *barely violent* caused the building to fall, then by the exclusion principle its *violence* didn't do anything. But that is certainly objectionable. For it commits us to saying that while the earthquake was violent, in the circumstances the violence of the earthquake had no role to play in the building's toppling over.

How to respond to this objection to the exclusion principle? In my view, the most plausible response here involves recalling a point made in our discussion of necessitation dualism in Chapter 8. This is that there are various notions of distinctness: numerical distinctness, modal distinctness, metaphysical distinctness, and so on. Obviously, the exclusion principle appeals to *some* notion of distinctness, for the word 'distinct' occurs in the principle. But which notion of distinctness is at issue here? Well, Yablo's example seems to presuppose that what is at issue here is numerical distinctness, where a property F is numerically distinct from a property G just in case F is not identical to G. Being barely violent is *numerically distinct* from being violent because it is possible for something to be violent, but not barely so—a very violent earthquake, for example. But what if instead we operate with a different notion of distinctness—e.g. modal distinctness, where a property F is modally distinct from a property G just in case it is possible for F to be instantiated without G and vice versa. Now Yablo's example is beside the point. For being barely violent is not (e.g.) *modally distinct* from being violent because they are not modally independent; in particular, being barely violent necessitates being violent.

We may bring out this point more directly by drawing a distinction between two versions of the exclusion principle, as follows:

(7) For all events *e* and *e**, if *e* causes *e**, and if there is a property F which is causally efficacious in *e*'s causing *e**, then there is no property G such that
   (a) G is numerically distinct from F and
   (b) G is causally efficacious in *e*'s causing *e**.

(8) For all events *e* and *e**, if *e* causes *e**, and if there is a property F which is causally efficacious in *e*'s causing *e**, then there is no property G such that
   (a) G is modally distinct from F and
   (b) G is causally efficacious in *e*'s causing *e**.

Yablo's example threatens (7) but not (8). Being barely violent is numerically distinct from being violent, but it is not modally distinct. So if (8) is the correct version of the exclusion principle, that principle is compatible with its being the case, in Yablo's example, that the violence of the earthquake causes the building to topple over.

However, while the strategy of adopting (8) as the correct notion of exclusion avoids Yablo's counterexample, it also generates a series of points of concern when we turn back to the causal argument. The first is that it is now not clear that the causal argument is an argument for physicalism *as opposed to* various kinds of non-physicalism, e.g. necessitation dualism. As we saw in Chapter 8, the necessitation dualist has a distinctive version of non-physicalism according to which mental and physical properties are necessarily connected. If the exclusion principle is (8) rather than (7) however, the causal argument can tell us at most that mental properties and physical properties are necessarily connected. But since the necessitation dualist agrees with this, a philosopher who is a necessitation dualist need have nothing to fear from the argument. (One might appeal to a primitive notion of metaphysical distinctness here, and say that this notion is different from modal distinctness, but such a maneuver raises all of the issues we considered in Chapter 8.)

The second point has to do with the issue mentioned in Chapter 6 of whether physicalism should be formulated in terms of identity or in terms of necessitation—whether we should adopt the Identity View or the Necessity View, as I put it there. The causal argument is an argument (in the property case) that mental properties are identical to physical properties. But an identity version of physicalism is open to various objections, chief among which is the multiple realization objection. This suggests that we should interpret the causal argument so that it issues only in a necessitation version of physicalism. But then we get the problem that the argument does not discriminate between physicalism and necessitation dualism.

The final point concerns a famous development of the causal argument due to Jaegwon Kim (see Kim 1998). Kim suggests that the causal argument may be used not only as an argument for physicalism as opposed to dualism, but also as an argument for a reductive form of physicalism as opposed to a non-reductive form. (As we noted in Chapter 8, there are various things that 'reductive physicalism' could reasonably mean; I take it that what Kim has in mind is physicalism according to the Identity View.) Kim calls this "Descartes' Revenge," the idea being that the very same argument that the physicalist might use against the dualist may also be used against various forms of physicalism, in particular any version of physicalism which does not endorse the Identity View. In the light of our distinction between the two versions of exclusion, however, it is far from clear that Kim's development of the causal argument is correct. If we adopt (7) as our formulation of exclusion, then it is true that necessitation physicalism is in trouble; but as we have seen (7) is subject to counterexample. On the other hand, if we adopt (8) as our formulation of exclusion, necessitation physicalism has nothing to fear from the argument.

11.9 Problems with closure

We have been examining one line of response to the causal argument, a line that focuses on problems with the exclusion principle. I will close this chapter by looking a different line of response, a response that focuses on the causal closure principle, and connects that principle with the question of how to interpret physicalism.

In its property version, the causal closure principle was:

(4) For all physical events e, if there is an event e^* such that e^* causes e, then
   (a) e^* is a physical event and
   (b) there is a physical property F such that F is causally efficacious in e^*'s causing e.

How plausible is this principle? Clearly this depends on what 'physical' means. Moreover when we ask what it could mean, it emerges that the friend of causal closure faces an argument closely parallel to the one that we have already looked at in the case of physicalism. The argument can be set out as follows:

P1   In formulating causal closure, we must operate either with the Starting Point View or with some liberalized version of the Starting Point View.

P2   If we operate with the Starting Point View, it is possible to articulate a version of causal closure that deserves the name, but that version is false.

P3   If we operate with some liberalized version of the Starting Point View, it is possible to articulate a version of causal closure that is true; but that version does not deserve the name, because either
   (a) it is true at possible worlds where no version of causal closure should be true or
   (b) it is false at possible worlds where no version of causal closure should be false.

C   There is no version of causal closure that is both true and deserving of the name.

This argument, just like the original argument that we formulated at the end of Chapter 4, is valid. So, if its premises are plausible, any genuine version of causal closure is false.

But the premises of the argument *are* plausible; indeed they are plausible for reasons that parallel those that support the premises of the original argument. P1 is plausible on the assumption the concept of a physical property (and, one might add in this context, the concept of a physical event) is a cluster concept. P2 is plausible because any version of causal closure that operates with the Starting Point View will tell us in effect that the domain of the intuitively physical is causally closed. But this is false—events and properties described in terms of common sense physics certainly have causes that are not described in the language of common sense. And P3 is plausible because any version of causal closure that operates with a liberalized version of the causal closure principle will either end up being false at the twin-physics world, or else end up being true at the classical dualist world, and this goes against what is intended by a proponent of the causal argument.

Hence, once we factor issues of interpretation into the argument, causal closure is subject to the same sort of objection as physicalism itself.

One might object that it makes no sense to speak of a thesis of causal closure 'deserving the name' even if it makes sense to speak of a thesis of physicalism 'deserving the name' as we did in the original argument. There is an established practice of talking of physicalism or materialism, one might think, but there is no similar practice of talking about causal closure, which is a notion introduced by a proponent of the causal argument. However, while there is certainly some truth to this, I doubt it will affect the plausibility of the objection to causal closure that we are considering. For it seems possible to adjust the argument to avoid this issue. One might for example, speak not of causal closure deserving the name (or failing to) but of its not being a thesis intended by proponents of the causal argument. Or again, one might speak not of causal closure itself deserving the name but of causal closure generating a version of physicalism that does.

Alternatively one might object that there is a difference between this argument and the original argument, viz. that the sub-premise P3-a in the argument above is false. It is certainly true that if *physicalism* is defined with respect to the physics that is true at the actual world, then it will be false at a non-actual possible world at which a different physics is true, e.g. the twin-physics world. That indeed was the rationale behind the sub-premise in our original argument about physicalism that is the counterpart to P3-a in the argument about causal closure. But things are different for causal closure. For this thesis is in an important sense conditional: in effect it says that if there are any physical events, then such and such. However, such a conditional thesis will not be false at the twin-physics world, even if 'physical event' is defined with respect to the actual world. What will be true instead is that there are no physical events. And in turn this will permit causal closure to be true at the twin-physics world in the light of its conditional nature. However, while there is again truth to this objection, I again doubt it will affect the plausibility of the objection to causal closure we have set out. While the physics that is true at our world is distinct from the physics that is true at the twin-physics world, they nevertheless overlap—starting point physical properties (and events) will count as physical according to both; hence it is plausible to suppose that there are some physical events in the twin-physics world, even if our physics is not true there. Indeed, it is quite objectionable to say that there are no physical events at the twin-physics world. After all, when Smart waves his hand, this is presumably a physical event; so too, when twin-Smart waves his.

11.10 The role of physicalism in the causal argument

So the causal closure thesis, and indeed the causal argument, faces a problem that is parallel to the problem about physicalism. But on reflection this should have been expected. For according to the metathesis that we considered at the end of Chapter 4, and then again in Chapter 9, there is no thesis of physicalism that is both true and deserving of the name. If that metathesis is true, then we know that the causal argument for physicalism is no good, for the causal argument is an argument for the truth of physicalism. Indeed, if the metathesis is true, the question should not be 'is the causal argument sound?' but rather 'where exactly is its mistake?' If we waive the problems about exclusion that we considered earlier, it would seem natural enough to pin the mistake on the thesis of causal closure and in particular on the fact that there are various interpretations of that thesis. Some of these interpretations will permit us to formulate an argument for a thesis that deserves the name of 'physicalism' and other interpretations will permit us to formulate an argument for a thesis that is potentially true. But no interpretation will permit us to formulate an argument for a thesis that is both true and deserving of the name. For if the metathesis is true, there is no such thesis.

At this point, however, it is natural to look again at the strategy we formulated at the end of chapter 9, i.e. the strategy of asking whether the reference to physicalism is essential in the various pieces of reasoning in which it occurs. In the previous chapter we applied this strategy to the conceivability argument, and noted that it is possible to suppose that the conceivability argument is really about the question of whether mental facts, and facts about consciousness in particular, are fundamental or not. In the case of the causal argument for physicalism, it seems reasonable to make a parallel suggestion, namely, that while the causal argument is certainly presented as an argument for physicalism it is not clear that this is central to the main idea behind it. The main idea behind the argument seems to be to show, not so much that mental properties are physical, but that they are not modally distinct from all other instantiated properties.

How would this idea work out in detail? Well, suppose we take the premises of the causal argument, adjust them in the light of our discussion of exclusion, and replace 'physical' with 'non-mental'. The result would be:

(9) For all events e and and all non-mental events $e*$, if there is a property F such that F is causally efficacious in e's causing $e*$ then F is a non-mental property.

(10) For all mental events e, there is a non-mental event $e*$ such that e causes $e*$ and there is a mental property F such that F is causally efficacious in e's causing $e*$.

(11) For almost all events e and $e*$, if e directly causes $e*$, and if there is a property F which is causally efficacious in e's causing $e*$, then there is no property G such that
    (a) G is modally distinct from F and
    (b) G is causally efficacious in e's directly causing $e*$.

On this interpretation, the causal argument is an argument for the thesis that mental properties are necessitated by non-mental properties. This is, I think, a plausible conclusion and the argument is a plausible argument for that conclusion. But of course the reason for its plausibility at least in part is this: the argument now has nothing to do with physicalism, and so is not affected by skepticism about that thesis.

Summary

In this chapter, we have been considering two arguments in favor of physicalism: the impressionistic argument and the causal argument. The impressionistic argument is not persuasive as an argument for physicalism (though it might be more persuasive as an argument for something else). Likewise, the causal argument is less persuasive than it sometimes seems. In the first place, reflection on the exclusion principle suggests that the causal argument, even on its own terms, does not support physicalism as opposed to necessitation dualism. In the second place, when we ask what 'physical' might mean in the argument, there is nothing really it could mean. At this point the proponent of the argument can replace 'physical' with 'non-mental.' But in that case we don't have an argument for physicalism, what we have is an argument for the view that there are no mental properties that are modally distinct from every other property. That is an interesting and plausible conclusion, but it is not physicalism.

Recommended reading

The literature on the causal argument is huge, and we have covered only a part of it here. Jaegwon Kim is the philosopher who has done most with the argument; his best discussion to my mind is Kim 1998. Papineau 2001 connects the causal argument with issues of the interpretation of physicalism somewhat in the way that I have done here, as does Sturgeon 2000. Papineau's paper is also an excellent source of information about the historical background to physicalism. For the exclusion thesis see Yablo 1992 and Bennett 2003. Stoljar 2008 connects the causal argument with the question of distinctness.

CONCLUSION

We may bring our discussion to an end by indulging in a little counterfactual history. I noted in the introduction that towards the end of the nineteenth century almost all professional philosophers were idealists of some stripe or other, but that idealism was overthrown and that later analytic philosophy became predominately physicalist in the materialist sixties—that is, the *nineteen*-sixties. Now I ask you to imagine that idealism was not overthrown. I don't want you to imagine that the idealism of the nineteenth century lasted longer than it did. That form of idealism seems to me at least quite remote, largely because its intellectual culture doesn't show the self-conscious influence of logic in quite the way that analytic philosophy does. What I want you to imagine rather is that idealism, and not physicalism, became the Weltanschauung of modern analytic philosophy, but that developments in logic, and in science more generally, remained pretty much as they are.

Now, in the circumstances I am asking you to imagine, your typical idealist philosopher holds, not simply that everything is mental (for the reasons given in Chapter 2), but rather that every instantiated property is necessitated by, and not metaphysically distinct from, some mental property. To clarify their position further the idealist would be required to say, first, what it is for a property to be a mental property and, second, what it is for one property to be necessitated by, and not metaphysically distinct from, another. As regards the second question, the issues seem the same as those examined in Chapters 6 to 8. What about the first question? What does the idealist mean by a 'mental property'?

Well, to answer this question the idealist might begin by pointing out that we do have an intuitive conception of various mental events and states, such as itches or the belief that Beijing is the capital of China. And he or she might then introduce the notion of a mental property by saying that mental properties are the distinctive properties of such intuitively mental events and states.

But there are problems ahead for this sort of procedure. Some problems are clearly specific to the idealist case. For example, logically speaking, the bearers of mental properties are subjects in the way that the bearers of physical properties need not be. There is always someone (in the typical case, some person or animal) who is itchy or believes that Beijing is the capital of China, but there need not be someone who (e.g.) weighs three hundred pounds—a mere physical object is perfectly acceptable. How the idealist is going to weave this fact into their view seems to me very much an open question. However, even if we waive the difficulty about subjects, the idealist in our counterfactual circumstances faces a different sort of difficulty as well. The problem—at least if we hold the development of science and logic constant—is that modern psychological theories tend to go beyond the distinctive properties of intuitively mental states and events. Suppose—to adopt an absurdly simplified example—that psychologists and neuroscientists tell us that to believe that Beijing is the capital of China it is required that one be in a sub-personal, computation-cum-representational state called 'COMP'. Such a state is not identical to the state of believing that Beijing is the capital of China but it is something that explains or constitutes believing this. Now, is COMP a *mental* state or not? At this point, the issue becomes potentially embarrassing for the idealist. For whatever else one says, COMP is certainly not an intuitively mental state like an itch or a belief; likewise, its distinctive properties are not the distinctive properties of intuitively mental states. But if itches (etc.) are our model for what mental states are, then COMP is not a mental state; likewise, its properties are not mental properties. On the other hand, if COMP is not a mental state, and if its properties are not mental properties, then idealism is false, and, moreover, is false for empirical reasons. (It may seem strange that idealism could be false for empirical reasons, but remember the sort of idealist I have in mind is the thoroughly modern sort, the kind who assumes that idealism is an abstract but contingent doctrine that no small amount of experiments can force us to give up. Presumably actual idealists don't hold anything like this, but this is no problem for *counterfactual* history.)

In order to avoid this result, the idealist is obliged to interpret the notion of a mental property broadly, i.e. in such a way that it is not limited to the distinctive properties of intuitively mental states and events. For example, she might well say that a mental property is not simply a property distinctive of intuitively mental events and states but is instead, or in addition, a property expressed by a predicate of a theory introduced to explain those intuitive mental events and states. On such a liberalized conception, COMP may perfectly well count as a mental state and its properties as mental properties, and so the potential empirical refutation of idealism is avoided. But by the same token, the idealist who takes this road will now have considerable difficulty articulating a version of idealism that plays the theoretical role that idealism traditionally plays. In particular, if the theory in question is a merely possibly true theory, any resulting version of idealism will be true in cases in which it palpably is not; but if the theory in question is an actually true theory, any resulting version of idealism will be not be true in cases in which it palpably is.

If this is right, the idealist is at this point in the same sort of bind that afflicts the physicalist, and which we looked at in detail in Chapters 3 to 5. The problem is that the natural way of introducing the key notion into their views—the notion of a mental property and physical property respectively—is subject to a certain kind of empirical pressure. In order to alleviate the pressure, the actual physicalist, and my imaginary idealist, is forced to weaken the conditions on what counts as a mental or physical property. However, once this is done it becomes very difficult to get the cases right, that is, to properly account for the range of cases in which philosophically speaking the notion needs to apply. But this suggests that there is no thesis of either physicalism or idealism that is both true and deserving of the names.

I doubt most people will be sympathetic to our counterfactual idealist. While idealism has some extremely able contemporary defenders, most philosophers these days think it false. Why do they think it false? I am not sure about others, but my own view is that, at least as it is initially developed, idealism is false because it assumes that the basic forms of reality are in important ways deeply similar to the ones we come to know when we stub our toes. When you stub your toe you feel pain, and in the normal case come to know about pain, i.e. you become acquainted with certain distinctive properties of the pain. Now, the idealist thinks that the basic properties of the world are of the same kind as these distinctive properties. So what the idealist is saying is that when you stub your toe you are acquainted with a fundamental property of the world. But—and now I am just speaking personally—I just cannot bring myself to believe that this is so. Finding out about the basic forms of reality is *hard*. Even to formulate a reasonable partial hypothesis about that kind of thing you would need, if human history is anything to go by, something like three hundred years of funding, a lot of cooperation, some incredibly insightful people, considerable social freedom, and a lot of luck. Stubbing your toe is *not* one of the methods likely to produce success. So it seems to me that the most straightforward version of idealism cannot be right. God did not bring us into existence—if indeed he did bring us into existence—to find out about the fundamental facts that easily. What about a more sophisticated version of idealism, in which the notion of a mental property is liberalized? Well such a version might well avoid the result that stubbing your toe acquaints you with the fundamental facts of nature, but it is quite unclear that this liberalized version of idealism will preserve the basic impulse of the simple version of the view.

So my view is that lack of sympathy is the right attitude to take to the idealist. But if that is so, it is hard to see that it is not the right attitude to take to the physicalist as well. When you stub your toe, you feel a distinctive sort of pain, but you are also confronted with a distinctive sort of object, the physical object on which you stubbed your toe—a doorframe, as it might be. So what the physicalist (or at any rate the starting point physicalist) is saying is that when you stub your toe you are acquainted with some of the basic forms of reality. However—and again I am here just speaking personally—I cannot bring myself to believe that this is so. As before, finding out about fundamental properties is hard, and stubbing one's toe is not a method likely to produce success. So it seems to me that the most straightforward version of physicalism—starting point physicalism—cannot be right. What about a more sophisticated version of physicalism, in which the notion of a physical property is liberalized? Well such a version might well avoid the result that stubbing your toe acquaints you with some of fundamental facts of nature, but it is quite unclear that it will preserve the basic impulse of the simple version of the view—that indeed is what we have been seeing throughout this book.

We may bring out the problem for both the idealist and the physicalist in a different way by noting that both views date from a period of human history when common sense reigned supreme. (Indeed, this is true of all of the views that have dominated Western philosophy, idealism, physicalism and dualism.) Once we agree that the true description of the world goes beyond common sense categories, it is difficult to hold to any of these traditional world-views. Of course this means that starting point physicalism is false. But it also means that any thesis with one foot in common sense and another in a scientific attempt at understanding the world that eschews common sense is bound to come unstuck. What we have been doing is largely seeing how and why physicalism and other traditional world-views have come unstuck.

At this point we may drop the counterfactual history and refocus our attention on physicalism. As we saw in Chapter 1, and then again in Chapter 9, physicalism is interesting not only as a philosophy of nature, it is interesting also as a philosophy of philosophy, i.e. a thesis whose main role is in the spelling out of philosophical questions, and in particular metaphysical questions about the presuppositions of everyday life. If physicalism were merely a philosophy of nature, then any problem presented by the formulation problem could very likely be minimized. A physicalist could always tell us what he or she thinks the world is like and not use the word 'physicalism' or indeed related words. So it is in its role as a philosophy of philosophy that the formulation problem really becomes acute. In particular, if the skeptic about physicalism is right, and there is no version of physicalism that is (a) true and (b) deserves the name, then we lose both attractive features of that philosophy of philosophy: the idea that in many cases problems about the presuppositions of everyday life can be construed as placement problems, and the related idea that a large class of such problems can be thought of as being highly unified.

It is this situation that leads to the stand-off between the skeptic about physicalism and the true believer: the skeptic about the existence of such problems says that they don't exist; the true believer responds that, since the existence of such problems is not in doubt, it must be that the formulation problem is solved. But as we saw in Chapters 10 and 11, this stand-off can be avoided by construing the various pieces of philosophical reasoning in which physicalism appears as not really about physicalism. In that sense, the nature of many philosophical problems seems in reality to be quite distinct from what you would predict from the standard picture. Not only are these problems not all about how various things fit or find a place in the physical world, it is not even true that they are all of a similar type. So in that sense the standard picture of philosophy is a casualty of the interpretation problem for physicalism.

One might think that this result is a rather unwelcome one. The standard picture represents a lot of philosophical problems as being highly unified. If our discussion in Chapters 10 and 11 is right, however, it turns out that they are in fact very different from each other, and the unity of philosophical problems is lost. No doubt from an aesthetic point of view this is a disadvantage. My own view, however, is that unity is much better dispensed with. If we think of philosophical problems as being similar to one another, then we will be inclined to think that the solutions to philosophical problems will likewise be similar. But this blinds us to offering different kinds of solutions. For example, as I noted in Chapter 10, my own preferred response to the CA is the epistemic view. The epistemic view is quite implausible if you try to apply it (e.g.) to the problem about intentionality that is generated by the idea that intentionality is a relation. If these problems were both fundamentally placement problems that would seem to be an objection to the epistemic view; but if they are both fundamentally different it is pretty much what you would expect. Philosophical problems are very different from each other, and there is no easy inference from the treatment of one to the treatment of another.

There is however a final twist to the story. One motivation for the standard picture, as I have been emphasizing, is that it portrays many philosophical problems as highly unified. But unification is only one motivation for the standard picture, and arguably the least important one. The more important one was that the standard picture provides an answer, or at least a partial answer, to the question of what philosophy is about, the problem posed vividly in the passage from Rorty that I quoted in the introduction. If we lose the answer that physicalism gave us, then it is unclear that we can answer the objection. How then to answer this objection?

It is too late to give this issue the attention it deserves, but I think the discussion we have been having throughout this book provides some direction here. For lying behind the problem of philosophy is the idea that we need to place (or fit, or find, or ...) philosophy or philosophical problems in a space of intellectual concerns which are antecedently regarded as raising no problems of their own. But it is not at all obvious that this is true. This is not to say of course that there is no difference between scientific, philosophical, and literary concerns. Anyone who indulges in any of these pursuits seriously can hardly doubt that the differences are real enough. But the idea that we have a clear enough conception of what a scientific problem is, or what a literary problem is, and that we can, in the light of these conceptions, criticize or defend a view about what a philosophical problem is, seems to me to seriously overstate our current level of insight into the possibilities of human inquiry. It may be that the ideal theory of the various forms of intellectual problems humans can raise for themselves draws a three-fold distinction in this way, but it is premature at this point for us to suppose so. And if it does not then the problem of philosophy should be dismissed as having a false presupposition. It is not clear that we have a uniform conception of a philosophical problem. But it is also not clear that in order to defend or explain the nature of philosophical problems we require one.

GLOSSARY

causal closure   In events, the principle that for all physical events e if there is an event $e*$ which causes event e, then $e*$ is physical; in properties, the principle that for all physical events e if there is an event $e*$ which causes event e, then $e*$ is physical and there is a physical property F which is efficacious in $e*$s causing e.

cluster concepts   Concepts that can be associated with, and defined in terms of, a range or cluster of features.

coherentism   A view according to which there might be various but incompatible world-views; in this book, a coherentist holds a coherence theory of truth.

conceivability   In one sense, it is conceivable that p just in case it is imaginable that p or it appears possible that p; in another sense, it is conceivable that p just in case it is not a priori that not p.

conceptual analysis   The project of giving non-circular and perfectly general necessary and sufficient conditions for the application of a concept.

consciousness   Roughly, a property of a mental state according to which there is something it is like to be in the mental state. This is sometimes called 'phenomenal consciousness' or just 'experience'. (There are other notions of consciousness, but these are not discussed in this book.)

dualism   (Roughly) the view that there are psychological properties and events which are not necessitated by and are metaphysically distinct from, physical properties and events. Dualism comes in a number of different varieties—substance dualism versus property dualism, interactionist, epiphenomenalist, and overdeterminationist dualism.

epiphenomenalism   A version of dualism according to which mental events and properties have no causal role in the production of physical events.

exclusion principle   In events, the principle that for all events *e* if there is an event *e** which causes event *e*, then no distinct event also causes *e*; in properties, the principle that if a property *F* is causally efficacious in *e*'s causing *e**, then no other property is causally efficacious.

fundamental properties   A special sort of property which is (to put it metaphorically) one of the key ingredients of the world. The notion figures prominently in David Lewis's philosophy.

Fundamental Properties View   The view that physicalism is the thesis that every instantiated fundamental property is a physical property.

Hempel's dilemma   An argument given by Carl Hempel, usually interpreted as suggesting that physicalism is either defined by reference to contemporary physics in which case it is false (since no one thinks that contemporary physics is complete) or else it is defined by reference to ideal physics in which case we don't know what it says (for who knows what the ideal physics will say?).

Hume's dictum   The thesis that there are no necessary connections between distinct existences.

idealism   (Roughly) the thesis that everything is mental or spiritual. Idealism stands in need of clarification just as much as physicalism.

Identity View   The view that physicalism is the thesis that every property is identical to some physical property.

intentionality   The aboutness of a mental state, sentence, speech act or sign.

interactionist dualism   A version of dualism according to which mental events and properties produce physical events in just the way that mental events and properties do. The interactionist dualist denies causal closure.

Kripkean necessitation   See necessitation.

materialism   A traditional name for physicalism; I use 'materialism' and 'physicalism' interchangeably in this book.

metaphysical distinctness   There are various ways of developing this idea. On some views, metaphysical distinctness is the same as modal distinctness; on other views it is taken as a primitive.

metaphysical necessitation   See necessitation.

method of cases   The method of considering imagined case or possibilities to decide on the conditions under which a particular concept or word or thesis applies.

modal distinctness   A property F is modally distinct from a property G just in case it is possible for F to be instantiated and G not to be instantiated and vice versa.

naturalistic platonism   Roughly, the thesis that every property is necessitated by some property distinct from the sort presented in common sense, or in unaided thought and perception.

necessitation   (In properties) a property F necessitates a property G just in case in all possible worlds, if F is instantiated, so is G.

necessitation dualism   The thesis that mental properties and physical properties are metaphysically distinct and yet necessarily connected.

Necessity View   The thesis that physicalism is true just in case every property is necessitated by a physical property

neutral monism   The thesis that every property is necessitated by some property which is neither mental nor physical.

nomological necessity   An event occurs or a property is instantiated by nomological necessity, if it occurs or is instantiated in all possible worlds that exhibit the same laws of nature as the actual world.

numerical distinctness   A property F is numerically distinct from a property G just in case F has a property that G does not, i.e. F is not identical to G.

phenomenal concept   (Roughly) a concept of an itch or pain or other conscious experience.

physicalism   (Roughly) the thesis that everything is physical; in this book, it is clarified to the thesis that every instantiated property is necessitated by, and not metaphysically distinct from, some physical property.

pluralism   A development of dualism which holds that many properties stand to the physical as the psychological properties do.

property   An attribute or characteristic of a thing; properties may be instantiated in particulars and other properties; on the other hand, it makes no sense to say that particulars can be instantiated.

property dualism   The view that while every particular is physical some properties are not necessitated by, and are metaphysically distinct from, any physical properties.

realization   Usually, a property F is realized by a property G just in case F is a second-order property of having some property that does such and such, and G is the property that does such and such.

Realization View   The view that physicalism is the thesis that every property is either identical to a physical property or is identical to a second-order property which is realized by a first-order property (see second-order property).

second-order property   In this book, a second-order property is the property of having some property that meets a certain condition.

Semantic View   The view that physicalism is a semantic doctrine according to which every statement is synonymous with some physical statement. Carnap held this view.

standard picture   A picture of physicalism and its role in philosophy held by many contemporary philosophers, both physicalist and non-physicalist alike.

Starting Point View   An initial characterization of what a physical property is, and what physicalism is.

substance dualism   The view that, while there are physical particulars, there are also non-physical particulars, such as souls, which are metaphysically distinct from any physical particular.

supervenience   (Roughly) one set of properties supervenes on another just in case there can be no difference in the first without a difference in the second.

Theory View   The thesis that a property is physical just in case it is expressed by a predicate of a physical theory. This idea can be developed in various ways depending on whether the relevant theory is actually true, possibly true, true in the ideal limit or currently believed to be true.

Weltanschauung   A world picture. See the epigraph from Freud at the beginning of the book.

REFERENCES

Alter, T. and Walter, S. (eds) (2007) *Phenomenal Concepts and Phenomenal Knowledge*. New York: Oxford University Press.

Appiah, A. (1991) "Racisms." In D.T. Goldberg (ed), *The Anatomy of Racisms*. Minneapolis: University of Minnesota Press, pp. 5–7.

Armstrong, D. (1968) *A Materialist Theory of the Mind*. London: Routledge & Kegan Paul.

—— (1999) *A World of States of Affairs*. Cambridge: Cambridge University Press.

Bennett, K. (2003) "Why the exclusion problem seems intractable and how, just maybe, to tract it." *Nous*, 37/3: 471–97.

Bickle, J. (2008) "Multiple realizability." In *The Stanford Encyclopedia of Philosophy* (Fall 2008 edn, ed. E.N. Zalta). Available at <http://plato.stanford.edu/archives/fall2008/entries/multiple-realizability/>.

Block, N. (1981) "Psychologism and behaviorism." *Philosophical Review*, 90: 5–43.

Block, N. and Stalnaker, R. (1999) "Conceptual analysis, dualism and the explanatory gap." *Philosophical Review*, 108/1: 1–46.

Boghossian, P. (1989) "The rule-following considerations." *Mind*, 98/392: 507–49.

Boyd, R. (1980) "Materialism without reductionism: what physicalism does not entail." In N. Block (ed.), *Readings in the Philosophy of Psychology*, vol. 1, Cambridge, MA: Harvard University Press, pp. 67–106.

Broad, C.D. (1925) *The Mind and its Place in Nature*. London: Routledge & Kegan Paul.

Broad, C.D. (1960) *Lectures on Psychical Research*. London: Routledge & Kegan Paul.

Byrne, A. (1999) "Cosmic hermeneutics." In J. Tomberlin (ed.), *Philosophical Perspectives*, 13: 347–83.

—— (2004) "Inverted qualia." In *The Stanford Encylopedia of Philosophy*, <http://plato.stanford.edu/entries/qualia-inverted/>.

Campbell, K. (1976) *Metaphysics: An Introduction*. Encino, CA: Dickenson.

Carnap, R. (1959) "Psychology in physical language." In A.J. Ayer (ed.), *Logical Positivism*. New York: The Free Press, pp. 165–98. First publication 1932/33.

—— (2003) *The Logical Structure of the World*. Chicago: Open Court Classics. First publication in German, 1928.

—— (1947) *Meaning and Necessity: A Study in Semantics and Modal Logic*, 2nd edn. University of Chicago Press.

Cartwright, N., Cat, J., Fleck, N., and Uebel, T. (1996) *Otto Neurath: Philosophy Between Science and Politics*. Cambridge: Cambridge University Press.

Chalmers, D. (1996) *The Conscious Mind*. New York: Oxford University Press.

—— (1999) "Materialism and the metaphysics of modality." *Philosophy and Phenomenological Research*, 59: 473–93.

—— (2002) *Philosophy of Mind: Contemporary and Classical Readings*. New York: Oxford University Press.

—— (2002) "Consciousness and its place in nature." In S. Stich and T. Warfield (eds), *Blackwell Guide to the Philosophy of Mind*. Oxford: Blackwell, pp. 102–42. (Also printed in D. Chalmers (ed.), *Philosophy of Mind: Classical and Contemporary Readings*, New York: Oxford University Press, 2002, pp. 247–72).

—— (2007) "Phenomenal concepts and the explanatory gap'. In T. Alter and S. Walter (eds), *Phenomenal Concepts and Phenomenal Knowledge*. New York: Oxford University Press, pp. 167–94.

Chalmers, D. and Jackson, F. (2001) "Conceptual analysis and reductive explanation." *Philosophical Review*, 110/3: 315–60.

Chomsky, N. (2000) *New Horizons in the Study of Language and Mind*. Cambridge: Cambridge University Press.

—— (2009) "The Mysteries of Nature: How Deeply Hidden?" *Journal of Philosophy*, Vol. CVI, No. 4, April 2009, 167-200.

Crane, T. and Mellor, D.H. (1990) "There is no question of physicalism." *Mind*, 99: 185–206.

Daly, C. (1998) "What are physical properties?" *Pacific Philosophical Quarterly*, 79/3: 196–217.

Davidson, D. (1970) "Mental Events." Reprinted in *Essays on Actions and Events*, New York: Oxford University Press, 1980: 207–24.

Descartes, R. (1641) "Meditations on first philosophy." In J. Cottingham, R. Stoothoff, A. Kenny, and D. Murdoch (eds and trans.), *The Philosophical Writings of René Descartes*, Cambridge: Cambridge University Press, 1985.

Devitt, M. (1996) *Coming to Our Senses: A Naturalistic Program for Semantic Localism*. Cambridge: Cambridge University Press.

Dijksterhuis, E.J. (1961) *The Mechanization of the World-Picture*. Oxford: Clarendon.

Dowell, J.L. (2006a) "Formulating the thesis of physicalism." *Philosophical Studies*, 131/1: 1–23.

—— (2006b) "The physical: empirical, not metaphysical." *Philosophical Studies*, 131/1: 25–60.

Dupré, J. (1993) *The Disorder of Things*. Cambridge, MA: Harvard University Press.

Dyke, H. (2009) (ed) *From Truth to Reality*. London: Routledge.

Eddington, A.S. (1928) *The Nature of the Physical World*. London: J.M. Dent & Sons.

Evans, G. (1983) *The Varieties of Reference*. Oxford: Oxford University Press.

Feigl, H. (1958) "The 'mental' and the 'physical'." In H. Feigl, M. Scriven, and G. Maxwell (eds), *Concepts, Theories, and the Mind–Body Problem*, Minnesota Studies in the Philosophy of Science, vol. 2. Minneapolis: University of Minnesota Press, pp. 370–97.

Feinberg, G. (1966) "Physics and the Thales problem." *Journal of Philosophy*, 63/1: 5–17.

Field, H. (1972) "Tarski's theory of truth." *Journal of Philosophy*, 69, 347–75.

—— (1992) "Physicalism." In J. Earman (ed.), *Inference, Explanation and Other Frustrations*. Berkeley: University of California Press, pp. 271–87.

Fine, K. (1994) "Essence and modality." In J. Tomberlin (ed.), *Philosophical Perspectives 8: Logic and Language*: 1–16.

Fodor, J.A. (1974) "Special sciences (or, The disunity of science as a working hypothesis)." *Synthèse*, 28: 97–115. Reprinted in N. Block (ed.), *Readings in the Philosophy of Psychology*, vol. 1. Cambridge, MA: Harvard University Press, pp. 120–33.

—— (1987) *Psychosemantics*. Cambridge, MA: MIT Press.

—— (1994) "Fodor, Jerry A." In Samuel Guttenplan (ed.), *A Companion to the Philosophy of Mind*. Oxford: Blackwell, pp. 292–300.

Foster, J. (1982) *The Case for Idealism*. London: Routledge.

van Fraassen, B.C. (2002) *The Empirical Stance*. New Haven, CT: Yale University Press.

Freud, S. (1995) *The Freud Reader* (ed. Peter Gay). London: Vintage.

Friedman, M. (1975) "Physicalism and the indeterminacy of translation." *Nous*, 9/4: 353–74.

Gates, G. (2001) "Physicalism, empiricism, and positivism," in C. Gillett and B. Loewer (eds), *Physicalism and Its Discontents*. Cambridge: Cambridge University Press, pp. 251–67.

Gendler, T.Z and Hawthorne, J. (eds) (2004) *Conceivability and Possibility*. Oxford: Oxford University Press.

Gillett, C. and Loewer, B. (eds) (2001) *Physicalism and Its Discontents*. Cambridge: Cambridge University Press.

Gillett, C. and Witmer, D.G. (2001) "A 'physical' need: physicalism and the via negativa." *Analysis*, 61: 302–9.

Goodman, N. (1978) *Ways of Worldmaking*. Cambridge, MA: Harvard University Press.

Harman, G. (1977) *The Nature of Morality: An Introduction to Ethics*. Oxford: Oxford University Press.

Haugeland, J. (1982) "Weak supervenience." *American Philosophical Quarterly*, 19: 93–103.

Hawthorne, J. (2002) "Blocking definitions of materialism." *Philosophical Studies*, 110/2: 103–13.

Heil, J. and Mele, A. (eds) (1995) *Mental Causation*. Oxford: Oxford University Press.

Hellman, G. (1985) "Determination and logical truth." *Journal of Philosophy*, 82/11: 607–16.

Hempel, C. (1949) "The logical analysis of psychology." In H. Feigl and W. Sellars (eds), *Readings in Philosophical Analysis*. New York: Appleton-Century-Crofts, pp. 373–84. (Reprinted in N. Block (ed.), *Readings in the Philosophy of Psychology*, vol. 1, Cambridge: Harvard University Press, 1980, pp. 14–23).

—— (1969) "Reduction: ontological and linguistic facets'. In S. Morgenbesser, P. Suppes, and M. White (eds), *Philosophy, Science and Method: Essays in Honor of Ernest Nagel*, New York: St. Martin's Press, pp. 179–99.

—— (1980) "Comments on Goodman's *Ways of Worldmaking*." *Synthése*, 45: 139–99.

Horgan, T. (1983) "Supervenience and microphysics." *Pacific Philosophical Quarterly*, 63: 29–43.

—— (1993) "From supervenience to superdupervenience: meeting the demands of a material world." *Mind*, 102: 555–86.

Huttemann, A. and Papineau, D. (2005) "Physicalism decomposed." *Analysis* 65: 33–9.

Jackson, F. (1982) "Epiphenomenal qualia." *Philosophical Quarterly*, 32: 127–36.

—— (1998) *From Metaphysics to Ethics: A Defense of Conceptual Analysis*. Oxford: Clarendon.

—— (2006) "On ensuring that physicalism is not a dual attribute theory in sheep's clothing." *Philosophical Studies*, 131: 227–49.

Johnston, M. (1992) "How to speak of the colors." *Philosophical Studies*, 68: 221–63.

Kaplan, D. (1989) "Demonstratives." In J. Almog *et al.* (eds), *Themes From Kaplan*. Oxford: Oxford University Press, pp. 565–614.

Kim, J. (1993) *Mind and Supervenience*. Cambridge: Cambridge University Press.

—— (1998) *Mind in a Physical World*. Cambridge: Cambridge University Press.

—— (2007) *Physicalism, or Something Near Enough*. Princeton, NJ: Princeton University Press.

Kripke, S. (1980) *Naming and Necessity*. Cambridge, MA: Harvard University Press.

—— (1982) *Wittgenstein on Rules and Private Language: An Elementary Exposition*. Oxford: Basil Blackwell.

Lange, F. (1925) *The History of Materialism and Criticism of its Present Importance*, trans. E.C. Thomas. London: Routledge & Kegan Paul. First published in German, in 3 vols, 1875.

Lenin, V.I. (1908) *Materialism and Empirio-Criticism: Critical Comments on a Reactionary Philosophy*. Available at <www.marxists.org/archive/lenin/works/1908/mec>.

Leuenberger, S. (2008) "Ceteris absentibus physicalism." In D. Zimmerman (ed.), *Oxford Studies in Metaphysics*, vol. 4. Oxford: Oxford University Press, pp. 145–70.

Levine, J. (2007) "Phenomenal concepts and the materialist constraint." In T. Alter and S. Walter (eds), *Phenomenal Concepts and Phenomenal Knowledge*. New York: Oxford University Press, pp. 145–166.

Lewis, D. (1980) "Mad pain and Martian pain." In N. Block (ed.), *Readings in the Philosophy of Psychology*, vol. 1. Cambridge: Harvard University Press, pp. 216–22.

—— (1983) "New work for a theory of universals." *Australasian Journal of Philosophy*, 61/4: 343–77. Reprinted in D. Lewis, *Papers in Metaphysics and Epistemology*, Cambridge: Cambridge University Press, 1999, pp. 8–55; references to the reprint.

—— (1986a) *On the Plurality of Worlds*. Oxford: Blackwell.

—— (1986b) "Introduction." In D. Lewis, *Philosophical Papers*, vol. II. Oxford: Oxford University Press.

—— (1988) "What experience teaches." *Proceedings of the Russellian Society*, 13: 29–57. Reprinted in D. Lewis, *Papers in Metaphysics and Epistemology*, Cambridge: Cambridge University Press, 1999, pp. 262–90; references to the reprint.

—— (1994) "Reduction of mind." in S. Guttenplan (ed), *A Companion to the Philosophy of Mind*, Oxford: Blackwell, pp. 412–31. Reprinted in D. Lewis,

Papers in Metaphysics and Epistemology, Cambridge: Cambridge University Press, 1999, pp. 291–324; references to the reprint.

Lewis, D. (2002) "Tharp's third theorem." *Analysis* 62/274: 95–7.

Loar, B. (1997) "Phenomenal states." In N. Block, O. Flanagan, and G. Guzeldere (eds), *The Nature of Consciousness: Philosophical Debates*. Cambridge, MA: MIT Press, pp. 597–616.

Ludlow, P., Nagasawa,Y., and Stoljar, D. (eds) (2004) *There's Something about Mary: Essays on Phenomenal Consciousness and Frank Jackson's Knowledge Argument*. Cambridge, MA: MIT Press.

Mackie, J.L. (1973) *Truth, Probability and Paradox*. Oxford: Oxford University Press.

McGinn, C. (1989) "Can we solve the mind–body problem." *Mind*, 98: 349–66.

McLaughlin, B. (1992) "The rise and fall of British emergentism." In A. Beckerman, H. Flohr, and J. Kim (eds), *Emergence or Reduction? Prospects for Nonreductive Physicalism*. Berlin: De Gruyter, pp. 49–93.

McLaughlin, B. and Bennett, K. (2005) "Supervenience." *The Stanford Encyclopedia of Philosophy* (Fall 2005 edn, ed. E.N. Zalta). Available at <http://plato.stanford.edu/archives/fall2005/entries/supervenience/>.

Mellor, D.H. (1973) "Materialism and phenomenal qualities." *Proceedings of the Aristotelian Society, Supp. Vol.*, XLVII: 107–19.

Melnyk, A. (1997) "How to keep the 'physical' in physicalism." *Journal of Philosophy*, 94: 622–37.

—— (2003) *A Physicalist Manifesto: Thoroughly Modern Materialism*. Cambridge: Cambridge University.

Montero, B. (1999) "The body problem." *Nous*, 33: 183–200.

—— (2001) "Post-physicalism." *Journal of Consciousness Studies*, 8/2: 61–80.

—— (2009) "What is the physical?". In B. McLaughlin, A. Beckermann, and S. Walter (eds), *Oxford Handbook of Philosophy of Mind*, Oxford: Oxford University Press, pp. 173–86.

Montero, B. and Papineau, D. (2005) "A defense of the via negativa argument for physicalism." *Analysis*, 65/3: 233–7.

Nagel, T. (1974) "What is it like to be a bat?" *Philosophical Review*, 4: 435–50.

—— (1983) *The View from Nowhere*. Oxford: Oxford University Press.

Neurath, O. (1931a) "Physicalism: the philosophy of the Vienna Circle." In R.S. Cohen and M. Neurath, (eds), *Philosophical Papers 1913–1946*. Dordrecht: D. Reidel, 1983, pp. 48–51.

—— (1931b) "Physicalism." In R.S. Cohen and M. Neurath, (eds), *Philosophical Papers 1913–1946*. Dordrecht: D. Reidel, 1983, pp. 52–7.

—— (1931c) "Sociology and physicalism." In A.J. Ayer (ed.), *Logical Positivism*. Glencoe: The Free Press, 1959, pp. 282–317.

—— (1932/33) "Protocol sentences." In A.J. Ayer (ed.), *Logical Positivism*. Glencoe: The Free Press, 1959, pp. 199–208.

—— (1934) "Radical physicalism and the 'real world'." In R.S. Cohen and M. Neurath, (eds), *Philosophical Papers 1913–1946*. Dordrecht: D. Reidel, 1983, pp. 100–14.

—— (1946) "The orchestration of the sciences by the encyclopedism of logical empiricism." *Philosophy and Phenomenological Research*, 6: 496–508. Reprinted in R.S. Cohen and M. Neurath, (eds), *Philosophical Papers 1913–1946*, Dordrecht: D. Reidel, 1983.

Nietzsche, F. (1973) *Beyond Good and Evil*. Penguin: Harmondsworth.

O'Neill, J. (2004) "Ecological economics and the politics of knowledge: the debate between Hayek and Neurath." *Cambridge Journal of Economics*, 28: 431–47.

Papineau, D. (2001) "The rise of physicalism." In C. Gillett and B. Loewer (eds), *Physicalism and Its Discontents*. Cambridge: Cambridge University Press, pp. 3–36.

—— (2007) "Must a physicalist be a microphysicalist?" In Jesper Kallestrup and Jakob Hohwy (eds), *Being Reduced: New Essays on Causation and Explanation in the Special Sciences*. Oxford: Oxford University Press, pp. 126–48.

Pettit, P. (1994) "A Definition of Physicalism." *Analysis*, 53: 213–26.

Poland, J. (1994) *Physicalism: The Philosophical Foundations*. Oxford: Clarendon Press.

—— (2003) "Chomsky's challenge to physicalism." In L.M. Antony and N. Hornstein (eds), *Chomsky and His Critics*. Oxford: Blackwell, pp. 29–48.

Price, H. (1997) "Naturalism and the fate of the M-worlds.' *Proceedings of the Aristotelian Society, Supp. Vol.*, LXXI: 247–67.

Putnam, H. (1975) "Philosophy and our mental life." In H. Putnam, *Mind, Language and Reality: Philosophical Papers*, vol. 2. Cambridge: Cambridge University Press, pp. 291–303.

Quine, W.V. (1954) "The scope and language of science." In W.V. Quine, *The Ways of Paradox and Other Essays*. Cambridge, MA: Harvard University Press, 1976, pp. 228–45.

—— (1960) *Word and Object*. Cambridge, MA: MIT Press.

—— (1969) *Ontological Relativity and Other Essays*. New York: Columbia University Press.

—— (1976) "Whither physical objects?" In R.S. Cohen, P.K. Feyerabend, and M.W. Wartofsky (eds), *Essays in Memory of Imre Lakatos*. Dordrecht-Holland: D. Reidel, pp. 497–504.

—— (1979) "Facts of the matter." In R.S. Shahan and C. Swoyer (eds), *Essays on the Philosophy of W.V. Quine*. Norman: University of Oklahoma Press, pp. 155–69.

Ravenscroft, I. (1997) "Physical Properties." *Southern Journal of Philosophy*, XXXV: 419–31.

Rayo, A. and Uzquiano, G. (eds) (2006) *Absolute Generality*. Oxford: Oxford University Press. Rosen, G. (2010) "Metaphysical dependence: reduction and grounding." In B. Hale and A. Hoffmann (eds), *Modality: Metaphysics, Logic and Epistemology*. Oxford: Oxford University Press.

Russell, B. (1917) "Physics and sense data." In B. Russell, *Mysticism and Logic*. Penguin: Harmondsworth, 1963.

—— (1925) "Preface." In F. Lange, *The History of Materialism and Criticism of its Present Importance*, trans. E.C. Thomas. London: Routledge & Kegan Paul.

—— (1927) *The Analysis of Matter*, London: Kegan Paul.

Ryle, G. (1949) *The Concept of Mind*. London: Hutchinson.

Schaffer, J. (2003) "Is there a fundamental level?" *Nous*, 37/3: 498–517.

—— (forthcoming) "Limning the true and ultimate structure of reality".

Schlick, M. (1932/3) "Positivism and realism." Reprinted in A.J. Ayer (ed.), *Logical Positivism*. Glencoe: The Free Press, 1959, pp. 82–107.

—— (1934) "The foundations of knowledge." Reprinted in A.J. Ayer (ed.), *Logical Positivism*. Glencoe: The Free Press, 1959, pp. 209–27.

Searle, J.R. (1980) "Minds, brains, and programs." *Behavioral and Brain Sciences* 3/3: 417–57.

—— (1992) *The Rediscovery of the Mind*. Cambridge, MA: MIT Press.

Sellars, W. (1956) "Empiricism and the philosophy of mind." In H. Feigl and M. Scriven (eds), *Minnesota Studies in the Philosophy of Science*, vol. 1. Minneapolis: Minnesota University Press.

—— (1962) "Philosophy and the scientific image of man." In R. Colodny (ed.), *Frontiers of Science and Philosophy*. Pittsburgh: University of Pittsburgh Press, pp. 35–78. Reprinted in W. Sellars, *Science, Perception and Reality*, London: Routledge & Kegan Paul, 1963, pp. 1–40.

Shapiro, L. (2000) "Multiple realizations." *Journal of Philosophy*, 97: 635–54.

Shoemaker, S. (1982) "The inverted spectrum." *Journal of Philosophy*, 79: 357–81.

—— (2007) *Physical Realization* Oxford: Oxford University Press.

Smart, J.J.C. (1959) "Sensations and brain processes." *Philosophical Review*, 68: 141–56.

—— (1963) *Philosophy and Scientific Realism*. London: Routledge.

—— (1963a) "Materialism." *Journal of Philosophy*, LX/22: 651–62.

—— (1978) "The content of physicalism." *Philosophical Quarterly*, 28: 239–41.

Soames, S. (2007) *Reference and Description: The Case Against Two-Dimensionalism*. Princeton, NJ: Princeton University Press.

Spelke, E. (1994) "Initial knowledge: six suggestions." *Cognition*, 50: 443–47.

Stalnaker, R. (1996) "Varieties of supervenience." *Philosophical Perspectives*, 10: 221–41.

—— (2008) *Our Knowledge of the Internal World*. Oxford: Oxford University Press.

Stebbing, L.S (1958) *Philosophy and the Physicists*. New York: Dover Publications. First published 1937.

Stern, D. (2005) "Wittgenstein, the Vienna Circle, and physicalism: a reassessment." In A. Richardson and T. Uebel (eds), *The Cambridge Companion to Logical Empiricism*. Cambridge: Cambridge University Press, pp. 305–31.

Stoljar, D. (2005) "Physicalism and phenomenal concepts." *Mind and Language*, 20/5: 469–94.

—— (2006) *Ignorance and Imagination: The Epistemic Origin of the Problem of Consciousness*. New York: Oxford University Press.

—— (2008) "Distinctions in distinction." In J. Kallestrup and J. Hohwy (eds), *Being Reduced: New Essays on Causation and Explanation in the Special Sciences*. Oxford: Oxford University Press, pp. 263–79.

—— (2009a) "Hempel's dilemma." In H. Dyke (ed.), *From Truth to Reality: New Essays in Logic and Metaphysics*. London: Routledge, pp. 181–97.

—— (2009b) 'Physicalism' In The *Stanford Encyclopedia of Philosophy* (http://plato.stanford.edu/archives/fall2009/entries/physicalism/).

Stove, D. (1991) *The Plato Cult and Other Philosophical Follies*. Oxford: Blackwell.

Strawson, G. (2003) "Real materialism." In L.M. Antony and N. Hornstein (eds), *Chomsky and His Critics*. Oxford: Blackwell, pp. 49–88.

—— (2006) "Realistic Monism – Why Physicalism Entails Panpsychism." *Journal of Consciousness Studies* 13 (10-11):3-31.

Stroud, B. (1986) "The physical world." *Proceedings of the Aristotelian Society*, LXXXVII: 263–77.

Stubenberg, L. (2008) "Neutral monism." *The Stanford Encyclopedia of Philosophy* (Fall 2008 edn, ed. E.N. Zalta). Available at <http://plato.stanford.edu/archives/fall2008/entries/neutralmonism/>.

Sturgeon, S. (2000) *Matters of Mind: Consciousness, Reason and Nature*. New York: Routledge.

Sussman, A.N. (1981) "Reflections on the chances for a scientific dualism." *Journal of Philosophy*, 78/2: 95–118.

Swinburne, R. (1997) *The Evolution of the Soul*. Oxford: Clarendon. First published 1986.

Thau, M. (2002) *Consciousness and Cognition*. New York: Oxford University Press.

Trusted, J. (1999) *The Mystery of Matter*. Basingstoke: Palgrave Macmillan.

Tye, M. (2009) *Consciousness Revisited: Materialism without Phenomenal Concepts*. Cambridge, MA: MIT Press.

Unger, P. (1998) "The mystery of the physical and the matter of qualities: a paper for Professor Shaffer." *Midwest Studies in Philosophy*, 23: 75–99.

Vitzthum, R.D. (1995) *Materialism: An Affirmative History and Definition*. New York: Prometheus Books.

Williamson, T. (2008) *The Philosophy of Philosophy*. Oxford: Blackwell.

Wilson, J. (2005) "Supervenience-based formulations of physicalism." *Nous*, 39/3: 426–59.

—— (2006) "On characterizing the physical." *Philosophical Studies*, 131: 61–99.

—— (forthcoming) "What is Hume's Dictum and Why Believe it?" *Philosophy and Phenomenological Resesarch*.

Yablo, S. (1992) "Mental causation." *Philosophical Review*, 101: 245–80.

INDEX